FOUNDÂTION®

A Hands-on Introduction to Business Fundamentals

Edition 1 Revision 1

Unforgettable Business Learning

Capsim Management Simulations, Inc.
55 East Monroe, Suite 3210
Chicago, Illinois 60603
+1(312) 477-7200
www.capsim.com

Table of Contents

Module 5

Module 6

Module 7

Module 8

Appendix 1

Appendix 2

Appendix 3

Index

Introduction

Learning Objectives:

After reading this module and completing the associated exercises, you will be able to:

LO1: Describe the basic resources businesses need to effectively function and compete.

LO2: Discuss the importance of deep practice for developing your business acumen.

LO3: Describe the "do's and don'ts" of using deep practice in the simulation.

LO4: Describe your roles in the simulated company.

LO5: Discuss your company's products, departments, and facilities.

LO6: Navigate capsim.com and the Foundation Simulation.

LO7: Find and open the Online Simulation Guide and the Web Spreadsheet.

Key terms to look for:

- *Board of Directors*
- *Management*
- *Ideas*
- *Money*
- *People*
- *Deep practice*

An Experience

One way to learn about business is to read the textbooks, learn the definitions, discuss case studies, and pass the exam. In *Foundation: A Hands-on Introduction to Business Fundamentals* we take a less theoretical and more hands-on approach. We're going to learn business by managing a business.

The approach makes sense for two reasons. First, business itself is practical. If there were a single true theory of business success, then every person who started a business and followed the theory would be able to create a profitable and sustainable enterprise. Unfortunately, it's not that simple. Business requires the practical application of people, skills, ideas, and money and it requires some trial-and-error before you succeed. Second, it is in that process of trial-and-error that mastery is developed. If you want to *master* the basics of business, rather than learn only the theory, this program is for you.

Foundation uses a simulation to give you hands-on experience in running a company. It provides the opportunity to work with all the essential managerial functions including marketing, production, and finance, and to experience the interactions and interrelationships that businesses must engage in – internally and externally – to succeed.

It starts with an idea . . .

Every business requires three basic resources to function and compete: ideas, people, and money. In the world of business, those resources are configured and reconfigured over and over again to satisfy the needs and wants of the market.

Sometimes businesses are based on a brilliant idea that completely changes how we do something – such as the way smart phones revolutionized the way we find, manage, and communicate information. Sometimes businesses find a new way to make us want more of what we already have – like the fashion industry urging us to update our wardrobe every season. Some businesses continually improve on a basic product – whether it is cars, light bulbs, fabricated steel, or dishwasher detergent. Sometimes we're being sold an emotion – by the entertainment industry, for example – or a service, like haircuts or gym memberships. Whatever the business, it begins with an idea.

. . . Add some good management

Individual brilliance, great ideas, even a revolutionary technology, however, are only parts of the equation. The real art of business is to take the basic resources – ideas, people, and money – and get them working together as a growing, functional operation. Building a business requires the ability to understand and manage the network of interrelationships that delivering your product or service to the market requires.

And to do that, every single business relies on some standard elements and practices. For example, accounting to keep track of the money, marketing to entice customers to buy, and production to get your product or service into the customers' hands. Put simply, businesses need effective management.

The roots of the word *manage* come from the Latin word *manus agere* (to lead by hand) or *mansionem agere* (to run the house for the owner). The dictionary defines management as *"the person or persons controlling and directing the affairs of a business or institution."* It is the people who have their hands on the

It starts with an idea......

Smart phones have stimulated many new business ideas. Jack Dorsey is responsible for a few of them and has created two start-ups offering products we didn't know we needed or wanted until we had them. Twitter is one. Dorsey co-founded the social networking chat site in 2006. When the possibility of an IPO for Twitter was canvassed in early 2013, the company was valued (by one of its investors) at close to $10 billion.

Square is another of Dorsey's ideas. Square is a small credit card reader that plugs into a smart phone or tablet, replacing card-processing equipment and making it simple for any merchant to accept credit cards. The card reader allows shoppers to swipe a credit or debit card and sign on-screen with a finger. Square launched in the United States and has expanded to Japan, where low credit card usage has been attributed to the difficulty small merchants have accepting cards.

Uber, another San Francisco start-up, launched a smart phone ride-on-demand app that has made traditional taxi unions, city governments and transport providers more than uncomfortable about their business models. Uber allows you to order a car, track its progress to your location, call and talk to the driver, plus pay for the ride when it's done – all on one app. Uber has spread quickly to 35 markets including Seoul, Taipei, Mexico City, and Zurich but was followed into the market by both Lyft, and SideCar from Google Ventures. With the ride-on-demand market heating up quickly, Lyft had a reported valuation of $275 million in mid-2013. The taxi and limo companies are fighting back and can be referred to as "rent seekers" in the market, attempting to maintain the status quo through regulation and litigation.

Twitter, Square, Uber, Lyft and others are great ideas that were turned into businesses but will require excellent, fleet-footed management to become established and remain relevant.

How many other businesses can you come up with that offered new products we didn't know we needed until we saw them?

controls of the organization. In *Foundation*, you will get your hands on some critical management tools and begin to build your skills using them. Those tools include accounting statements, forecasts, teamwork tactics, and more – all applied to the task of creating and managing a successful enterprise.

The forms that businesses take might be limitless, but the essence of how to run a company remains the same. The company you will run in this course designs, builds, and sells electronic sensors, but our goal is not to learn about sensors, it's to build the skills you need to effectively manage a business – any business organization at all.

... And develop mastery!

The good news is that brilliant and successful business people – whether it's Mukesh Ambani, Bill Gates, Rupert Murdoch, or Mark Zuckerberg - were not born with a "business success" gene. Their success is not simply due to an inbuilt talent, and this means any one of us could be successful in business one day.

The bad news is that like all successful business people, we need to devote thousands and thousands of hours to our goal - trying and failing, learning from our mistakes, and trying again - because it turns out that while many of us have the right attributes to be successful in business, not all of us are willing to invest the time.

To become expert in any field, we need to engage in what is called "deep practice."

Deep practice

This is not to say genetics is always irrelevant – if you want to be a world-class basketball player, it helps to be tall – but few occupations require specialized characteristics such as height. Most require a combination of skills that can be developed and honed through practice, and this is especially true for business acumen.

Success is often embedded in environmental influences. For example, the presence or absence of a great coach or mentor matters significantly. The presence of a role model in the culture also influences success. The opportunity to develop a skill matters most of all. One cannot become a pianist when there are no pianos.

After only 100 hours of deep practice, a person becomes noticeably better at a subject than ordinary people. At 1000 hours, he or she becomes highly skilled in that subject, and it does not stop there. Thus, "talent" becomes somewhat predictable and measurable. One can say that a person with 100 hours of deep practice is less competent than a person with 1,000 hours of deep practice.

Viewed in this way, talent becomes a choice. Every person must trade off the time to develop one talent for time spent on another. The more time spent focused on a single talent, the less time can be given to others.

Business acumen is a function of deep practice; talent has little to do with it.

Sensors: a fast-growing sector

Electronic sensors – the product you will be designing, producing, marketing, and selling during your simulation – exist in many applications. One crucial sector is the fast-growing consumer electronics market.

With "wearables" a hot trend in electronic devices, the health-conscious, tech-savvy buyers in the "quantified-self" market are being offered devices to measure their energy input and output against personal fitness goals. Wearables all require sensors.

Jawbone (the industrial design company that brought us sleek, in-ear Bluetooth devices) launched its fitness-tracking device, a wrist band called Up, in late 2011. Jawbone had to withdraw Up after a month due to technical problems. Nike+ took advantage of Up's withdrawal to promote its FuelBand in early 2012. By the end of that year, Up was back, and the two products continue to compete as they provide their unique approaches to measuring everything from how many steps taken to how many calories consumed in a day.

FuelBand offers immediate feedback on the device and works with a proprietary Nike Fuel Points system you can share (if you choose to boast) on Facebook or Twitter. Up has to be plugged into a mobile device (Apple or Android) to provide feedback, but offers expert advice on how to improve your fitness regimen, plus – looking more like a fashion accessory – it wins design accolades. Both products have one major shortcoming however: Placing sensors at the wrist means they cannot measure energy expended on activities that don't require much arm movement, like cycling.

Sporting a FuelBand on his own wrist, Apple CEO Tim Cook told the All Things Digital Conference in May 2013 that the problems to be solved in building wearable electronics were not trivial – but they would be good news for the sensor industry: "The whole sensor field is going to explode," Cook said. "It's already exploding. It's a little all over the place right now, but with the arc of time, it will become clearer I think."

Simulations and deep practice

Simulations are designed to offer focused opportunities for deep practice. That is why they are often more effective than passive tools such as textbooks, videos, or lectures.

By the way, "deep practice" is very different from "ordinary practice." After all, automobile commuters accumulate thousands of hours of driving, but that does not make them expert drivers. The key to deep practice is self-awareness. That is, paying attention to what you are doing well *and* not so well. This is so important to learning that scientists use a specific term for it: "metacognition," or thinking about the way you think and learn.

Deep practice has these characteristics:

- It is intentional. You are consciously seeking improvement as you practice.
- It is at the limits of your present capability.
- You fail. Often. If you did not, you would not be at the limits of your capability. You try again.
- You are seeking incremental improvement in each practice session, not breakthroughs.
- You are practicing the right things, not the wrong things. This often requires a coach.
- You have a feedback system in place, one that tells you when you are right and when you are wrong.
- You spend between half an hour and three hours a day in deep practice. If you spend more, you are getting diminishing returns. There is only so much you can accomplish in one day.

Simulations work because they are hands-on experiences that mimic the real world. Well-designed simulations, such as *Foundation Business Simulation,* present problems at the limits of your capabilities, offer positive and negative feedback, have a "coach," and work your brain in a way that builds your business skills. Throughout the training, you can witness the incremental improvements in yourself over time.

Here is a list of "do's and don'ts" that will enable you to use this simulation to develop your business acumen, in much the same way that you might use a gym to build muscle.

Do's:

- Feedback is critically important to deep practice. The simulation delivers it via your online interface and in your reports. Both positive feedback and negative feedback are important. When the results come in, compare your expectations with the actual results. Why were you right? Why were you wrong? This applies when your results are both better than expected and worse than expected.
- Focus on your portion of the company's decisions each round. In sports, a player may spend a day of practice on only one skill. This same principle applies to business acumen and management skills.

- Add a new skill each round such as pricing for products, sales forecasting, production analysis, financial modeling, and so forth.
- Practice the old skills as well as the new skill.
- Use your coaches. These include your instructor, of course, but also the automated coaches that produce the Analyst Report, the Balanced Scorecard Report, and the Rubric Report. If you encounter something you do not understand, the answer is probably in the online support

system, or you can contact *Help@Capsim.*

Don'ts:

- Do not treat failure as a bad thing. Failure is a good thing. It means that you are practicing at the limits of your ability. It has been estimated that Olympic ice skaters fall 20,000 times on their way to the gold. The skaters practice at their limits, focusing on the movements that make them fall. Failure is also feedback. An emergency loan, a stock-out, a capacity shortage – simulations are designed to highlight mistakes such as these – but the important questions are, "What led to the failure?" and "How can I avoid this in the future?"

- Do not ask others to do it for you. Do the work yourself. Do not seek help from past or present students. This is the equivalent of going to the gym to watch other people work out.

- Do not be concerned with the confusion you will feel at the beginning of the simulation. Of course you are confused – you have never run a multimillion-dollar company before. Trust the process. The confusion will fade.

- Do not focus on your mistakes. That angst locks you in place and prevents growth. As difficult as it is to accept, if you are not looking bad, you are not growing.

So let's begin.

Each module in this course includes a chapter introduction, followed by the opportunity for experience in running a company, and deep practice exercises designed to improve key skills.

There will be constant opportunities to practice what you are learning, to try, fail and try again in your business, with your own results.

And so: good luck!

You – in the executive suite!

When a monopoly sensor manufacturer was broken up, six companies were formed from the existing company, with each new company being the same size and configuration. The new companies were registered as Andrews, Baldwin, Chester, Digby, Erie, and Ferris.

In your simulation experience, you will have the chance to run one of these companies, either by yourself or as part of a management team, depending on how your instructor has set up your course.

Before you can run the whole company, however, you will need a period of orientation to get to know the company and the market in which it operates. Imagine the Andrews Board of Directors has just hired you. A Board of Directors is a body of appointed or elected members that represents the owners' (the shareholders') interests by overseeing the activities of the company. You will start work on a job rotation track. That means the Board wants you to cycle through each of the key management roles at the company in order to gain experience in each area of the business.

The preparation exercises that follow will help you to understand your market and your customers. In all of the exercises in this book, try to focus on cause and effect. Constantly ask yourself "what is the true impact of the decision I made?" and look deeper than the most obvious answer

Exercise #1: Meet Your Company

Your Product

First things first, what does your company do? Andrews Corporation designs, manufactures, and sells electronic sensors. Sensors are devices that observe and measure physical conditions. They are used in products ranging from a game controller to sophisticated aeronautics. Your company sells sensors to other manufacturers who use them in their products. That means you are in a "business to business" market, selling to Original Equipment Manufacturers (OEMs) not directly to individual consumers. But what do your sensors look like?

Your company makes one sensor called Able. It has a plastic housing with mounting brackets that contains the sophisticated processors. It has connectors that allow it to be integrated into your customers' products. You have been told the market is developing quickly and that your product will have to get smaller and the processor will have to get faster to meet ongoing demands.

When you were preparing for your interview with the Board of Directors, you read that NASA was using solar radiation sensors that incorporated one of your products. You look that up in your company's information system and find your sensor is the centerpiece of the product ... pretty cool!

Your Management Team

Your company's organizational chart includes four major departments:

Marketing is responsible for understanding what your customers want and creating value for them. Marketing sets the prices of your products and manages sales and promotions budgets.

Production is responsible for the efficient manufacturing of your products.

Research & Development is responsible for designing new products and redesigning existing products.

Finance ensures that all company activities – operations and investments – are fully funded. Finance includes the **Accounting** team, which is responsible for developing and communicating financial information to inform your decision making.

There are also two other departments, **Human Resources** and **Quality Management.**

Your Facilities

You take a walk around the plant, and you're impressed. The factory and warehouse are located on one campus. There is currently one production line, but you are told the company could add as many as four on its current site, so there is plenty of room to grow.

Andrew's Company Headquarters. You are shown to your office, get a parking pass, find the cafeteria and rest rooms and begin to settle in.

Factory. The factory currently has capacity to make 800,000 units (sensors) a year per shift. Last year the factory employed 154 production workers in the first shift and another 94 in the second shift. The factory works on two 12-hour shifts, seven days a week. You take a good look around and note that the production machinery is not as technologically sophisticated as you thought it would be.

Warehouse. This facility stores the:

- Component parts inventory (the pieces that are combined to produce your product) and
- Finished goods inventory (the number of units of your product Able that are available for sale).

Exercise #2: Gearing Up for the Simulation

Now it is time to familiarize yourself with the online resources available to help you get up to speed on your company and begin to run it.

Activities: Approximately 60 -90 minutes to complete.   COMPLETED

A-1: Get familiar with the website: www.capsim.com. This website provides the interface you will use to enter all the decisions you are going to make about your company. Your first step is to log onto www.capsim.com – using the login information provided by your instructor – and go to "Getting Started" which is the first link on the welcome page.   ☐

A-2: Introductory Video: Under Getting Started, the first option on the left menu bar, you will find the Introductory Lesson video. Please view the video. You can also access it via this code.

Throughout this book, QR codes like this one can take you directly to online material via your smart phone or tablet. If you don't have a QR reader, just search for and download the QR reader app for your device.   ☐

A-3: Read the following text to the end of the module. Complete all of the required tables and watch the videos. This is your orientation as Sales and Marketing Manager of Andrews Company.   ☐

A-4: **Familiarize yourself with the Summary Guide – Appendix 1.** In Appendix 1 we have included a condensed version of the rules and parameters of the model. Please read **The Course Roadmap** on 193. You will find a more comprehensive guide at the second tab on your online Foundation interface, under Getting Started. Take a look through the topics in the Guide so you'll know where to find the information you need to help you as you progress.   ☐

A-5: **Open the Web Spreadsheet – Please see full instructions in the box below.** This interface provides a model of your company and enables you to:

- Make decisions in each department: Research and Development, Marketing, Production, Finance, Human Resources and Total Quality Management

- Access pro forma accounting documents (e.g., the Balance Sheet, Income Statement, and Statement of Cash Flows). These pro forma statements are projections of what may occur for the coming year based upon the decisions you have made.   ☐

- View reports such as the FastTrack and Annual Report. These report the actual results of last year's decisions and establish the starting conditions for the year in which you are making decisions.

A-6: **Print a copy of the Foundation FastTrack** from the Reports tab in the interface – you will need it for Module 1 Exercises.   ☐

FOUNDATION
Rounds of the Simulation

Throughout your course, your instructor will guide you through rounds of the simulation. You will begin with practice rounds, where you can 'test drive' your corporation. Practice rounds give you the opportunity to play with the software, test some assumptions, see how the model responds to various inputs and make as many mistakes as you like – because it's just practice!

Following the Practice Rounds come the Competition Rounds where you have the opportunity to run your company in a competitive marketplace against up to five additional Foundation companies.

Your instructor will provide you with a schedule for the practice and competition rounds of Foundation Business Simulation.

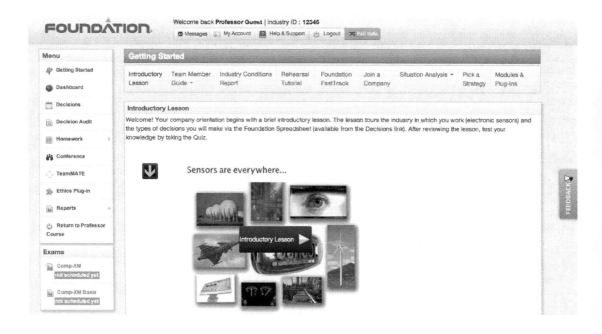

1 What is a business and how does it work?

Learning Objectives:

After reading this module and completing the associated exercises, you will be able to:

LO1: Define what a business represents and why businesses exist.

LO2: Define essential business concepts including products, services, profits, and stakeholders.

LO3: Describe the major functions of business.

LO4: Discuss the role of management in business success.

LO5: Differentiate between performance effectiveness and efficiency.

LO6: Describe the enterprise system and how it relates to business.

LO7: Differentiate between internal and external stakeholders.

LO8: Discuss key market concepts such as specialization, uncertainty, and risk.

LO9: Compare and contrast economic and opportunity costs.

LO10: Describe the differences between financial and managerial accounting.

Key Terms To Look For:

- *Business functions*
- *Decision making*
- *Demand*
- *Enterprise system*
- *Innovation*

- *Management*
- *Markets*
- *Products*
- *Supply*
- *Stakeholders*

An Overview of Business Basics

What is a business?

A business can be defined as any organization that provides products, services or both to individual consumers or to other organizations. The essential role of a business is to create products or offer services that satisfy customer needs or wants. Whether is it creating smart phones or offering home delivery of groceries, businesses could not exist without someone desiring their products or services.

Let us start with some basic definitions of essential concepts:

PRODUCT: a good that has tangible characteristics and that provides satisfaction or benefits (e.g., an automobile).

SERVICE: an activity that has intangible characteristics and that provides satisfaction or benefits (e.g., a mechanic performing automotive repair)

PROFIT: the basic goal of most businesses. Profit is the difference between what it costs to make and sell a product or service and what the customer pays for it.

STAKEHOLDERS: groups of people who have a vested interest (a "stake") in the actions a business might take. There are four major groups of stakeholders: (1) owners, (2) employees, (3) customers, and (4) society. The specific interests of each of these stakeholder groups may sometimes conflict with each other.

To summarize, a business sells products or services with the specific goal of making a profit, and in the process has an impact on various stakeholders. Business, however, is much more interesting than its definitions.

As described in the introduction, every business requires three basic resources – people, ideas, and money – that are configured and reconfigured over and over again to satisfy the needs and wants of customers. In that process there may be winners and losers, there may be cheaters, heroes, hard work, laughter, tears – the theory of business may be straightforward, but the experience of business is an exciting, ever-changing story, as you will discover in the Foundation Business Simulation. Let's look at the way businesses deploy their three important resources.

Business Functions and Functioning

Each business must employ people to entice customers, produce its products or services, organize workflow, plan to fund or pay for its operations, and more. Whatever type of business it is, the work that has to be done will typically fall into four basic "business functions."

MARKETING is all the activities designed to provide the goods and services that satisfy customers. These activities include market research, development of products, pricing, promotion, and distribution.

PRODUCTION refers to the activities and processes used in making products or delivering services. These activities involve designing the production processes (investments in facilities and equipment) and the efficient management and operation of those processes.

ACCOUNTING is the process that tracks, summarizes, and analyzes a company's financial position.

FINANCE refers to the activities concerned with funding a company and using resources effectively.

There is no one simple formula for successful business functioning or performance. Put simply, ideas (innovation + product development) + people (marketing + operations + leadership) + money (finance + accounting) *does not equal* a well-functioning business. Business is all about complex interactions – external interactions with customers, competitors, communities, and regulators – and internal interactions between all the people who operate the functions of the business itself. Engineers, computing wizards, accountants, human resource professionals, creative designers, marketers, and sales people – they may all be necessary to a business, but they are not sufficient to guarantee success.

To be successful, businesses need good managers who are able to see the big picture and understand how all the individual business functions work together. Fortunately, we know a lot about what goes into good management.

Managing a Business

As we discussed earlier, without customers a business would not be sustainable. This fact also applies to managers – without managers a business would wither and die. Successful management requires individuals who juggle the trade-offs and compromises necessary to keep a complex business moving along a clear strategic track. These individuals must also display intellectual flexibility to adjust to changing customer demands, and be able to harness the impact of creative abrasion that results from dealing with various business stakeholders who often have colliding agendas that must be met in the drive for success, profitability, and sustainability.

However, when we say "success," what do we really mean? One useful way to think about success in management is that it entails the two "E's" of performance: effectiveness and

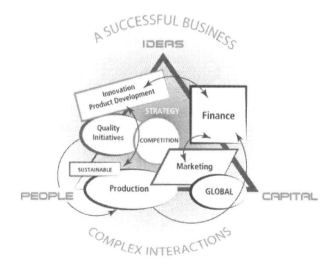

efficiency. Performance effectiveness means *doing the right thing*. Performance efficiency means *doing things right*.

Being **effective** involves committing to a course of action that allows you to accomplish your goals. It is a measure of how appropriately and successfully your actions achieve your goal. Being **efficient** refers to employing the right processes to achieve the goal. Efficiency is measured by comparing the resources invested with the outcomes achieved.

Decisions that shape the marketing, production, and financial functions of a business are often made in environments that are specialized, complex, uncertain, and risky. Managing these functions requires planning, organiz-ing, leading, and controlling all the important variables.

PLANNING: Determining what the organization needs to do and how to get it done.

ORGANIZING: Arranging the organization's resources and activities in such a way as to make it possible to accomplish the plan.

LEADING: Enacting the plan, including guiding and motivating employees to work toward accomplishing the necessary tasks.

CONTROLLING: Measuring and comparing performance to expectations established in the planning process and adjusting either the performance or the plan.

The critical ingredient – good management

 There are many reasons why good businesses go bad, but compare lists of "why businesses fail" and the most consistent cause is poor management. It may be defined as an inability to manage costs, poor planning, insufficient marketing, not anticipating shifts in the market – but who is responsible for all these things? Managers.

The gaming business, for example, is full of winners and losers but how could a company responsible for such ubiquitous products as the "Ville" series (FarmVille and its spin-offs) and the "With Friends" series (from 'Words with Friends' to 'Running with Friends') become a loser?

One key reason is that Zynga, maker of these games, did not anticipate the speed with which gamers were transitioning from web-based to mobile applications. Zynga management was not swift enough to implement the necessary research and development for new product implementation.

In December 2011 Zynga was valued at $9 billion. By its second quarter as a publicly traded company, Zynga's earnings were labeled "disastrous". Just over a year later, shares in the company were trading at 80% below their original value, and by February 2013 the company's valuation had plummeted to $2 billion.

The migration of gamers from computer screens to mobile devices shifted customer demands dramatically underneath Zynga's feet, but there were also shifting sands inside the company. In its first year, the company lost its Chief Financial Officer (CFO), Chief Mobile Officer (CMO), Chief Operating Officer (COO) plus its Chief Creative Officer (CCO). In 2013 it was the Chief Games Designer followed by Chief Executive Officer (CEO) Mark Pincus, who moved aside to be Chairman and Chief Product Officer.

Research Zynga and you will find a disproportionate number of articles about the company's management problems and instability in the senior executive ranks. In June 2013 Zynga cut 520 people – 18% of its workforce – and closed offices in New York, Los Angeles and Dallas. Take a look at the company today. Has it recovered from its management challenges?

Regardless of the business functions or the types of managerial decisions to be made, effective and efficient management cannot be achieved without leadership. At higher levels of responsibility, people who may be referred to as chief executives or senior managers fill leadership roles. Of course, the more people, functions, and processes a company has, the more its senior management will need to align and coordinate management activities. You will have the opportunity to experience a plethora of management challenges in your simulated company, particularly if you are operating in a team where each team member, depending on his or her business function, will pursue different interests.

The Big Picture: The Enterprise System

Now that we've discussed some basics about business, business functions, and management, let's look a little closer at the economic forces that impact business functioning.

Businesses operate within an overall economic system. There are at least three key terms to understand when thinking about overall economic systems.

> MARKET: a mechanism that facilitates the exchange of goods and services between buyers and sellers.

Stakeholders' changing needs and demands

The Easy-Bake Oven may have been a favorite toy of American children for more than 50 years, but in recent years Hasbro, its manufacturer, has had to respond dramatically to stakeholders including both customers and government regulators.

The toy, launched in 1963, is a working oven in which mini-portions of cake mix and other treats are fed on small trays into a slot and emerge cooked. In 2003 it was voted Parenting magazine's Toy of the Year. In 2006 it was inducted into the American Toy Hall of Fame. Since then, however, Hasbro has dealt with health and safety concerns, environmental legislation, and claims of sexism related to the Easy-Bake design.

In early 2007 nearly a million of the pink-and-purple ovens were recalled. Hasbro had received 249 reports of children getting their hands or fingers caught in the oven's opening, including 77 reports of burns, 16 of which were reported as second- and third-degree burns, with one leading to a partial finger amputation for a 5-year-old girl.

After the recall, a redesigned oven was launched, powered by the heat source the Easy-Bake used from the beginning – an incandescent bulb. Environmental legislation announced by President George W. Bush that same year, however, required a phase-out of incandescent bulbs by 2012. In 2011 Hasbro launched a new oven, powered by a heating element.

The next year, a New Jersey teen, McKenna Pope, collected 40,000 signatures – including those of several celebrity chefs – asking Hasbro to launch an Easy-Bake that was gender neutral. McKenna claimed the oven's feminine-looking pinks and purples alienated her younger brother. At the 2013 Toy Show, Hasbro launched an oven in black and silver. Responding to this pressure may have proved controversial internally, however, because it was not Hasbro's first attempt to appeal to boys. In 2002 it had launched the Queasy Bake Cookerator, making "boy friendly" treats such as Chocolate Crud Cake and Dip 'N Drool Dog Bones. The product failed to reach adequate sales and was withdrawn.

It can be difficult – even for an established product such as the Easy-Bake and an established manufacturer such as Hasbro – to keep up with the various pressures from different stakeholders.

DEMAND: the quantity of goods and services that consumers are willing to buy at different prices.

SUPPLY: the quantity of goods and services that businesses are willing to provide at those prices.

The terms of a sales transaction, or the quantity of goods traded and the trading price, are determined by the supply of and demand for any particular good or service.

Economic systems are typically, but not always, embedded in a framework of activities that are carried out by mostly democratic elected representatives (the government) of a society within its geographic boundaries. Activities that serve the society by fulfilling basic needs (e.g. roads, defense, security) or needs that no other business can serve (e.g. judicial branches) are performed by *public enterprises.*

Unlike public enterprises, the simulated company you will run in the Foundation Simulation is a *private enterprise.* In private enterprise systems individual citizens (rather than governments) own and operate the majority of businesses. Private enterprise systems require four essential conditions:

1. Private property
2. Freedom of choice

Innovation sparks growth

He has been called the "Steve Jobs of yogurt". Hamdi Ulukaya, a Turkish immigrant to the United States, built the Chobani yogurt company that made him a billionaire (according to Forbes magazine) in six years due to obsessive focus on brewing the perfect cup of yogurt.

Ulukaya's first business in the U.S. was a small cheese factory in New York that he opened because his father, on a visit from Turkey, could not find any decent feta in the local stores. Ulukaya's feta factory survived, but when he switched to yogurt, he thrived. In 2005 he bought an almost defunct yogurt factory Kraft was trying to sell in New Berlin, N.Y., with a U.S. Government small business loan (private enterprise loans, guaranteed by a public enterprise: the U.S. Small Business Administration). In 2007 he launched an innovation into the already crowded yogurt market: low-fat, sugar-free, Greek-style yogurt with a taste customers loved.

As Ulukaya told USA Today: *"I literally lived in the plant for 18 months to make that perfect cup. And then five years after, it just exploded. I did not have all the ideas right from the beginning. I just jumped in and learned the swimming right in there."*

Chobani went from six employees to 3,000 in five years and added a second plant in Twin Falls, Idaho, in 2012. Chobani was shipping 19.2 million containers of yogurt a week by mid-2013. Ulukaya said that when he launched Chobani, Greek yogurt was 1% of the yogurt market in the United States, but within five years it was almost 60%. *"So we take quite a bit of credit for that. What we did was make it for everyone, and we made it delicious. And when people tasted it for the first time, this wow effect came in."*

Innovation, however, was not restricted to the mass-production of Greek-style yogurt. Other new businesses followed. As Ulukaya told USA Today: *"That old plant that we turned back to life opened four different other factories somewhere else because of the butterfly effect. So you open the Greek yogurt factory. Then somebody has to make a cup factory. Somebody has to make a foil factory. Somebody has to make a fruit factory. Then the farmers have to add more cows. Then the people have to work on the farms. Then the trucks have to go up to those factories. All of that contributes to billions and billions of dollars invested and thousands of jobs created."*

3. The right to keep profits
4. An environment where fair competition can occur

The theory underlying the private enterprise system is that competition among businesses will produce an efficient allocation of resources across the economy. Goods and services are desired where they produce the greatest benefit or are used most productively. Throughout this economic process, pressure is exerted from several areas. For example, there is pressure to lower prices and pressure to innovate through technological and procedural improvements.

When businesses compete in a private enterprise system, value is created for consumers. Customers are offered additional choices because businesses are motivated to innovate,

Stakeholders in an oil spill

On April 20th 2010, an explosion on the Deepwater Horizon oil rig, operated by British Petroleum in the Gulf of Mexico, triggered the largest marine oil spill of its type in U.S. history.

The rig sank, 11 people were killed, 17 were seriously wounded and oil flowed underwater from the well, discharging more than 200 million gallons before it was declared fully capped in September. On April 30th President Barack Obama said: *"This oil spill is the worst environmental disaster America has ever faced ... Make no mistake: We will fight this spill with everything we've got for as long as it takes. We will make BP pay for the damage their company has caused. And we will do whatever's necessary to help the Gulf Coast and its people recover from this tragedy."*

The scale of the disaster resulted in adverse effects on a very wide range of stakeholders. Owners saw their investment in BP halved as the market capitalization of the company plunged from $180 billion in April 2010 to $90 billion by June of that year. Employees suffered not only from the direct and indirect effects of the deaths and injuries, but from the impact of working for the world's largest oil producer one day, and its most infamous the next. Customers felt less inclined to buy BP products with BP-branded gas stations in the U.S. (most of which are not owned by BP) suffering losses of between 10% and 40% of sales.

It was, however, society that felt the largest impacts. In Louisiana, for example, 17% of all jobs are related to the oil industry. Job losses in the state followed a moratorium on offshore drilling, implemented while investigations were underway. Jobs were lost in tourism (the industry reports losing $23 billion in the region) and fishing (reported losses of $2.5 billion), as the effects of the spill and cleanup efforts devastated both industries. Health issues included 143 cases of chemical poisoning in the first two months of the disaster alone, with the American Journal of Disaster Medicine suggesting *"cancers, liver and kidney disease, mental health disorders, birth defects and developmental disorders should be anticipated among sensitive populations and those most heavily exposed."* The oil spill area included more than 8,000 species of fish, birds, mollusks, crustaceans, sea turtles and marine mammals, with effects on these animals including death from oil or the cleanup chemicals, disease, birth defects and mutations, and lesions and sores.

By mid-2013 BP had paid out or earmarked more than $42 billion for cleanup, compensation, and environmental fines, selling assets to help cover the cost. The company was charged with 11 counts of manslaughter under U.S. law for the deaths of workers and it is being tried under provisions of the Clean Water Act. The U.S. Government National Commission investigation into the disaster placed blame for the spill squarely at the feet of BP and its contractors Halliburton and Transocean, citing cost cutting and insufficient safety procedures. The disaster is one of the most vivid examples in recent history of how errors in business can negatively and dramatically impact a wide range of stakeholders.

often through technological advancements to improve their offerings and make them more attractive. *Innovation* of processes, products, and services also motivates businesses to price their offerings attractively to position themselves for future and sustainable success.

Internal and External Stakeholders

Within an economic system are various groups with a stake in the way businesses operate. Earlier, we defined these different groups as business "stakeholders". All businesses will have stakeholders from the four categories we discussed. One way to think of these stakeholders is in terms of their being either internal or external to a business.

The key *internal* stakeholders are owners (stockholders/shareholders), who derive economic benefits when the business makes a profit, and whose investments lose value when it doesn't, and employees, who also derive economic benefits through wages but can experience additional benefits (such as training and experience) or disadvantages (exposure to toxins/accidents). The key *external* stakeholders are customers, who want the best product or service possible for the lowest possible price, and the society at large that may also be benefited (more jobs for more people leading to more tax revenue) or disadvantaged (toxic waste in the water system/market failures).

The private enterprise system needs laws to make corrections when markets do not produce outcomes desirable for the people who live in a society. The laws are set by governments elected to act on behalf of the whole society – and they are designed to protect all stakeholders according to a mutual sense of justice. In this sense, governments establish rules for the overall economic system designed to balance the needs of the society with the drivers of profit.

All areas of law or regulation that influence business practice contribute to our shared definition of fairness. Examples include establishing standards of conduct in negotiating contracts with a company's buyers or suppliers, providing information (advertising) to consumers, providing information to potential investors, and negotiating with employees or their representatives.

To summarize, we have an overall economic system based on privately owned businesses, regulated to ensure the rights of all stakeholders are protected, and fueled by transactions between buyers and sellers in various markets. Next we will look at the notion of a market.

Markets – The Engine that Keeps it All Running

A market – according to our definition – is a mechanism that facilitates the exchange of goods and services between buyers and sellers. From cavemen trading stone tools for bison meat, to the NASDAQ (an electronic market for buyers and sellers of stock), informal and formal markets have existed as long as human demand has been able to find a source of supply.

Some terms you'll come across in relation to markets are *specialization, uncertainty,* and *risk*.

In an economic context, *specialization* is a measure of how broadly or narrowly the range of activities performed by a business is defined. A bicycle shop, for example, is a more specialized retail store than Wal-Mart because the bicycle shop focuses on a narrow and deep range of products. Specialization creates an opportunity for greater efficiency and increased productivity. The division of tasks that comes with specialization introduces a need for coordination of those specialized tasks. These different levels of specialization and different kinds of coordinating mechanisms create a complex economic environment.

Markets are also characterized by *uncertainty* and *risk*. Uncertainty is not knowing an exact outcome or not being able to predict the exact consequences of a choice in a decision situation. The greater the uncertainty, the less you can know about the results of a particular choice. Decision makers must work to reduce uncertainty by compiling as much relevant information as possible about a decision situation. Risk is also associated with the consequences of choice; therefore risk is a measure of the significance of those decisions.

Decision Making – The Critical Skill

When planning, organizing, operating, and controlling a company, decisions are constantly made and the quality of those decisions determines, to a large extent, whether and how the company will achieve its goals. In today's world of work, teams make the vast majority of strategic, high-impact decisions. These teams can range from product development teams and quality control teams to top management teams comprised of executives from each business function.

The process of defining problems and opportunities that merit attention, generating and evaluating alternative courses of action, and committing to the action that is most likely to produce the optimal result is one way to describe the decision-making process.

Decision making also involves comparing the economic and opportunity rewards (benefits) and sacrifices (costs) involved in a course of action and committing to the one that best meets your goals. The objective is to make the parties involved "better off" than they were before the transaction took place. Typically, good decisions are commitments that help you accomplish your goals in whatever way you define them. Business decisions primarily focus on gaining economic rewards, which means there is an assumption that we only engage in transactions that offer the potential to improve our "position." When we choose a course of action, it requires a sacrifice to obtain the reward. In economic terms, this sacrifice is called a "cost." When evaluating alternative choices, a decision maker considers two kinds of costs, the economic cost and the opportunity cost:

An *economic cost* is the money spent implementing the decision.

An *opportunity cost* is the cost of what you gave up doing when you committed to the course of action you chose.

Everyday Life: Opportunity Cost

Consider being offered two jobs. One offers $10,000 more in base salary but few prospects for promotion. The other offers less money but has more opportunities for promotion and future training. You have two choices: Take the higher paying job, or the lower paying job. The economic cost of taking the second job is $10,000. The opportunity cost of taking the first job is the chance for promotion, future training, and higher pay in the future. In the long run, opportunity costs are often more important than economic costs, but economic costs are generally easier to determine than opportunity costs.

Assessing opportunity costs is important to determine the *true cost* of any decision. Opportunity cost can measure anything that is of value. The opportunity cost is not the sum of the available alternatives, but rather the benefit of the best single alternative. If there is no explicit accounting or monetary cost attached to a course of action, ignoring opportunity costs may create an illusion that the benefits cost nothing at all, turning them into a *hidden cost* associated with that action. The opportunity cost of a company's decision to build a new plant on vacant land the company owns, for example, is the loss of the land for another purpose, such as using it to build

a facility to be leased to another business, or to have access to the cash that could have been generated from selling the land. Only one set of choices is possible. Only one set of benefits is attainable.

Accounting – Keeping Track of Financial Outcomes

Every business keeps track of its financial health through accounting. Accounting is a set of rules applied to a company's financial records that allows owners and managers to monitor, analyze, and plan the finances of the business. In short, accounting deals with the business resource of "money" we discussed at the beginning of this chapter.

Whatever business you are in, the stakeholders in your business – and that, as we know, might be owners and shareholders, potential buyers, customers, or even the government's tax office – need to have a consistent frame of reference for assessing the financial health of your company. That consistent frame of reference is the company's financial reports. To understand the financial reports, however, we need to understand some of the basic principles that underpin the rules and principles of accounting.

There are two major types of accounting: *Financial Accounting* and *Management Accounting*.

Financial Accounting produces the balance sheets, income statements, and cash flow statements that ensure external stakeholders can access the information they need. These stakeholders are usually people and groups outside the company who need accounting information to decide whether or not to engage in some activity with the company. That might include individual investors; stockbrokers and financial analysts who offer investment assistance; consultants; bankers; suppliers; labor unions; customers; local, state, and federal governments; and governments of foreign countries in which the company does business.

Management Accounting provides vital information about a company to internal users. Because it is for internal use, it does not have to conform to the restrictions of outside regulation and can be expressed in whatever way is most useful for managers. Information can be reported in dollars, units, hours worked, products manufactured, number of defective products, or the quantity of contracts signed. The job of a management accountant is to produce information that is relevant to specific segments of the company's products, tasks, plants, or activities. The goal of that information is to enable managers to make more informed and effective decisions.

The reports a management accountant produces might forecast revenues, predict costs of planned activities, and provide analysis based on those forecasts. By describing how alternative actions might affect the company's profit and solvency, forecasts and analyses help managers plan.

We'll talk in greater detail about financial accounting and reports such as income statements, cash flow statements, and balance sheets in Modules 4 and 5. More detail will be provided on managerial accounting including budgets, cost analysis, and management reporting in Modules 2 and 3, which cover marketing and production.

Chapter Review Questions

Business Basics

1. What are the four main business stakeholder groups?

2. What are the primary functions of business?

3. What are the four major activities involved in managing a business?

4. What is the difference between performance effectiveness and performance efficiency?

The Private Enterprise System

5. How would you define supply?

6. How would you define demand?

7. How would define a market?

8. What are the four conditions that must exist for the free enterprise system to exist?

9. What are the implications of the relationship between supply and demand?

10. What are the differences between internal and external stakeholders?

11. What is specialization?

12. How would you illustrate the concept of "uncertainty"?

13. How would you illustrate the concept of "risk"?

Decision Making

14. What is the difference between an economic cost and an opportunity cost?

15. What is the main purpose of the accounting function of a business?

16. What are the differences between financial and managerial accounting?

You – in the executive suite!

Sales and Marketing Manager

Let's start putting all that theory into practice. The web-based simulation you are about to begin allows you to apply all of the important business concepts we've discussed. You will address marketing, production, accounting, and finance issues and manage your company's production and sale of goods. With less than perfect information, you will have to decide what volume of product to produce, how to promote your products, how much to invest in your sales activities, how to finance your expenses, and how to assess your financial performance.

However, you are not expected to be able to do it all right now!

As we discussed in the introduction, you will begin your career in the sensor industry on a job rotation track.

In the Introduction chapter, we took a look at Andrews Corporations' structure (R&D, Marketing, Production, Finance, Human Resources and Quality Departments) and at your facility, which currently has one production line.

Now let's take a look at the industry in which your company operates and begin your first rotation: as *Sales and Marketing Manager.*

Activities: Approximately 60 minutes to complete.

COMPLETED

A-1: Go to http://capsim.com/go/v/fft. This is a video about the Foundation FastTrack. The FastTrack is the report that you are using in all of these exercises.

While some of the information in the FastTrack may be obscure at the moment, take a look at this 5 minute video to appreciate what it will offer you as you begin to run your company. ☐

A-2: In the Summary Guide at Appendix 1 read The Reports on page 194. ☐

A-3: Read the following text to the end of the module. Complete all of the required tables and watch the videos. This is your orientation as Sales and Marketing Manager of Andrews Company. ☐

Exercise #3: Building understanding of your industry and customers

Understanding Your Sensor Industry

Why does a business exist? To create wealth. How does it do that? By satisfying customers. So your first step, as you get to know your company and market, is to understand your customers and what they want. On your desk you find a Customer Report that shows that the sensor industry in which you operate has two major market segments. The customers you are hoping to attract are looking for either low tech sensors or high tech sensors – two different segments of the same market. Your product, Able, sits in the middle of the two segments, which suggests to you that it's not completely satisfying either market.

Let's take a look at the two market segments – low tech and high tech – by seeing what the Foundation FastTrack report can tell us.

Go to the copy of the FastTrack you printed out at the end of the Introduction Preparation Exercises OR look it up online (log onto www.capsim.com with your user name and password and follow the instructions for "How to Launch the Spreadsheet" in the Introduction Preparation Exercise. The FastTrack is under the Reports tab in the online interface.)

FOUNDĀTION.

Why is every company the same?
You'll notice that each company – Andrews, Baldwin, Chester, Digby, Erie, and Ferris has exactly the same numbers. That's because, when the monopoly was broken up, all six companies were created equally. The numbers in this report will begin to change dramatically as soon as you make your first decision.

The FastTrack presents statistics from last year – you'll see that it is dated December 31st of the preceding year (top right header). Each year, you will use last year's information to help inform your decisions for the coming year.

Every year your customers' requirements, the tactics of the companies in the market and, therefore, the market itself, are changing. The information in the FastTrack is old news – it's last year's results. One of the critical skills you will develop is how to use historical information to study emerging patterns, to understand cause and effect relationships between decisions and outcomes, and project the best course of action for the future.

You will need *Page 4: Low Tech Market Segment Analysis* and *Page 5: High Tech Market Segment Analysis.* Let's look at the statistics box in the top left corner of pages 4 and 5 of the Foundation FastTrack.

This box shows the total industry unit demand (for last year), the actual sales (for last year), the percentage of total industry for each segment (70% for low tech, 30% for high tech), and next year's segment growth rate (10% for low tech, 20% for high tech). You see that the low tech sector is much larger than high tech, but the growth rate for high tech is twice that of low tech. Think about that for a moment. It might have very interesting implications for new product development, pricing policies, production schedules – a whole range of decisions you will make in the future.

Because the market is growing, you will need to multiply the FastTrack "Unit Demand" from last year by the growth rate every year. To visualize the size of the market in the future, take a couple of minutes to calculate its growth for the next eight years. Low tech is growing at 10%. To "grow" a number by 10%, multiply that number by 1.1. High tech is growing at 20%. To grow by 20%, multiply by 1.2. Complete Table 1 - Segment Growth - below and use it for future reference.

Table 1 - Segment Growth

Segment	Current	Growth	Year 1	Year 2	Year 3	Year 4	Year 5	Year 6	Year 7	Year 8
Low Tech	5,040	10%	5,544	6,098						
High Tech	2,160	20%								
Total	7,200									

Understanding Your Customers

What differentiates a low tech buyer from a high tech buyer? Obviously it is the type of product they are looking for, but it's also the criteria they use to make their buying decisions.

When you buy yourself a shirt, for example, you have your own buying criteria. The shirt has to be in your size, in a color you like, in a style that pleases you - plus it has to be the right price. So you can list your buying criteria as size, color, style, and price. But you might have those criteria prioritized differently. Price might be most important, for example, and color least important. It's the same for your sensor buyers.

All customers in the sensor market decide which product to buy based on four criteria:

PRICE: The statistics box we have been looking at in the FastTrack shows price expectations for low tech customers are $15 to $35 and for high tech customers $25 to $45. That is a big spread for pricing! You begin to consider what factors will make a customer pay top dollar and what factors you will have to control if you want to keep prices low.

AGE: Customers want to know how long ago the product was released or revised. Low tech customers are satisfied with older, proven products while high tech customers are looking for the latest release. Your customers have to consider their own designs and processes – a brand new, high tech sensor design may require upgrades to their own products to make them compatible.

RELIABILITY: This is measured as Mean Time Between Failure (MTBF) or how long the sensor will perform before it fails. Achieving a higher MTBF requires more expensive components.

POSITION: Position refers to where the product is graphed on a *perceptual map.* Your company uses perceptual maps (or a product attribute graph) to determine where the greatest concentration of buyers will be in a market. The map we are using has Size on the X axis and Performance on the Y axis. In other words, what combination of size and performance defines the product? Customers have certain combinations in mind to fulfill their needs – and those combinations are changing every month. For example, some customers look for increasingly miniaturized sensors with better and better performance while others are satisfied with larger products and average performance that improves more slowly. The second group still expects your sensors to get better, but at a slower rate so that their own manufacturing processes can keep up.

The Customer Report tells you that your customers not only have different expectations for products, but they place a different importance on each buying criterion.

It says:

1. Customers' expectations for price range, age, and reliability are relatively consistent over time, although there is a range of options for price and reliability.

2. Customers' expectations for position (size-performance) change constantly (month-to-month) as customers look for continuous improvement.

3. Low tech customers have different expectations (for position, price, age, and reliability) than high tech customers.

4. Low tech and high tech customers place different importance on each characteristic – for example, price is top priority for low tech buyers but age is the top priority in the high tech market.

The FastTrack gives you all the necessary detail in the statistics box we have been studying at the top left of pages 5 and 6.

Table 2 - Customer Buying Criteria

Low Tech Market Segment (page 5)	High Tech Market Segment (page 6)
1. Price: $15.00–35.00 (41%)	1. Ideal Position Pfmn.: 7.4 Size 12.6 (33%)
2. Ideal Age: 3.0 (29%)	2. Ideal Age: 0.0 (29%)
3. Reliability/MTBF: 14,000–20,000 (21%)	3. Price: $25.00 - 45.00 (25%)
4. Ideal Position Pfmn.: 4.8 Size 15.2 (9%)	4. Reliability/MTBF: 7,000–23,000 (13%)

To help you be very clear on what each customer wants from your products, take a moment to fill out the **Table 3** – Constant Customer Buying Criteria.

Table 3 - Constant Customer Buying Criteria

	Low Tech	High Tech	Overlap
Price			
Age			
Reliability			

Now let's look at the 4th criterion, **position**. Your company keeps track of customers' ex-
pectations by using a perceptual map, as you know. The map is a way to visualize how customers tend to cluster around certain product features in the marketplace.

First look at Page 8 of the Foundation FastTrack for the current perceptual map. As all of the six companies are the same at the moment, their products are graphed at exactly the same spot on the map. Customers in both market segments have only one option – until the competition heats up! Here is a perceptual map a little further along in a simulation, showing a range of different products:

Figure 1. From FastTrack Report - Perceptual Map

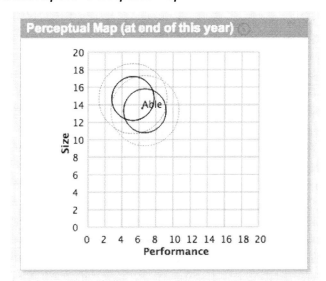

Positioning and the Perceptual Map

Product positioning on the perceptual map is an important concept that will help with your research and development, and your marketing decisions. To help build your understanding, please work through the Perceptual Map Demonstration at the website:

Select Help > Manager Guide > Demonstrations > Perceptual Map

There are three things you need to remember about the perceptual map:

1. Size and performance are interrelated product characteristics. A small sensor that is slow has little value in the market. Similarly, a high performance sensor that is large attracts no buyers. The Perceptual Map helps you visualize the interrelationship between performance and size.

2. Customers expect size and performance to improve constantly. From month-to-month and year-to-year, the size/performance combinations that your customers demand in each market segment will change.

3. All acceptable combinations of size and performance are not equally attractive to customers; each market segment has an "ideal" combination. We call this the "ideal spot" or the "sweet spot" in the market.

Market Expectations: Performance and Size

The circle that describes the market segment defines the acceptable combinations of performance and size. The circle in our perceptual map has a radius of 2.5 units – every combination of size and performance in that circle is acceptable to our customers. As we also know however, there is an ideal spot that represents the ideal combination of size and performance that customers would choose if they could – that is if the price was right, there was enough supply in the market, and the products were easily accessible.

In the low tech segment, the center of the market segment and the ideal spot are the same set of coordinates – 15.2 for size and 4.8 for performance at the beginning of the simulation. The biggest concentration of buyers, therefore, is around the central point of the circle.

In the high tech segment, the ideal spot is 1.4 units smaller and 1.4 units faster than the segment center. The biggest concentration of buyers in that market is at the leading edge. Because you know the segment center for each of the eight rounds, you can also determine the ideal spot.

Performance and Size Expectations by Round

On Table 4 - Performance and Size Expectations by Round, you can see the year-by-year progression of coordinates for the center of the market segment in both low tech and high tech. As you know, the segment center and the ideal spot are the same for low tech.

As you also know, the ideal spot for high tech is 1.4 units smaller and 1.4 units faster than the segment center. Please list the coordinates for the ideal spot in the high tech segment for the next eight years.

Table 4 - Performance and Size Expectations by Round

Round	Low Tech Segment Center / Ideal Spot		High Tech Segment Center		High Tech Ideal Spot	
	Perf.	Size	Perf.	Size	Perf.	Size
0	4.8	15.2	6.0	14.0		
1	5.3	14.7	6.7	13.3		
2	5.8	14.2	7.4	12.6		
3	6.3	13.7	8.1	11.9		
4	6.8	13.2	8.8	11.2		
5	7.3	12.7	9.5	10.5		
6	7.8	12.2	10.2	9.8		
7	8.3	11.7	10.9	9.1		
8	8.8	11.2	11.6	8.4		

Customers expect products to be smaller and faster every year (.5 units for low tech; .7 units for high tech). The expectations change every month – low tech by .042 (.5/12) and high tech by .058 (.7/12).

The monthly change for Low Tech is shown in Table 5 - Size and Performance Expectations by Month.

Table 5 - Size and Performance Expectations by Month for Low Tech

	Jan	Feb	Mar	April	May	June	July	Aug	Sept	Oct	Nov	Dec
Size	15.16	15.12	15.08	15.03	14.99	14.95	14.91	14.87	14.83	14.78	14.74	14.70
Perf.	4.84	4.88	4.93	4.97	5.01	5.05	5.09	5.13	5.18	5.22	5.26	5.30

This table should give you a strong understanding of the constant rate of change for customer expectations. Nothing in business is static!

Understanding Price

Now you have a good idea of the size and growth of your industry and you have looked at your customers' requirements. You have learned about your customers' buying criteria and how specifications such as size and performance can be interrelated and change over time.

Now let's investigate another important interrelationship: between customer demand and pricing.

Let's go back to the example of buying a shirt. If price is your top buying criterion, you are likely to look for the shirt at a discount retailer – either in a store or online. You might have to sacrifice choice of color or style to get the right price. If the latest style and a designer label are more important to you, you are most likely to shop at a high-end department store or a designer-branded store. You will sacrifice price for style. In other words, you are making trade-offs based on your criteria. The retailers are also making trade-offs. The discount retailer is geared toward making lots of sales for a lower price whereas the high-end designer store knows it will sell fewer items but will make more money on each.

As a business manager you will also be required to balance the trade-offs between price and other considerations in the business and the marketplace.

At this stage you cannot modify your product's size, performance, or MTBF – that comes when we move to Research & Development Manager. Experimenting with various prices, however, will demonstrate the elasticity of pricing and its effect on demand.

Our goal is to:

- Examine how price affects demand
- Identify price ranges for the low tech and high tech markets
- Provide an opportunity to use the Foundation FastTrack
- Become familiar with the Foundation interface

You will be entering your pricing decisions in the Foundation spreadsheet. To access the Foundation spreadsheet, log in to your account on www.capsim.com and select "Foundation". Click on "Decisions" from the menu on the left-hand side of the screen, then locate "Launch the Web Spreadsheet" from the middle of your browser. Now click on the pop-up option to "Continue Draft Decisions" which will open your spreadsheet.

Pricing

You will be pricing the product "Able" and observing the impact that price has on the Benchmark Prediction. To accomplish

this task, click on the "Decisions" and then "Marketing" menu at the top of your Foundation spreadsheet.

FOUNDATION. Coach ▾ File ▾ Undo ▾ Decisions ▾ Proformas ▾ Reports ▾ Help ▾

Recalculate   ᴹ Marketing   Teamname: Andrews | SimID: F63301 | Round: 1 | Year: 2015

Name	Price	Promo Budget	Sales Budget	Benchmark Prediction	Your Forecast	Gross Revenue	Variable Costs	Contrib Margin	Less Promo/Sales
Able	$ 34.00	$ 1000	$ 1000	1,122	0	$ 38,138	$ 30,452	$ 7,685	$ 5,685
NA	$0.0	$ 0	$ 0	0	-	$ 0	$ 0	$ 0	$ 0
NA	$0.0	$ 0	$ 0	0	-	$ 0	$ 0	$ 0	$ 0
NA	$0.0	$ 0	$ 0	0	-	$ 0	$ 0	$ 0	$ 0
NA	$0.0	$ 0	$ 0	0	-	$ 0	$ 0	$ 0	$ 0
Total		$ 1,000	$ 1,000	1,122	0	$ 38,138	$ 30,452	$ 7,685	$ 5,685

In the first white cell, you can adjust Able's price and observe the impact on the Benchmark Prediction. Did it go up, down, or stay the same? By what percentage did it change?

*Note: the Benchmark Prediction is a helpful tool for estimating sales of your product with the assumption that all of your competition is mediocre. This can be used for understanding how price will modify your demand.

 Let's take a look at the *Price Video* to briefly review the material:

Before adjusting Able's price, refer to customer buying criteria on pages 5 and 6 of the Foundation FastTrack. As you know, there are price ranges for both the low and high tech segments. Observe the importance each segment's customers place on price; that is, think about how much they *care* about price. Another important item to consider is where the product is positioned in the market. The best

way to observe this for now is on the R&D page of your spreadsheet. At the top of the screen, click: "Decisions" then "R&D". The top right graph displays the perceptual map, both market segments, and where your product is positioned. Take the positioning into consideration when you price your product.

As you change the price of your product, click the Recalculate button in the top left of the screen to refresh the charts. When you are satisfied with the sales price for Able, save your decisions. To do so, navigate to the top menu to: File > Update Official Decisions. Then select the "Marketing" option, and click "Save". Do not choose "Save Draft." Be sure to always "Update Official Decisions" from the File menu.

FOUNDATION. Coach ▾   File ▾   Undo ▾   Decisio

| Recalculate | | | |

Update Official Decisions
Save Draft
Exit

Name	Price ⓘ	Promo Budget ⓘ	
Baker	$ 35.00	$ 1000	$ 1000
NA	$0.0	$ 0	$ 0
NA	$0.0	$ 0	$ 0
NA	$0.0	$ 0	$ 0

2 Identifying, enticing, and adding value for customers

Learning Objectives:

After reading this module and completing the associated exercises, you will be able to:

LO1: Describe the role of a marketing manager.

LO2: Describe the key activities of marketing research.

LO3: Discuss the seven steps of information gathering for market research.

LO4: Define and differentiate the "4P's" of marketing.

LO5: Discuss the importance of market segmentation.

LO6: Describe the purposes and goals of marketing strategy.

LO7: Define "diminishing returns" and discuss why this matters to marketing.

LO8: Compare and contrast the concepts of risk, ambiguity, and conformance with regard to marketing.

Key Terms to Look For:

- *Ambiguity*
- *Conformance*
- *Customer*
- *Diminishing returns*
- *Forecast*
- *Interpreting data*
- *Marketing strategy*

- *Organizing information*
- *Place*
- *Price*
- *Product*
- *Promotion*
- *Research*
- *Risk*

Customers are Heard, but Often Not Seen

No matter how good a firm is at offering its products and services, it has to strive for constant improvement because satisfying the customer is a never-ending process. From buying a bottle of shampoo or ordering a cup of coffee, to choosing a health-care provider or setting up a retirement plan, the abundance of choice in the market makes decision making increasingly complex for consumers. The same is true for customers in business-to-business markets, like the electronic sensor market.

For any company, understanding the relationship its customers have with the company and its product, and how those relationships are enhanced or deteriorate over time, is critical to the long-term profitability and sustainability of the firm.

Today's customers have access to a wealth of information, as well as many choices in the marketplace. Acquiring and retaining customers can, therefore, be challenging. But a satisfied and/or loyal customer -a "captured" customer - is, in simple economic terms, an asset that yields future cash-flows and contributes to a firm's future growth.

Without unlimited resources, it is impossible for any firm to excel in every aspect of its product: that is, to provide the highest quality, fastest delivery and widest variety at the lowest price. Therefore, firms must make tradeoffs on the basis of what they do best, what their competitors are offering, and what criteria they think matter most to their customers. Managers often struggle to determine the "best" configuration of product-service offerings that will appeal to their chosen target markets and to potential customers.

The Marketing Manager's Role

Ideally, all company activities should satisfy customer needs. The role of a marketing manager is to focus the company's efforts on identifying, satisfying, and following up on its customers' needs - all at a profit. The marketing manager has to understand how:

- To clearly define, describe and forecast the needs of its customers by using data *(Market Research)*,
- To determine how to select specific markets and satisfy customer needs through balancing products, services, and benefits *(Marketing Mix)*,
- To analyze its competitive advantages, plans, and actions *(Marketing Strategy)*

Market Research

A successful marketing manager cannot afford to implement best-practice initiatives for all possible product offerings to ensure the company can be "everything to everybody." Nor can they use "spray and pray" tactics until they find the most popular product that will stick. With limited resources available, a marketing manager's first step is to view the business from a customer's perspective.

Most marketing managers combine the customer perspective with their sense of the market that comes from experience. However, experience is not always a good thing. Experience may include information acquired over a number of years that has become outdated and is no longer timely or relevant to today's decisions. Sometimes industry folklore – stories repeated often but without a firm factual foundation – can create misleading impressions that may lead an organization in the wrong direction. Timely market research to ensure you have an up-to-date understanding of your market and customers helps keep decision making on track.

Organizing Information

Any research assignment is a systematic gathering, recording, and analyzing of data related to a subject or problem you would like to understand. In particular, market research is simply an orderly and objective way of learning about the group of people who buy from you or who are most likely to do so.

Market research is not a perfect science because it deals with people and their constantly changing likes, dislikes, and behaviors – all potentially affected by hundreds of influences. It is an attempt to learn about markets scientifically and to gather facts and opinions in an orderly and objective way. Market research seeks to find out how things are, not how you think they are or would like them to be, and can define what specific products or services people want to buy, rather than focusing on what you want to sell them.

Market research answers the questions every business must ask to succeed, such as:

- Who are my customers and potential customers?
- What kind of people are they?
- Where do they live?

- Can and will they buy from my business?
- Am I offering the kinds of goods or services they want at the best place, at the best time, and in the right amounts?
- Are my prices consistent with buyers' opinions of the product's value?
- Are my promotional programs working by creating awareness in the marketplace?
- Are my sales programs working to create accessibility for my product through the distribution channels?
- What do customers think of my business?
- How do our *value propositions* (a product or a service that creates value for the customer) compare with those of our competitors?
- Are there specific reasons customers would make the decision to purchase from our business rather than from competitors?

Information Gathering

We often engage in information gathering to allow us to systematically organize knowledge. It ensures that such knowledge and information is timely and meaningful. Sound information gathering provides what you need to:

- Identify problems and potential problems in your current market that you can solve in a unique manner
- Acquire facts about your market to develop a strategy and implement action plans
- Assist you in making better decisions and correcting problems as needed
- Reduce implementation risks
- Discover unknown opportunities

Many managers conduct informal research every day. In their daily managerial duties, they check returned items to see if there is a pattern of dissatisfaction. They meet a former customer and ask why they have not been in lately. They look at a competitor's ad to see what they are charging for the same products. These activities help provide a framework that enables managers to objectively evaluate the meaning of the information they gather about their business.

A more formal information gathering or research process may include the following seven steps:

1. Defining the problem or opportunity
2. Assessing available information
3. Reviewing internal records and files; interviewing employees
4. Collecting outside data (primary research)
5. Organizing and interpreting data
6. Making a decision and taking action
7. Assessing the results of the action

Defining the Problem or Opportunity. Defining the problem or assessing the opportunity is the first step of the research process. This process is often overlooked, yet it is the most important step. You have to be able to see beyond the symptoms of a problem to get at its cause. Labeling the problem as "a decline in sales" is not defining a cause, but identifying a symptom.

You must establish an outline of the problem that includes causes that can be objectively measured and tested. Look at your list of possible causes frequently while you are gathering your facts, but do not let it get in the way of the facts. To define your problem, list every possible influence that may have caused it. For example, if sales have declined:

- Have your customers changed?
- Have customer tastes changed?

- Have customers' buying habits changed?
- Do our services still meet our customers' needs?
- Is our product still relevant?

Assessing Available Information. Once you have formally defined your problem, assess the information that is immediately available. You may already have all the information you need to determine if your hypothesis is correct, and solutions to the problem may have become obvious in the process of defining it. Stop there. You have reached a point of diminishing returns (we'll talk about this term in depth a little later). You will be wasting time and money if you do further marketing research that doesn't offer additional insight.

If you are uncertain whether you need additional information, weigh the cost of more information against its usefulness. This presents a dilemma similar to guessing, in advance, what return you will receive on your advertising dollar. You do not know what return you will get, or even if you will get a return. The best you can do is to balance that uncertainty against the cost of gathering more data to make a more informed decision.

Everyday Life – available information

Imagine you sell tires. You might guess that sales of new cars three years ago would have a strong effect on present retail sales of tires. To test this idea, you might compare new car sales of six years ago with replacement tire sales from three years ago. What if you discovered that new tire sales three years ago were 10 percent of the new car sales three years before? Repeating this exercise for previous years reveals that in each case tire sales were about 10 percent of new car sales made three years before. You could then logically conclude the total market for replacement tire sales in your area this year will be about 10 percent of new car sales in your locality three years ago.

Begin by "thinking cheap and staying as close to home as possible." Before considering anything elaborate, such as market surveys or field experiments, explore your own records and files. Look at sales records, complaints, receipts, and any other records that can help you better understand where your customers live, work, what they buy, and how they buy.

Naturally, the more localized the figures you can find from published sources, the better. For instance, there may be a national decline in new housing starts, but if you sell new appliances in an area in which new housing is booming, you need to base your estimate of market potential on local, not national conditions. Newspapers and local radio and television stations may be able to help you find this information.

Keep in mind that there are many sources of published material and much of it is free. You can find it online, in libraries, newspapers, magazines, and in trade and general business publications. Trade associations and government agencies are also rich sources of information.

Interviewing Employees. When you have finished reviewing the available information in your records, turn to that other valuable internal source of customer information: your employees. Employees may be the best source of information about customer likes and dislikes. They hear customers' complaints about your products or services, they are aware of what customers are looking for but you are not offering, and can probably supply good customer profiles from their day-to-day contacts whether it's face to face, on the phone, or online.

Beyond Search Engines – Gathering Primary Information. Once you have exhausted the basic sources for information about your market, the next step is to collect information not commonly available in published form.

Primary research is the collection of original data. Primary research can be as simple as asking customers or suppliers how they feel about your store or service firm, or as complex as the surveys conducted by sophisticated professional marketing research firms. Primary research includes among its tools direct mail questionnaires, telephone or on-the-street surveys, experiments, panel studies, test marketing, behavior observation, and more.

It is critical to ask the right questions and to avoid creating a bias in the responses. If the questions are not carefully crafted, people may answer the way they think they are expected to answer, rather than telling you how they really feel about your product, service, or business.

Interpreting Data. After collecting the data you must organize it into meaningful information. Go back to your definition of the problem, compare it with your findings, and prioritize and rank the data.

- What marketing strategies are suggested?
- How can they be accomplished?
- How are they different from what I am doing now?
- What current activities should be increased?
- What current activities must I drop or decrease in order to devote adequate resources to new strategies?

Making Decisions and Taking Action. Prioritize each possible tactic from the standpoint of determining the:

- Immediate goal to be achieved;
- Cost to implement;
- Time to accomplish, and;
- Measurement of success.

If your market research suggests 10 possible strategies, select two or three that appear to have the greatest potential impact or are most easily achievable and begin there. For each strategy, develop tactics, which may include:

- Staff responsibilities
- Necessary steps
- Budget allocations
- Timelines with deadlines for accomplishing strategic steps
- Progress measurements

Research can take you only so far...

The Internet makes collecting information for market research easier than ever before. The Internet, however, also makes a clear vision of the future harder to define because of the precarious uncertainties it has introduced for many traditional industries and institutions.

The most research-driven institutions in the world, universities, are watching their entire business model change – and all their expertise in the scientific method cannot produce a clear conclusion about their own future. In the United States for example, Congress, concerned the nation's universities were at risk from a range of forces, asked the National Academies for a full report on the future. The Academies produced a list of 10 actions necessary to secure the university sector including policy, funding, productivity, and partnership priorities in the U.S. It could not, however, predict *how* a new university sector might *look*. A recent Ernst and Young report on universities concluded: "the dominant university model ... will prove unviable in all but a few cases over the next 10-15 years", but could not confirm what would take its place.

Innovators in higher education are offering their own solutions. Western Governors University, for example, an online university created by several U.S. state governments, offers competency-based programs that are, unlike existing university programs, low-cost and self-paced. Coursera, an education technology company, gives millions of people access to teaching from highly respected professors through Massive Open Online Courses (MOOCs). Founded by Stanford University professors, Coursera has more than four million users and is working with the American Council on Education to offer the equivalent to university credits.

The traditional news media – newspapers delivered to your door, with television and radio bulletins delivered at scheduled times – also saw its business model collapse as the Internet delivered a 24-hour news cycle and user-generated content. When Amazon's Jeff Bezos purchased the *Washington Post*, commentators suggested a "back to the future" model would follow in which wealthy, tech-savvy individuals would buy and transform traditional media outlets. The news website BuzzFeed was already offering a new model for news: user-generated content mixed with material by staff journalists and organized by what's "viral" on the web at any moment. Announcing that his company had made its first profit in September 2013, BuzzFeed CEO Jonah Peretti said: *"We don't have the trust the traditional news brands have won over the past 100 years, but we are working hard to earn it, and it won't take us 100 years to get there."*

But where exactly, is "there"? Universities and news media have total access to information for data-driven decision making. No amount of data, however, can guarantee the future. Information can tell you how things are today, but cannot make the decision for you on what you should do about it tomorrow.

Based on this information, make a final decision on the strategies and go to work on the tactics.

Assessing the Results of the Action. Analyze your progress against success measures. If adjustments are appropriate, make them. At the conclusion of the time you have allotted for accomplishing your goal, take a hard look at the results.

- Did you achieve your goal?
- Should the decision be renewed on a larger scale?

If you are disappointed in the results, determine why the plan went awry.

The Possibilities Revealed

Market research should also identify trends that may affect sales and profitability levels in the future. Population shifts, legal developments, and the local economic situation should be monitored to enable early identification of problems and opportunities. Competitor activity should also be monitored. Competitors may be entering or leaving the market, for example. To provide competitive

The Four P's Go Viral

California start-up Dollar Shave Club took on the market powerhouses in the shaving business not just with an alternative value proposition (razors delivered to your door through a monthly subscription), but also with a quirky video ad that went viral on YouTube and won marketing awards for its creativity.

Dollar Shave Club's value proposition started as home delivery of razor blades for as low as $1 a month (plus shipping) then expanded with a range of personal grooming products for men – included wet wipes for (ahem) the other cheeks.

The company's online ad "Our Blades Are F***ing Great" features founder and Chief Executive Michael Dubin riding on a forklift, lobbing stray tennis balls, dancing with a fuzzy bear, and poking fun at the high-priced, complex razor products sold by his competitors. It won Best Out-of-Nowhere Video Campaign at the 2012 Ad Age Viral Video Awards plus two 2013 Webby Awards.

When the company launched publicly in March 2012 it attracted close to $10 million in venture capital. In June 2013, *Forbes Magazine* said: "*The company's millions are dwarfed by those earned by Gillette or Schick, but its deft understanding of marketing's 4P's (product, price, place, and promotion) showed that big-name consumer brands are vulnerable.*"

Some big-name brands, however, have shown they can also play the YouTube game. Dove's "Real Beauty Sketches" campaign had more than 114 million total views in its first month in early 2013 and was labeled the most viral ad release of all time.

In the Dove video, an FBI-trained sketch artist draws women who are hidden behind a curtain, first based on their own self-description, and then based on the way a stranger describes them. In each case, the picture drawn from the stranger's description is more attractive and closer to the way the participants actually look – making the point that women are too critical of their appearances and don't see their true beauty.

Two brilliantly successful marketing campaigns in the personal products market, one from a start-up focused on men and another from an established brand (Dove by Unilever), both achieving outstanding awareness of their brand from professionally produced ads that ran on YouTube.

Thinking about the 4 Ps, however, what is the biggest difference between the two campaigns?

insight, it is also very useful to understand the strategies your competitors have chosen.

Good information about the market is critical. Research provides knowledge that can disclose problems – and a lack of knowledge can be easily remedied through research. The success of any business is based on its ability to build an increasing pool of satisfied customers. Customers buy something because they believe they will be "better off", in some way, as a result of the transaction. It is critical, therefore, that every business works out exactly who its customers are and how to create value for them. That is the role of Marketing.

The Marketing Mix

The 4 P's of Marketing

Marketing defines your actions for competing in the marketplace. At the simplest level, a high-end vehicle manufacturer such as Rolls-Royce spends its marketing budget enticing high-net-worth individuals, while the value marketing programs of a manufacturer such as Hyundai appeal to a much broader audience. Rolls-Royce and Hyundai do not compete in the same market "segment", which means their customers are looking for cars, but different types of cars. Their marketing programs, therefore, are very different. Hyundai, however, competes with KIA and Suzuki in the same small-vehicle market segment. All three are competing for the same customers, so their challenge is to design marketing programs that make them stand out from the others - to *differentiate* their offering in the market.

Traditionally marketing covers the 4 P's of *Product, Price, Promotion* and *Place*, and the way a company configures these elements is the marketing mix.

Product

What are you selling and how can you manipulate it to deliver better value for your customers? Does the business concentrate on a narrow product line, developing highly specialized products or services? Does it offer different versions of its products or services to different types of customers? Adjustments to the offerings - through research and development, revised designs, new packaging, etc. - are all a key part of the marketing mix.

Price

Price and pricing policies are vital to business revenues. Each product or service must be priced to satisfy customers and deliver on the company's profit target. But pricing also includes determining a credit policy: Do you allow your customer to pay for the product *after* they receive it, or do they need to pay for it *when* they receive it? The timing of payment by customers will have an impact on the cash available to the business at any given time.

Promotion

No business can expect customers to just stumble across their offering and buy. Each business needs to create awareness for the value proposition they are offering. This can be done by taking advantage of resources such as the Internet, advertising campaigns, sales efforts, special financing deals, or any other creative promotional or sales activities the company can imagine and implement. The cost of these activities, however, also has to be factored into the price of the products or services.

Place or Distribution Channel

The way you get your product or service into your customers' hands or lives is equally important. Businesses need to make their value propositions accessible. A manufacturer might work through established distributors or agents, for example, to get their products to the right place. A retailer has to consider cost vs traffic flow for their store – a high-traffic location will have higher rent but a low-cost, low-traffic location will require more expenditure on promotions to bring people in. Online retail requires search engine optimization. Making the product accessible is critical to the marketing mix.

Place might be as simple as displaying products that are often bought on an impulse, such as flavored popcorn, candy, or magazines, in a highly visible spot in a high-traffic area of a store (checkout line), or as complex as developing an Internet-based marketing plan to reach customers anywhere around the world.

There are more than four P's to great marketing campaigns, however. Precision, for example – identifying precisely who your cus-

Shifting viewer preferences a threat to cable TV?

 Netflix and other online video streaming services including Hulu and Amazon Prime are beginning to threaten the business model of cable television by capitalizing on a shift in customer demands and focusing almost exclusively on marketing.

With access to Netflix content via phone, tablet, laptop, PC ... oh, *and* television, cable subscribers who were also using Netflix reported in late 2013 they were twice as likely to downgrade, if not cancel, their cable TV subscription than a year before, according to research by The Diffusion Group.

TDG Senior Analyst Joel Espelian says the future of broadcasting is about marketing, not technology. "Today the clearest example of this phenomenon is Netflix, which doesn't broadcast anything. Nevertheless, the *marketing function* of broadcasting (i.e., getting new content in front of viewers at a single point in time) is highly relevant to Netflix."

At the Emmy Awards for television in September 2013, a program called *House of Cards* won the Best Director category, making it the first television series *never* seen on a television channel to win an award. *House of Cards* is an exclusive Netflix drama.

In August 2013 *The Economist* asked "Is Netflix killing cable television?" The answer was "not quite yet" as just 1% of US cable subscribers had "cut the cord". However: *"'Cord nevers,' youngsters who start their own households without a subscription, and who may never get one, will continue to add to the number of cable defectors. So will ownership trends of 'smart televisions' which are internet-connected: people may be more likely to opt out of paying for cable when they can easily stream Netflix in their living rooms."*

The traditional business model of the cable television business was built on offering a broad range of content to a high number of subscribers. The customers who were taught by cable to expect content "on demand" now want it all the time, and everywhere – and for a better price!

tomers are and what they want. Preparation is another – doing the careful research and design work to satisfy your customers' needs. And what about pizzazz – getting customers excited about choosing your value proposition over a competitor's? Just like business itself, marketing is much more interesting than its basic definition. *Service* is another way that an organization can increase perceived value and differentiate itself from competitors offering similar or identical products. Whether it's a free massage when you sign up for personal training, a luxury car dealer offering roadside service, or a mass market retail store with greeters to help customers find what they need quickly, service enhancements are increasingly important in the mix.

Because the resources available for marketing in any organization will be limited, concentrating the company's marketing efforts on one or a few key market segments – or target marketing - is one way to use resources efficiently. Markets can be segmented in several ways:

GEOGRAPHIC: Focusing on understanding the needs of customers in a particular geographical area.

DEMOGRAPHIC: Focusing on the attributes of the market based upon gender, age, income, education, or other measurable factors.

PSYCHOGRAPHIC: Identifying and promoting to people most likely to buy the product based on lifestyle and behaviors. This may be based on interests, fears, behaviors, or actions that can be categorized into groups, e.g., young health-conscious professionals, retired couples on fixed incomes, families with new babies, etc.

Target marketing enables you to identify, access, communicate with, and sell to those who are most likely to purchase your products.

The Marketing Strategy

A company's marketing strategy has one goal: to deliver value to customers while making a profit. Business incorporates many trade-offs – balancing one need or demand with another – and this is the most important: delivering just enough value to the customer at a price that allows the business to meet its profit target. The profit target will depend on the type of business. Some businesses focus on selling a relatively small number of products but make a large profit on each one (aircraft engines, for example) others focus on selling huge volume for a smaller profit on each (canned soda, for example).

Setting a marketing strategy involves identifying customer groups, or target markets, that your business can serve better than your competitors, and tailoring your product offerings, prices, distribution, promotional efforts, and services toward that particular market segment.

Ideally, the marketing strategy should address unmet customer needs that represent adequate potential size and profitability. A good marketing strategy recognizes that a business cannot be all things to all people and must analyze its market and its own capabilities in delivering value. By focusing on a target market that your business can serve best, you increase the effectiveness of marketing activities and provide a better return on the marketing budget.

Marketing strategy is most successful when the company overall has a "marketing orientation". A marketing orientation requires managers to constantly gather information about their customers' needs through research, to share that information throughout the firm, and to use it to help build long-term relationships between the organization and its customers.

After marketing program decisions are made, owners and managers need to evaluate the results of their decisions. Standards of performance need to be set so results can be evaluated against them. Sound data on industry norms and past performance provide the basis for comparisons against present performance. Owners and managers need to audit their company's performance on a periodic basis, at least quarterly.

Spending more on marketing programs is not always better. The law of **diminishing return** states that investing additional resources may initially increase productivity, but after a certain point, spending more will result in a lower return per dollar invested. The concept of **diminishing returns,** or the **rate of diminishing returns,** states that adding additional investment beyond a certain threshold will not add proportional returns. Spending money beyond this point does not yield as much as the amount spent prior to that point.

Diminishing returns may also be associated with other aspects of business, such as hiring too many employees, and investing in additional plant and equipment that you will never use.

FOUNDATION.

In Foundation Business Simulation, the rate of diminishing returns applies to your promotion budget. The first $1,500,000 you invest buys 36% awareness for your product. Spending an additional $1,500,000, for a total of $3,000,000, creates 50% awareness. Therefore, the second $1,500,000 you invest buys only 14% more awareness. The investment beyond $1,500,000 yields a lower return per dollar invested compared to the initial $1,500,000. The return of your promotional dollars diminishes beyond the initial $1,500,000 and will impact your decision regarding spending beyond this amount. Investing beyond $3,000,000 in a single year is just not worth it.

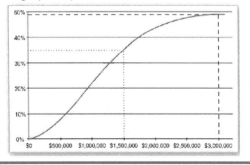

Marketing Reality

Irrespective of up or down economic cycles, today's business environment is more competitive than at any other time in recent history. To a certain extent, companies can re-engineer, restructure, and cut costs, but the heart of the business must be a sustainable and profitable business model that nurtures growth. Creating a sustainable and profitable business model can prove to be even more difficult than creating a product itself. Many "dot bomb" businesses were able to produce a product, but unable to back it up with a profitable business model.

In such a competitive business environment, managers must have a clear understanding of customer needs and their firm's own capabilities to grow revenue within the constraints of sustainability and profitability. While evaluating various possible market alternatives, managers typically refrain from implementing revolutionary changes in their product or service offerings and instead engage in evolutionary market moves. This makes sense, as it is always easier to modify the "core engine" of a product or service offering by adding one or many "engine variants", rather than introducing a "new core engine" that might capture new markets.

With limited resources at their disposal, it is imperative that managers understand the complexities of product or service "drivers" that truly reflect evolving customer needs and competitive activity, so their decisions return the most "bang for the buck."

In other words, to create, capture, and maintain demand for their product and service offerings, businesses have to perform a balancing act between the external environ- ment (changing customer demands) and the internal environment (the firm's given operational challenges) to maximize growth opportunities. It requires carefully calibrating the company's responses and approach to the following issues:

Ambiguity – What do our customers really want? Companies lacking a clear understanding of customer choices often take a shotgun approach, hoping that at least one of their offerings will succeed. Unfortunately, this approach is neither efficient nor profitable for most firms. Markets are often flooded with products and services that offer relatively little added value to customers and weaken the seller's bottom line.

Risk – Will our envisioned offerings be successful? Managers face complex choices

Profits are greater challenge than marketing for online businesses

The Internet has spawned a wide range of businesses that have overcome the traditional challenge of marketing – ensuring lots of people know about what they offer – but that have not overcome the critical challenge of business operations: bringing in more money than the company pays out to deliver their value proposition.

When Facebook paid a billion dollars for Instagram in 2012, the vastly popular photo-sharing site had yet to make one cent. Facebook put one of its rising star executives in charge of finding a way to turn Instagram's platform, with its high "cool" factor, into a money-making proposition. One of the problems for Instagram was to get large businesses – Nike, for example, or Lululemon Athletica – to pay for something that they, along with many other prominent brands, had been using for free, i.e., the Instagram platform for their viral ad campaigns. By mid2013 Mark Zuckerberg was still saying Facebook would generate "a lot of profit" from Instagram, but it had yet to happen.

In early 2013, Pinterest – the online scrapbooking site set up in 2010 – was valued at $2.5 billion even though, as its chief executive Ben Silbermann told the Wall Street Journal, the company was still "building foundations to monetize" its service. Like Facebook and Instagram, Pinterest's dilemma is matching its commercial imperative with the non-commercial elements users love about the site. The site was criticized for "lack of transparency" when users first discovered big retailers were compensating Pinterest based on the products users bought. In 2013 the company made it clear that it was developing tools to offer information on user activity to retailers.

Pinterest and Instagram both understand the value of information to drive new concepts in the marketplace. They and many other online businesses have Product, Place, and Promotion working for them. However, until they are successful with Price – and can bring in more than they spend – they do not have a true business model.

when deciding which product-service bundles to offer. Potential product/service drivers (e.g., price or specific product-service features) can have several variants, and managers often use experience, benchmarking analysis, or simply gut feel to decide what will be attractive to customers. On the one hand, such "informed guessing" might spur new and innovative ideas; it might also lead to depleted profits and chaos.

Conformance – Can we deliver what we promised? Although it is important for companies to understand market value drivers, they must also support customer preferences and align them with effective operations management. Even if firms succeed in identifying and delivering attractive product-service packages, their efforts may prove futile unless they can efficiently deliver on their promises under resource constraints.

In summary, the key questions to determine marketing performance include:

- Do the products and services the company is offering provide value to customers?

- Are existing and potential customers aware of the products and services available from the company?

- Is it easy for the customer to purchase what he or she wants and at a competitive price?

- Do the employees make sure the customers' needs are truly satisfied and leave them with the feeling that they would enjoy coming back?

The Sales Forecast

How will you know how much of your product to produce if you cannot make a reasonable prediction about how much you will sell?

One of the most critical aspects of marketing management is to create a sales forecast to predict how many units of a product will sell in the future.

The sales forecast process often begins by assessing how the total market will perform in a given period – one year, for example. From there, using all relevant information, you attempt to assess your performance and what market share your company will realize from that total forecast. To do this requires speculation on your competitors' performance as well. Forecasting sales is a challenging task due to the multiple variables involved in the process:

- What will the overall economic climate be like?

- Will consumers make decisions on the same basis they have in the past?

- At what level will our competitors perform?

- Will existing competitors introduce new products, and if so, when?

- Will there be new competitors, or will existing competitors drop out of the market?

- At what price can we sell our products given the many alternative product choices available?

Answering these questions provides insight for making better decisions for production schedules and allocating resources to attract new customers or retain existing customers. You will have the opportunity to practice sales forecasting and build skills in this area several times during the business simulation experience.

However, keep this in mind: What customers *prefer* is of interest, but what really matters is what customers *choose!*

Chapter Review Questions

Marketing

1. What are the three key responsibilities of a marketing manager?

2. What are the major components of marketing research?

3. What steps should you follow to collect information for marketing research?

4. What are the 4P's?

5. What are some other important factors beyond the 4P's?

6. How can one "segment" the market? Why is segmentation important?

7. What is marketing strategy?

8. When dealing with "marketing reality," what are the three questions that need to be addressed?

9. Why would a company need to forecast sales?

You – in the executive suite!

Sales and Marketing Manager, continued...

 In Module 1, you started your job rotation track as *Sales and Marketing Manager* and looked at the industry in which your company operates, the size and growth rates of the two market segments, and the criteria your customers use to make buying decisions.

Now it's time to focus on estimating how many customers you think will buy your products in the coming year – the sales forecast. Then we'll analyze the Customer Survey Score, from the Foundation FastTrack, to see how it can help your forecasting and decision making.

Activities: Approximately 90 minutes to complete.	COMPLETED?
A-1: Answer all **Chapter Review Questions** Your instructor will advise you on how to turn in your answers.	☐
A-2: In the **Summary Guide** at Appendix 1 read **Marketing Decisions**, 195.	☐
A-3: **Read** the following text through to the end of the module. **Complete** all of the required tables and watch the online videos.	☐

Exercise #4: Forecasting Sales

Industry Demand Analysis

The Industry Demand Analysis helps the Marketing Department, and later the Production Department, understand future demand. Marketing can use the total demand for each segment as it creates forecasts. Production can use the results when making decisions to buy or sell production capacity.

You will need the Segment Analysis reports (pages 5 - 6) of The Foundation FastTrack for Round 0 and the Industry Conditions Report.

On the form that follows, you will see the Total Industry Unit Demand number (Current or Round 0) for each segment at the start of the simulation and Next Year's Growth Rate (Growth) which is also found in the Statistics box.

The approximate demand for Round 1 (R1) is given. To get this number, we multiplied the Current demand (5,040 low tech and 2,160 for high tech) by the growth rates for the year (10% and 20% respectively).

If you prefer, you can use the following short-cut. First, convert the growth rate percentage to a decimal. For example, assume the Low Tech growth rate is 10%. Convert the percentage to a decimal:

Low Tech Segment Growth Rate = 10% = 0.1
Add 1 to the decimal: 1+0.1=1.1

Multiply the Round 0 Low Tech demand by 1.1. This will give you a close approximation of Total Industry Demand for Round 1.

Remember, the demand numbers are in thousands! For example, if the Round 0 Total Industry Unit Demand for the Low Tech segment reads 7,387, the Low Tech Segment demanded 7,387,000 units.

While you can calculate the demand for Round 1 from the information on hand, future growth rates are unknown.

Can you predict the market size for iPads in the future? No. On the other hand, you need something for planning purposes to address critical questions like, "How much production capacity will we need in the future?" "How much money do we need to raise?" "Is one segment more attractive for investment?"

Marketing and Strategic planners address this type of issue with scenarios. Typically there are three – worst case, average case, and best case.

The average case assumes that the current growth continues into the future indefinitely. Worst case assumes a lower growth rate and best case a higher growth rate. The true growth rate will unfold as the simulation progresses.

Next year's growth rate is published in the FastTrack on each Segment Page in the Statistics box.

For this exercise, complete the tables below with the "average" scenario.

Assume the Round 1 growth rates will continue into the future unchanged. This will give you some idea for potential market size. If you have time, try a worst case and best case scenario. For worst case assume, for example, half the growth rate. For best case assume, say, 1.5 times the growth rate. Consider developing a simple spreadsheet for this purpose.

Sales Forecasting

As Sales and Marketing Manager, one of the most important tasks to accomplish – and the most challenging – is forecasting how many units you think you are going to sell in the coming year.

Forecasting means projecting future sales based on past information. What makes forecasting so challenging is that you don't know what your competitors are going to do in the coming year. You can only make an educated guess based on data you are able to collect such as market size and growth, and how attractive your products are versus competing products.

Your sales forecast affects your production team because it determines how many units to build. It affects your research and development team because they manage product specifications – and that impacts customer demand. It affects your accounting and finance team because it helps develop financial forecasts. It affects human resources because the number of units in production determines staffing levels. In fact every part of the company can benefit from a good sales forecast, or suffer the consequences of a very poor forecast.

Before we begin, view the *Video on Sales Forecasting.*

So, how do we achieve a sales forecast?

First, keep the Foundation FastTrack, at Appendix 2, close by. There is a wealth of information about what happened last year in the FastTrack Report. The problem is that things change - and sometimes things change a lot. Let's start with all the information that is available to you from your report:

1. You have good information about the size of the market segments. You know exactly how much they will grow from year to year. (Statistics - reported on page 5 and 6 of the FastTrack Report and Table 1 from Module 1.)

2. You have good information about your customers' decision processes: how they evaluate your product and make their purchase decisions. (Customer Buying Criteria - reported on page 5 and 6 of the FastTrack Report and Tables 3 and 4 from Module 1.)

3. In "Units Sold," you know how many units your products sold and how many units your competitors' products sold last year in each market segment. You don't know how many you or your competitors will sell next year because the product offerings will change. (Top Products in Segment Table - page 5 and 6 of the FastTrack Report).

4. You have two valuable pieces of information in the market share report; how many units you sold as a percentage of the whole segment (Actual Market Share) and how many you would have sold if each customer had gotten his or her first choice (Potential Market Share). Why would a customer not have been able to get his or her first choice? Because you or your competitors did not produce enough units to meet the demand for the desired product (called "stocking out").

    In this example, Andrews deserved 20.61% of sales (potential), but only achieved 19.1% (actual). An estimated 1.5% of the market wanted to buy from Andrews but could not – why? Because Andrews did not produce enough product. If the market was 1,000,000 units, it means that Andrews could have sold 15,000 more units than they did (1,000,000 X 1.5%). Who got those sales? Andrews' competitors who, as you can see, had an "Actual Share" greater than their "Potential Share."

    The "Market Share Actual versus Potential" graph is available on pages 5 and 6 of the FastTrack Report. Detailed information about market share is provided on page 7 of the FastTrack Report.

5. Later on we will talk about the December Customer Survey. A Customer Survey Score provides good information about how well your product meets customers' expectations compared to all other offerings in the market. We'll look closely at this report in Exercise #5 below.

6. In the Production Information table (page 4 of the FastTrack Report), there is some limited information about new products entering the market in the next year. The problem is that it does not tell you whether the new products are launching into the Low Tech or High Tech segment. You will need to analyze your competitors' decisions to see if they demonstrate a strategic direction that allows you to assume where their new product will launch. The other important piece of information is the Revision Date. If the new product is similar to the existing product, the project time will be shorter. If the new product is very different, it will take longer to design and build.

From the example below, AceX – a new product from the Andrews Company – will take so long to build that it must be very different from Able. Since Able is Low Tech, you can assume AceX is probably designed for High Tech. Erie and Ferris's new products, East and Feast, are more similar to their existing products, so the new product might be in the same segment. You won't know for certain, however, until the products come out. There are two sources of "uncertainty" in this information:

1. *Some information has to be adjusted.* The FastTrack Report provides information about last year. Demand grows from year to year. Products age from month to month. Ideal positions drift.

2. *Some information is an estimate.* All you know is that just as you are trying to improve your products, your competitors are also trying to improve theirs. Sales levels depend on how much better or worse your product is relative to your competitors – and that is something you have to estimate.

Forecasting techniques are important because you will use your sales forecasts to:

- Set a production schedule.
- Establish a "worst case" scenario for sales so you can manage the risk of financing.
- Establish the need for investment in your capacity to manufacture products.

You have two goals for each of the forecasting techniques:

1. To master the technique of making a forecast – your educated guess.
2. To understand the quality of the forecast.

Table 1 - Product Overview

Name	Primary Segment	Units Sold	Units in Inventory	Revision Date	Age Dec 31
Able	Low	1,630	0	9-Nov-2013	3.1
Acex		0	0	17-Nov-2015	0.0
Eat	Low	1,201	93	15-Jan-2014	3.3
East		0	0	14-Mar-2015	0.0
Fast	High	1,134	207	10-Oct-2014	1.7
Feast		0	0	20-May-2015	0.0

Basic Forecasting

Basic forecasting involves two different techniques, "market growth" and "market share" forecasting.

Market Growth Estimate. The logic underlying the Market Growth forecast is that if the market will be 10% bigger next year, it is reasonable to assume your sales will be 10% bigger next year. To determine the forecast, take last year's sales and grow them by the growth rate of the market. To try this forecast, use the information for product Daze (a competing product offered by Digby) from Fast-Track Report pages 5 and 6: Market Segment Analysis. In the table:

- Enter the number of units sold and the growth rate for that Market Segment.
- Grow the number of units sold:
  Multiply Low Tech units sold by 1+ growth rate of 10%, which equals 1.1
  Multiply High Tech units sold by 1+ growth rate of 20%, which equals 1.2
- Add the two Market Growth estimates together.

Table 2 - Market Growth Estimate

	Units Sold	Growth	Future Market Size
Low Tech			
High Tech			
Total			

The limitation of this forecasting method is that it doesn't use any information except last year's sales and growth. It also ignores information about the coming year. Changes to your products, changes to competitors' products, or new product offerings could all significantly influence sales but are ignored by this method.

Market Share Estimate. The Market Share, Actual vs Potential chart on Page 7 of the FastTrack report should be studied whenever there is a difference between your potential and actual market share.

You know that both market segments will be bigger next year, so grow the reported demand (last year's) and get DEMAND (next year's demand). If you achieved 19.1% of last year's market, then it is reasonable that you would get 19.1% of next year's market. To try this forecast, use the information for product Able from FastTrack pages 5 and 6 - Market Segment Analysis and page 7 - Market Share Report.

For forecasting sales to the Low Tech market use information from FastTrack page 5:

- Calculate DEMAND for Low Tech products next year (last year's demand X 1.1).
- Enter it into both Tables 3 and 4.
- Enter Able's "Actual share" (from chart on page 5, or page 7) in the Actual Market Share Table 3.
- Multiply "Actual Share" by Demand to get the "Actual estimate" then enter it into Table 3.
- Enter Able's "Potential share" (from chart on page 5, or page 7) in the Potential Market Share Table 4.
- Multiply "Potential Share" by Demand to get the "potential estimate".
- Enter it into the Potential Market Share Table.

A forecast for High Tech market sales will use information from FastTrack page 6:

- Calculate Demand for High Tech products next year (last year's demand X 1.2).

- Enter it into both tables.
- Enter Able's "Actual share" (from chart on page 6, or page 7) in the Actual Market Share Table 3.
- Multiply "Actual Market Share" by Demand - to get the "actual share estimate" - then enter it into the Actual Market Share Table 3.
- Enter Able's "Potential share" (from chart on page 6, or page 7) in the Potential Market Share Table 4
- Multiply "Potential Market Share" by Demand to get the "potential share estimate".
- Enter it into the Potential Market Share Table 4.
- Add the two Actual Market Share estimates.

The Actual Market Share estimate and the Basic Forecasting (Market Growth) estimate would be very close because they do exactly the same thing; take what was sold last year and "grow" it at the same rate as the market grows. If you use either of those for a product that stocked out, you will most likely **underestimate** sales for the coming year.

The "Potential Market Share" is what your company would have sold if every customer could buy their first choice product. If you underestimated sales last year and didn't produce enough, then you "stocked out." In that case, your **potential** market share should be greater than your **actual** market share. In that situation, use potential market share for your sales forecast.

If a competitor stocked out, your potential share will be less than your actual share. In both cases, use the potential market share for your forecast.

If the "Actual" and "Potential" market share are exactly equal, this method offers no advantage over the Market Growth method (and would produce the same forecast).

Table 3 - Actual Market Share Estimate

ACTUAL	Demand	"Actual" Share	"Actual" Estimate
Low tech			
High tech			
Total			

Table 4 - Potential Market Share Estimate

POTENTIAL	Demand	"Potential" Share	"Potential" Estimate
Low tech			
High tech			
Total			

Worst Case / Best Case and the Pro formas

The model of your company at www.capsim.com allows you to enter your decisions in all of the functional areas of your business: R&D, Marketing, Production, and Finance. When you enter your decisions, the model adjusts the information it is providing to give you the "best guess" of the outcomes of your decisions. You only make one entry that is not a decision but a forecast, and that is Your Sales Forecast.

The decision screens for Foundation use the number in the "Your Forecast" cell to determine **projected** outcomes and to generate pro forma financial statements. In your simulation practice rounds, begin to use the sales forecast to help you make a variety of decisions, including how many sensors to have available for sale. The number of units available defines a range of acceptable sales levels to meet your inventory management goals.

While you are testing out your decisions, keep this in mind: Use the **lower end of your sales forecast range** (your worst case) before you make your **financing decisions**. This helps to ensure you have enough cash to support your operational decisions. However, use the **top end of the range** (your best case) to make your **production decisions,** which helps ensure you'll have enough stock on hand to satisfy your customers.

Exercise #5: The Customer Survey Score

Before we begin, view the video on *The Customer Survey Score*

You already have a very comprehensive model of how customers make their purchase decisions. Every month, customers identify the products that meet their minimum expectations (which your market research staff calls the "rough cut"). They then evaluate those products against their buying criteria (the fine cut). They make adjustments to their evaluation based on credit terms (Accounts Receivable, which we will address in a future chapter), Awareness, Accessibility, and any additional characteristics that might be outside the fine cut.

Sales levels are directly and closely correlated with how well your product is rated *relative* to how all of the other products are rated. This evaluation is captured in the monthly Customer Survey Score (CSS).

The FastTrack contains December's CSS (DCSS) for each product at the end of each year. You can use this information to forecast sales for the coming year. The logic of the calculation is simple. Your market share (percentage of the market that will buy from you) is your CSS as a percentage of the total CSS of all products in the market.

From the "Top Products in Segment" table at the bottom of pages 5 and 6 of the Fast Track report (Appendix 2):

- Enter Able's DCSS in Table 8.
- From those same tables, add the DCSS for all of the products and enter the total in the table.
- Divide Able's DCSS by the Total DCSS and enter it. This is your projected market share.
- From the "Statistics" table on pages 5 and 6, take last year's "Total Industry Unit Demand" and increase it by the "Growth Rate" (1.1 for Low Tech, 1.2 for High Tech).
- Enter these figures as Demand.
- Multiply Demand by your market share (percentage) and that is your estimate for your sales in each segment.
- Add the estimates together and that is your estimate for Able's total sales.

Unlike the basic forecasting methods, this method incorporates all of the changes to all of the products that occurred in the past year. It forecasts based on relative product attrac

Table 5 - December Customer Survey Score

	Able's DCSS	Total DCSS	Percentage (Able/Total DCSS)	Demand	Estimate
Low Tech					
High Tech					
Total					

tiveness at the time you are making your decisions – you are using information from December 31st of the year just ended to make decisions for the coming year. It does not, however, take into account changes in product offerings that will happen in the coming year.

To do that, you would have to do a month-by-month estimate of the CSS for all products in each segment and use that to forecast sales.

All of the forecasts you have made are based on past information - what has already happened. However, you are forecasting the future - what has yet to happen. You know that your competitors are going through the same process that you are.

Their Sales and Marketing people are following a strategy to entice customers to do business with them, and not you. They are seeking to capture resources and harness them so that they can compete more effectively. You have to adjust your forecast of the future to incorporate what you think will happen. This involves incorporating your improvements and your predictions of how your competitors will improve in the coming year(s).

3 How does a business create goods and services to sell?

Learning Objectives:

After reading this module and completing the associated exercises, you will be able to:

LO1: Differentiate between operations and production.

LO2: Describe the purpose of production schedules.

LO3: Discuss the importance of inventory control.

LO4: Describe an economy of scale.

LO5: Discuss the five components of supply chain management.

LO6: Discuss why it is important to manage quality.

LO7: Describe how to measure productivity.

LO8: Define the accounting equation.

LO9: Discuss the typical types of managerial accounting reports.

LO10: Describe how to calculate contribution margins and why these are valuable.

Key Terms To Look For:

- *Accounting equation*
- *Benchmarking*
- *Carrying cost*
- *Contribution margin analysis*
- *Economies of scale*
- *Fixed costs*
- *Inventory control*

- *Master production schedule*
- *Materials requirement planning*
- *Productivity*
- *Supply chain management*
- *Total Quality Management*
- *Variable costs*
- *Work-in-process inventory*

Production Basics

The story so far...

We know that a business exists to make a profit by offering goods and services that satisfy customer needs in a marketplace. We know that there are many types of markets – physical and virtual – and we have analyzed the market for electronic sensors in our Foundation Business Simulation. We have discovered how to define customer needs and how important it is to promote our products and to make them accessible to customers.

Now let's talk about production: creating something to sell at a cost and level of quality that allows the company to satisfy customer needs *and* make a profit.

Production is a process that uses resources – such as cash, labor, and raw materials – to create a value proposition that is attractive to a particular market.

If "profit" is the answer to "why does a business exist?" and "marketing" holds the answers to "who does the business sell to?" then "production" is the answer to the "how, what, and when" questions about business.

In Foundation, your Production Department decides how many products your company will produce (depending on demand and your assessment of how attractive your products are to the market), whether to add or reduce production capacity in line with your production schedule, and the level of automation on your production lines. Production decisions come with a high price tag because you are dealing with sophisticated machinery and robotics. Weighing the options and the tradeoffs in the context of the overall business is critical.

Let's begin with an overview of production management.

A production process can be defined as: *any activity that increases the similarity between the pattern of demand for goods and the quantity, form, and distribution of these goods to the marketplace.*

Inputs to outputs

Production is the act of making products that will be traded or sold commercially based on decisions about what goods to produce, how to produce them, the costs to produce them, and how to optimize the mix of resource inputs used in their production. Production information is combined with market information such as demand to determine the quantity of products to produce and sell at an optimal price point.

A business needs a production process whether it provides products *or* services. The production process involves planning, procuring goods or expertise to produce the product or service, plus assigning and organizing tasks to get the products or services to the market. It is important to differentiate "production" from "operations" in the business context.

OPERATIONS describe the full range of management activities that enable a company to be profitable and sustainable.

PRODUCTION involves the actual process of creating goods and services.

Production can take the form of mass production, where a large number of standard products are created in a traditional assembly line process; it can be a very specialized process with individual or small quantities of a good being created; or it might involve running the logistics necessary to deliver a service efficiently. Inputs, therefore, can be raw materials like steel and chemicals; human inputs like specialized computer programmers, designers, or engineers; and money from a few thousand dollars to start a home-crafts business to millions of dollars for sophisticated manufacturing equipment. The concepts are the same whatever the business may be.

Core Functions in Production Management

Production management seeks to develop an efficient, relatively low-cost, and high-quality production process for creating specific products and services. Good production management is important if business goals, for both manufacturing and service-oriented companies, are to be met. The profit and value of each company is determined, to some extent, by its production management process.

The primary resources that firms use for the production process include:

- HUMAN RESOURCES: employees and their skills as applied to the production process
- RAW MATERIALS: the cost of all the goods needed to create the products or services
- CAPACITY: the annual production capabilities of the facilities, technology, machinery, and equipment

Each of these resources costs money. Employees need to be paid, materials have to be purchased, plus there are buildings, production facilities, and computer systems that require time and money to be maintained for ongoing production. The objective of production management is to use these resources in the most efficient manner possible. This will enable the organization to take advantage of higher production levels by producing more units at a lower cost per unit.

Whatever the business is selling, its production process is the conversion of inputs (such as skills and raw materials) into outputs (goods or services) as efficiently as possible. The process can include sourcing, manufacturing, storing, shipping, packaging, and more. Because it is based on a flow concept (the steps have to flow in a logical order to get the product or service ready for sale) production is measured as a "rate of output per period of time."

In any manufacturing environment – and your Foundation Business Simulation is in the manufacturing business – it is the Production Manager who has responsibility for scheduling the production sequence, type of product to be produced, and the volume of production. The three elements of management we discussed in Module 1 - planning, organizing, and controlling - are clearly necessary for production management. Following are some key concepts you will need to understand, along with some of the functions performed in the production department.

Scheduling Production

A *master production schedule* determines when the products will be produced and in what quantities. Dates must be met, specified quantities must be produced on time, and costs controlled to ensure this process goes smoothly and meets commitments. One tool to help with this process is a *PERT* chart. PERT stands for "Program Evaluation and Review Technique." This is a graphical representation that tracks production events and their time frames from start to finish. A PERT chart maps out the production process, which can help to identify problems before the process even begins.

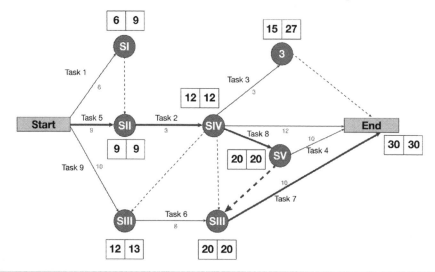

Is the BlackBerry season over?

Inventory management is critical to prevent stockouts and have smooth flow of product from your company to your customers. Production, however, is based on sales forecasts - and if the forecasts are not met?

RIM, maker of the BlackBerry, learned the answer to that question the hard way. In its disastrous second quarter results for 2013, the company announced a write-down of $934 million for unsold phones and cut 4,500 jobs, or about a third of its workforce. Sales for the period were about $1.6 billion, compared with the $3.03 billion analysts had expected.

As early as May 2012, business news site Bloomberg reported: *"stockpiles of BlackBerry smartphones and PlayBook tablets have swollen by two-thirds in the past year because of slumping sales".* Bloomberg data suggested the value of RIM's "in-house supplies" grew 18 percent in the first quarter of 2012 *"a faster rate than at any other company in the industry."*

In 2009, *Fortune* magazine named BlackBerry as the fastest growing company in the world. It held a 43% market share of the personal smartphone market at its peak in 2010. The competition from smartphones running Google's Android operating system and the Apple iPhone moved fast into BlackBerry's market. Management underestimated the impact of its competitors and over-estimated the popularity of its new product offerings. The BlackBerry Z10 phone, released in January 2013 to compete with the iPhone, did not excite buyers as expected. The result was close to a billion dollars in unsold BlackBerries left on the shelf.

Inventory Control

As goods are produced, they also need to be managed. Inventory control is the process of efficiently managing inventory. It is important to have enough products to sell, but not to have too many products unnecessarily sitting in the warehouse tying up cash. An efficient inventory control system minimizes the costs associated with inventory.

Companies must also manage inventory while it is in the process of being built. This is described as **work-in-process inventory,** or products that are only partially completed but have required an investment of some type of resource. Products cannot be sold until they are complete, and monitoring the status of products still involved in production is important.

Another cost directly associated with inventory is carrying cost. **Carrying cost** is the cost of maintaining completed products. Inventory ties up space, cash, and human resources. A popular method for reducing carrying costs

is the just-in-time (JIT) inventory system. This system is based on having just enough products on hand to satisfy consumer demand. Product should always be available, but not an overstock of what is needed for the near future.

The JIT system is often associated with a materials requirement planning system that ensures materials are available when needed. A **materials requirement planning** system or **MRP** helps determine when the materials to produce the product are needed to meet production deadlines. As a firm develops a forecast of the demand for its products, it determines the time at which the materials need to arrive at the production site to meet the anticipated market demand.

Economies of Scale

An **economy of scale** occurs when the cost of each good produced decreases as the volume produced increases. This reduction in cost per unit occurs because the initial investment of capital is shared with an increasing number of units of output. Variable costs

FOUNDATION.

Step fixed costs in Foundation.

In Foundation, you will encounter what is called step fixed costs, which is a business expense that is more or less constant over a low level shift in activity but changes incrementally when activity in the business shifts substantially. An example of a step fixed cost in your Foundation business is the need to buy new production machinery (e.g. capacity) to "step up" production to another level. Another example is investment in achieving a higher level of automation. Step fixed costs can be offset as production continues to expand, however, there are challenges assessing the impact on operating costs through the process of increasing activity levels in the business, and also the relationship with economies of scale. We will demonstrate how to calculate these impacts in the Module 3 Exercises.

Everyday life – economies of scale

You are setting up a small business in your local area and need a business card. The cost to print 50 business cards is $25, which is 50 cents per card. However, if you were to place an order for 500 business cards, the total cost is $50, reducing the cost to 10 cents per card. The more business cards printed in each print "run," the lower the cost per individual business card. The cost for the printing company is in setting the job up; the small additional cost in ink and paper to run a larger print run is marginal, so the cost per unit comes down.

(those that change with the number of goods produced) and fixed costs (costs that do not change regardless of volume) are monitored throughout this process. As output increases, fixed costs remain the same, and variable costs on a per-unit basis decline.

Economies of scale are particularly critical in industries with high fixed costs such as manufacturing. With an initial fixed investment in machinery, one worker, or unit of production, begins to work on the machine to produce a certain number of goods. If a second worker is added to the production line, he or she is able to produce an additional number of goods without significantly adding to the factory's cost of operation. If the number of goods produced grows significantly faster than the plant's cost of operation, the cost of producing each additional unit is less than the unit before, and an economy of scale occurs. This is one important reason why businesses always want to grow: Growth means you can reap the efficiency rewards offered by economies of scale.

Can Tesla achieve economies of scale and keep its promise?

Electric vehicles were first popular in the late 19th and early 20th centuries – before Ford Motor Company developed the production technologies to mass produce gasoline-fueled cars with internal combustion engines. For the next century and more, gas-powered cars ruled the highways with high-volume manufacturing providing the economies of scale to make them affordable. In the late 20th century, high oil prices, environmental concerns, and advances in battery technology brought electric cars back into the mainstream.

Most traditional car companies, including Ford, GM, BMW, Toyota, Honda, and Nissan, have released electric or electric/gasoline hybrid cars. By 2013, however, it was an automotive start-up, Tesla Motors from California, not only winning all the awards but also proving it had a profitable model for electric cars that might challenge the traditional car companies. Tesla opened a "new" market segment: luxury electric cars, with a longer battery life and range of up to 300 miles (480 kilometers), designed for discerning motorists and sold not through dealerships but their own, branded stores. It wasn't offering the battery version of a gas-powered car with fewer extras, but a new sought-after trend in upscale motoring.

When Tesla made its first profit in 2013, CEO Elon Musk said his company's goal had always been to mass-produce fully electric cars at a price affordable to the average consumer, and would do it *"within five years."* The current Tesla business model, however, makes the company a specialty car manufacturer (with the starting price on its Model S around $80,000), not a mass-market auto producer.

In Tesla's favor is the fact that as battery range increases, battery cost is likely to decrease; parts vendors – as they see the volumes increase on Tesla vehicles – are revamping their production and reducing the cost of parts; the company says it is steadily cutting the number of worker hours necessary to build each car; plus it is looking to buy additional production capacity.

The major car makers, however, are not sitting by while Tesla muscles into their space – they share all those advantages and have experience in mass manufacturing as well. Perhaps Tesla's biggest advantage is the extremely strong support it enjoys from its investors. In mid-2013, the Motley Fool site reported Tesla's market capitalization was almost $12 billion. *"That's about a fifth of BMW's, and BMW sold 1,845,186 vehicles last year. Tesla expects to sell 21,000 in 2013, and BMW will probably sell around 2 million."*

Forbes calls Tesla's share price *"a cult-like valuation",* and critics suggest that without generous U.S. Government loans and subsidies the company will not survive. Tesla's performance in the next few years will prove whether the beliefs of the Tesla faithful are well founded, or whether the challenge of economies of scale for mass market vehicles was too tough for the new market entrant.

Supply chain management

The collection of partners - manufacturer, wholesaler, distributor, retailer, on-line sales site - is referred to as the "supply chain." Efforts to improve the relationship between a company and its suppliers are referred to as *supply chain management (SCM).* The objective of SCM is to manage the connections between different businesses in the supply chain in order to enhance efficiencies and reduce costs.

Supply chain management involves these five basic components:

PLAN: The strategic plan to manage all of the resources needed to meet customer demand for your product or service

SOURCE: The selection of the supplies that will deliver goods and services (e.g., suppliers that can offer parts faster and/or cheaper)

MAKE: The manufacturing step involving scheduling, testing, packaging, and preparing for delivery

DELIVER: The logistics and timing of getting products and/or services through the relevant channels to the customer

RETURN: The "soft" link in the chain that supports customers who are returning products or have had problems with their product/service experience

Quality Control and Total Quality Management

Quality is the degree to which a product or service meets the company's internal or external standards *and* satisfies customer expectations. Quality control is the process of testing to ensure the product or service meets the organization's standards before it is sold. Techniques to monitor quality may include sampling, monitoring customer/user complaints, and planning to correct deficiencies.

National or international authorities often set standards in business. The International Organization for Standardization (ISO), founded in 1947 and made up of representatives from many national standards organizations, sets international quality standards. The ISO 9000 family of standards was designed to help organizations ensure they can meet the needs of customers and other stakeholders. The ISO 9000 standards are focused on a company's quality management systems. Certification requires a company to meet all of the requirements and pass a series of audits from independent certifiers. The benefits of compliance include internal management efficiencies – quantified by substantial research – and access to new business from companies that will work only with ISO-certified suppliers.

Companies are often required to adhere to standards set by national agencies or industry associations. In the United States, for example, standards agencies include the Food and Drug Administration (FDA) and the Consumer Products Safety Council (CPSC). The standards imposed by these entities affect design, performance, durability, safety, and many other attributes relating to performance and function. Quality is also used as a competitive advantage to provide "perceived excellence" compared with other choices in the market.

Whispers from the supply chain suggest a bullwhip

Apple Inc. is well known for extreme secrecy – particularly around new product offerings – but the company's silence creates an information vacuum that rumors race to fill. And Apple rumors are extremely popular on news websites, blogs, and in the general consumer and tech media.

A major source of information is Apple's supply chain – the many manufacturers that feed product components into the devices the world loves to buy.

A month after Apple released its new high-end 5S iPhone and lower end 5C iPhone in 2013, suggestions that the 5C was not selling as well as projected came from the supply chain. According to the *Wall Street Journal,* Taiwan-based iPhone manufacturers Pegatron and Foxconn both reported a cut in orders for the 5C. Retailers were reporting a much large inventory of 5C phones than 5S and some were cutting prices.

The lower than expected customer demand may have caused a "bullwhip effect" in the Apple supply chain. The bullwhip effect occurs when a change in customer demand for a product causes an increasingly large effect on suppliers the further along the supply chain it moves. Whereas Pegatron's order for the 5C phone was reportedly cut by 20% and Foxconn's order by around 33%, *"a component supplier was notified that the order for iPhone 5C parts would be cut by 50%, a source said."*

Information from the supply chain also suggested that Apple would revamp its device displays with new technology in 2014. In late 2013 NPD DisplaySearch, a company that provides analysis of the supply chain for computer displays, released data to suggest Apple *"intends to count on display technology for new product innovation".*

The information was based in part on the way Apple had approached various suppliers regarding samples and testing. A DisplaySearch analyst described the company's research method, which is to track *"the broadest bits of information throughout the supply chain and evaluate them over time to see what can be weeded out so that what is left is detailed, and hopefully, accurate indications of what is happening from a manufacturing and production standpoint."*

From current reports on Apple, can you verify if either of these supply-chain reports proved true? Did demand for the 5C phone decline? Did Apple release new display technology?

Several techniques are used to improve quality within an organization. **Quality Circles** are small groups of employees who meet regularly to attempt to identify and solve problems involved in quality improvement. A more formalized process is the concept of **Total Quality Management (TQM).**

Total Quality Management is the process of monitoring and improving the quality of products and services produced. This concept is primarily based on the work of W. Edwards Deming, an American statistician, professor, author, lecturer, and consultant. He is perhaps best known for his work in Japan. Beginning in 1950, Deming taught top man-

agement in Japan how to improve design and service, product quality, testing, and sales through the application of statistics and other methodologies. Deming offered 14 key principles to managers for transforming business effectiveness in his book **Out of the Crisis**. Although Deming does not use the term in his book, Deming is credited with launching the Total Quality Management movement. His work followed these objectives:

- To provide managers and other employees with the education and training necessary to excel in their jobs

- To encourage employees to take responsibility and to provide leadership

- To encourage all employees to search to improve the production process

Many firms create teams of employees to assess quality and to offer suggestions for improvement. This creates a form of cross-functional teamwork in which employees with different jobs, responsibilities, and perspectives work together to improve the production process through enhanced quality.

Benchmarking

The process called **benchmarking** is another quality-improvement technique. Benchmarking describes a method of evaluating performance by comparing it with another specified level achieved by another entity. Often, benchmarking involves studying highly successful companies in other industries. For example, Ford Motor Company in the U.S. studied and used the customer service performance levels of the American clothing company Eddie Bauer to improve its customer relations process. Benchmarking may also be used in conjunction with a TQM process.

Technology

Many production processes have been automated, and robotics has become a significant factor in manufacturing throughout the world. Machines and robotic equipment reduce the labor required in the production process. Good planning is required to make certain that the automation process, often requiring a substantial up-front investment in equipment, accomplishes the desired goals. This involves a thorough assessment of the required costs, savings, and benefits that may be realized, and the degree of "fit" within the organization and production process.

For example, automation is expensive and as you raise automation levels, it becomes more difficult for new product designs to be quickly created and produced. However, increasing automation carries the benefit of decreasing the labor costs associated with production.

Improving Productivity

Productivity is the ratio of output to inputs in production and is a measure of the efficiency of production. A common measure of productivity is dollars of output per hour worked. Production faces the standard challenges of increasing labor, material, and opportunity costs. It also must address the impact of uncertain world events, technological change, and the global labor market.

Interrelationship Between Production and Accounting

Accounting, as we discussed in Module 1, is the process that tracks, summarizes, and analyzes a company's financial position. Accounting provides information in a standard format so that stakeholders have a consistent frame of reference for assessing the company's financial health. Recall that we discussed two types of accounting:

FINANCIAL ACCOUNTING produces three key financial reports (the balance sheet, income statement, and cash flow statement). These three reports ensure that external stakeholders can access the information they need. External stakeholders might include investors and bankers; stockbrokers and financial analysts who offer investment assistance; suppliers; labor unions; customers; local, state, and federal governments; and governments of foreign countries in which the company does business.

MANAGERIAL ACCOUNTING provides vital information about a company to internal users. Because it is for internal use, it does not have to conform to the restrictions of outside regulation and can be expressed in whatever way is most useful for managers. Information can be reported in dollars, units, hours worked, products manufactured, numbers of defective products, or the quantity of contracts signed. The overall purpose of this information is to enable managers to make more informed and effective decisions.

There is another key difference between financial accounting and management accounting – financial accounting is always historical, in that it records past transactions in and through the company. Managerial accounting, however, is often forward-looking, using historical information to predict future outcomes and set expectations. For example, the reports a management accountant produces might forecast revenues, predict costs of planned activities, budget the amount of money the company will spend on various activities, and provide analysis based on that information. By describing how alternative actions might affect the company's profit and solvency, the information and analysis helps managers plan for the future.

Because managerial accounting pertains specifically to improving internal decision making, it has particular relevance to a company's production-related activities. So it is important to introduce you to some basic accounting concepts related to managerial accounting. We will look carefully at the reports related to financial accounting (balance sheet, income statement, and cash flow) in Modules 4 and 5.

The Accounting Equation and Managerial Accounting

Two key elements of the production function (those you will practice in Foundation) are increasing and reducing the capacity of production lines based on the sales forecasts for various products, and maintaining or increasing automation based on the technological advancement of products and how quickly the company can get them to market. The production department, therefore, builds up assets (production equipment) and accrues liabilities (loans to buy the equipment).

In reality, a production department is doing much more than dealing with assets and liabilities. It is managing staff, equipment, productivity, quality control, software, and so forth, but all the *accounting* department of the company is interested in is the way all those activities can be distilled into numbers that conform to accounting rules.

The Accounting Equation – which can be applied to every business – is:

$$\text{ASSETS} = \text{LIABILITIES} + \text{EQUITY}$$

In a corporation, "equity" means the money the owners have invested in it. As the accounting equation dictates, the equity must always be equal to the value of the company's assets, minus the value of its liabilities.

Companies typically use managerial accounting reports that fall into two broad categories:

BUDGET REPORTS: Budgeting is the process of quantifying managers' plans and showing the impact of these plans on the company's operating activities (and remember, the goal of operations is to make a profit.) Managers present this information in a budget (a "forecast"). Once the planned activities have occurred, managers can evaluate the results of the operating activities against the budget to make sure that the actual operations of the various parts of the company achieved the goals established in the plans. For example, a company might report a budget showing how many units of product it plans to sell during the first three months of the year. When actual sales have been made, managers will compare the results of these sales with the budget to determine if their forecasts were "on target" and, if not, they will investigate the discrepancy. Budgets are powerful planning and control devices.

COST ANALYSIS REPORTS: Cost analysis is the process of defining the costs of specific products or activities within a company. A manager will use a cost analysis to decide whether to stop or to continue making a specific product. The cost analysis shows a product's contribution to profitability at different levels of sales. Assigning (or defining) costs to products and activities is a complex activity. Every decision maker in the company has to be familiar with the way relevant costs are assigned in order to make appropriate decisions. Consistency in this reporting process is critical to ensure this information is accurate and understood by a company's various decision makers.

Management accounting reports, therefore, are produced to help managers monitor and evaluate the company's operations in order to determine whether its planned goals are being achieved. They can also highlight specific "variances," or differences, from plans, indicating where corrections to operations can be made if necessary.

FOUNDÁTION.

In Foundation, Plant and Equipment for your factory will be a significant number in your company's assets column, and the debt you take on to pay for it will be a significant number in the liabilities column.

Contribution Margin – a key to profitability

Contribution margin is the amount of money left over from the sale of your product after you have paid all the costs of producing that product. This money "contributes" to the running of the business.

When we say "costs" – as discussed earlier – we usually refer to either variable costs or to fixed costs. Costs that differ depending on how many products you produce (if you are producing a lot, you'll need more raw material and more labor so your costs will be higher) are called "variable" costs. Costs that don't change no matter how much you produce (whether you build one product or a million products you'll still have to pay the rent, the Corporate Office expenses, and other bills) are called "fixed" costs. The contribution margin represents the amount of money that is left over, after your products have been made and sold, to contribute to paying your fixed costs. The higher the contribution margin, the more profitable the business can be.

CONTRIBUTION MARGIN = PRICE – VARIABLE COSTS.

Calculating the contribution margin from each product line a company produces is a critical element of cost analysis.

In your Foundation Business Simulation you will have the opportunity to create your own managerial accounting reports. One of your most important managerial accounting calculations will be contribution margin.

This equation can help you work out how you might manipulate the contribution margin, by increasing or reducing the price and the variable costs of your products.

3D printers: changing the production paradigm?

3D printers use additive manufacturing techniques in which products are built up from a digital plan rather than pieced together by parts that are cut, machined, and drilled as in traditional manufacturing.

Companies such as **General Electric, Ford, Airbus,** and **Siemens** – companies that traditionally incorporate mass production throughout their operations – are all incorporating 3D printer manufacturing techniques in their production departments.

The technique makes mass *customization* possible, a concept that is valuable in areas like health care where each patient is different. For example, 3D Systems, a market leader in 3D printing, makes individual hearing-aid shells printed from scans of patients' ears, and transparent plastic "aligners" that progressively straighten teeth using molds from a patient's mouth. The disadvantages of additive manufacturing include the high price of many of the materials used for printing (from light-sensitive liquids to metallic powders) and the time it takes to produce individual items.

The advantages, however, as Richard A. D'Aveni suggests in the *Harvard Business Review*, may "change the world". They may certainly change production management. One implication is the potential for local or on-site manufacturing, reducing the value of centrally located plants offering mass production, and economies of scale. The higher cost per unit at a local 3D plant may be offset by lower transport costs. Printing on demand means inventory can be carefully managed. Repair shops could produce spare parts on-site. As D'Aveni suggests, *"assembly plants could eliminate the need for supply chain management by making components as needed."*

"These first-order implications," he said, *"will cause businesses all along the supply, manufacturing, and retailing chains to rethink their strategies and operations."*

Think about this issue and then list the implications 3D printing might have on topics discussed including Human Resources, Raw Materials, Capacity, Scheduling Production, Inventory Control, and Quality Control.

Actively monitoring the contribution margins of your various products will help to ensure your Foundation company is profitable and competitive. In Foundation there are several ways to improve your contribution margin, but each comes with trade-offs. For example, you can:

- *Raise prices:* But fewer people will purchase at a higher price.

- *Lower material costs:* Although you may make your product less attractive because it could be bigger, slower, or less reliable.

- *Reduce labor costs:* Increasing automation will cost money and can increase the length of time needed to update your products.

- *Economies of scale:* Reduce the cost of each good produced as the volume produced increases.

Chapter Review Questions

Production Basics

1. What is the difference between production and operations?

2. What are the primary resources used in the production process?

3. What does "economies of scale" mean, and why is that concept relevant in the production process?

4. What benefits does TQM offer an organization?

5. What does benchmarking accomplish?

6. How does supply chain management impact the production process?

7. What are the potential benefits of effectively managing quality control?

Linking Production to Accounting

8. Who relies on accounting information?

9. What is the accounting equation?

10. What is cost analysis?

11. What are some ways to increase your contribution margin?

You – in the executive suite!

Production Manager and Research & Development Manager

In Module 2, you completed your job rotation track as *Sales and Marketing Manager*, and learned about sales forecasting. If assigned, you also completed the Customer Survey Score exercise at Appendix 3 to gain further insight into your forecasting and decision making.

Now we switch gears to become, first, the *Production Manager,* and second, the *Research and Development Manager.*

Activities: Approximately 120 – 150 minutes to complete	COMPLETED
A-1: Answer all **Chapter Review Questions** Your instructor will advise you on how to turn in your answers.	☐
A-2: In the **Summary Guide** at Appendix 1 read **Research & Development Decisions** 200 and **Production Decisions** 202.	☐
A-3: **Read** the following text through to the end of the module. **Complete** all of the required tables and watch the online videos.	☐

Exercise #6: Production and Inventory Management

Production management requires two different kinds of decision making:

OPERATIONS: Operational decisions involve making your best effort to meet your goals with available resources in the current year. Some decisions you make won't have an impact in the current year – you cannot build a new factory or develop a completely new product within the year, for example.

INVESTMENT: Investment decisions are longer range because they help you build capacity and the systems you need to create the company you have visualized for next year and into the future.

Both operational and investment decisions are dependent upon one thing; accurate sales forecasting.

The sales forecast, as we discovered in Module 2, is an *uncertain* prediction. However, the sales forecast is also an *important* prediction because you will use it to make decisions with significant consequences. The sales forecast:

- Determines the production schedule (how many units of each product to produce)

- Determines capital investments (when and how much to invest in capacity)

- Establishes the financing requirements to operate and grow your business

- Is used to test the sensitivity of the company's overall performance in the market to different levels of sales.

Decision making under conditions of uncertainty and risk is the essence of operating in a competitive environment. Fortunately, there are tools to help you manage the riskiness of each decision.

These exercises will explore these areas:

- Inventory management goals
- Production schedule
- Investment decisions in capacity.

 Before we begin, view the *Video on Production*

Sales Forecasting and Inventory Management

Your company manufactures electronic sensors, so determining how many sensors you are going to produce is your single most important operational decision. Why is it so important?

If you don't produce enough sensors, you will sell everything you produce and "stock out". On the surface, that may sound like a good thing. But it means disappointed customers and lost revenue.

On the other hand, if you produce many more sensors than you sell, then you have a large buildup of sensors (inventory) in the warehouse. The cost of carrying inventory for a year is 12% of its value, and that is an expense that reduces profitability. The biggest reason to manage inventory levels, however, is that inventory *ties up cash*.

At the most simple level, the production process turns cash into electronic sensors. You take cash and purchase materials and labor. The materials and labor are combined in the factory to produce product. Your product inventory represents cash that you cannot use (because it is sitting on the shelves in the warehouse) until you sell it and turn it back into cash.

Inventory Management Targets. How much is the right amount of inventory to have at the end of the year? As Production Manager, you have been told that the Board has two inventory management goals for you to meet.

1. Never stock out; have at least one unit of inventory left at the end of the year.

2. Do not have more than 60 days of inventory on hand at the end of the year.

What is 60 days of inventory? It is the amount of inventory you would sell in 60 days. Because you don't have control over how many you will actually sell, however, we are going to talk about 60 days of production instead.

To help visualize 60 days of production, a simple example is provided on the next page. Assume you want to produce 1,200 units of the product Able in 12 months, so you'll produce 100 units a month.

Table 1

Jan	Feb	Mar	April	May	June	July	Aug	Sept	Oct	Nov	Dec
100	100	100	100	100	100	100	100	100	100	100	100

Since a month has (on average) 30 days, 60 days of inventory is about 2 months. In this example, 2 months of inventory would be the 100 units produced in November and the 100 units produced in December. If you have 1,200 units available for sale, 60 days of inventory would be 200 units. Sixty days is 2/12 of a year. For ease of calculation, 2/12 is 1/6 of a year. A convenient inventory management tools is this simple table.

Table 2

Year End Inventory	Production
1	1,200 - 1 = 1,199
1,200 / 6 = 200	1,200 - 200 = 1,000

To meet your inventory management goals:

- What is the least you can have in year-end inventory? Since you never want to stock out, you want at least 1 unit left.
- What is the most you can have in inventory? Since you don't want more than 60 days or 1/6 of a year's worth of inventory, you don't want more than 1,200/6 or 200 units left in the warehouse at the end of the year.
- What is the most you can sell? If you have 1,200 available for sale and have one left in the warehouse, you will have sold 1,199.

The least you can sell? If you have 1,200 units available for sale and have 200 units left at the end of the year, you will have sold 1,000 units total. So, if you have 1,200 units available for sale, you will meet your inventory management goal if you sell at least 1,000 but not more than 1,199. If you have 1,200 units available,

you will meet your inventory management goal if you have at least 1 but not more than 200 in the warehouse at the end of the year.

Sales Forecasts and Production Schedules. There is one important concept that you have to understand to set your production schedule:

The number of units that you make available for sale should generate an inventory management range that captures your sales forecast(s).

Let's start simply with a fictional product named AceX. You analyze all of the information available to you and decide that your BEST estimate is that you will sell 1,100 units of the product next year, so how many do you produce?

You need a number that generates an inventory management range that is "centered" on 1,100 units. That way, if you sell more than you predict, you will still have some units left over. If you sell less than you predict, you won't have too many left over.

The inventory management range is two months' worth of inventory. If you want 1,100 to be in the "middle" of that range, you would to produce so that you would have made 1,100 units in 11 months. If you do that and you sell 1,100 units, you would still have one month's inventory left at the end of the year.

If you want an inventory management centered on 1,100 units; you would:

- Divide 1,100 (number to be in the center of the range) by 11 (number of months in which you want to produce your target).

The result is 100 (your 1 month "cushion")

- Add the 100 to 1,100 to get 1,200. This is the number you want to produce.

To check, generate an inventory management table based on having 1,200 units available for sale.

Table 3

Year End Inventory	Production
1	1,199
200	1,000

If you produce 1,200 units, your sales forecast of 1,100 units is right in the middle of the range (1,000 - 1,200). Your forecast is uncertain. If you have been too optimistic in your forecast, you can sell 100 units less (1,000) and still meet your goal. If you were conservative in your forecast, you can sell 99 units more (1,199) and still meet your goal.

Now let's look at a typical example you will come across in Foundation. Imagine that you have used the market growth forecast to predict sales of 1,232 in the Low Tech segment for your Able product next year, (1,120 x 1.1). Able sold 463 units in the High Tech market last year, but you know that those customers are going to have better options next year. You did another forecast, using the December Customer Survey, to predict that you will sell 418 units of Able to the High Tech market. Combining your forecasts (1232 + 418) gives you a best guess of 1,650 units. How many should you have available for sale?

As in the first example, you will need a number that ensures you have 1,650 available in 11 months. If you divide 1,650 by 11, you have a monthly production schedule of 150 units. If you make 150 units a month for 12 months, you would have 1,800 units available. (That is the same as adding 1,650 + 150).

Table 4

Year End Inventory	Production
1	1,799
1800 / 6 = 300	1,800 - 300 = 1,500

Your target of 1,650 is in the center of the "acceptable sales" range generated by having 1,800 units available for sale.

Now let's look at another important piece of information you need to note when you are scheduling production – the inventory on hand.

Figure 1

Schedule ⓘ	
	Able
1st Shift Capacity ⓘ	1,630
Buy/Sell Capacity ⓘ	123
Automation Rating ⓘ	1522
Production After Adj. ⓘ	1,507

We have been using the clumsy language "having 1,800 available for sale" rather than "making 1,800" because the actual production schedule must take into account the number of units left in inventory. In the case of the Able product in the example pictured right, you want 1,630(000) units available to meet the sales forecast. You start the year with 123(000) in the warehouse. So instead of scheduling production for 1,630(000) units, you schedule so that you would have 1,507(000) produced (1,630-123 = 1,507).

However, to really have 1,507 produced in a year, you have to schedule production for 1,522 – a little bit more – so that your "Production After Adjustment" will be your target of 1,507. There are several reasons you might not actually get all of the units you schedule out of your production facility on time. In the case of this example, it is because the company has a 30 day Accounts Payable lag – and at 30 days, the company's suppliers withhold about 10% of the components ordered from them. We will cover these issues in later modules. The key point right now is to remember to allow for "Production After Adjustment" in your production scheduling.

Capacity Decisions. All of the production decisions discussed above assume that you have a production line that has the capacity to produce as many products as you need. When you took your job with the Andrews company, the production line for your product Able had the capacity to produce 800(000) units running one shift for a full year, and 1600(000) units running a full second shift for a year.

It is critical to understand that additional capacity takes a year to build. If it is 2014 and you order additional capacity on your production line, that capacity will not be available until 2015. Look at the FastTrack (Appendix 2), page 4, Production Information. The second to last column is headed "Capacity Next Round". Of the six companies in the market, only Digby Company ordered additional capacity. Digby has 900(000) units of capacity available and, if it runs two shifts, can produce up to 1,800(000) units in the coming year, which is Round 2. All companies are completely out of stock (see column 4, Unit Inventory). You know that demand in the Low End will be 6098 next round (5,544 + 10% growth) and will continue to grow at that rate each year. If you believe you will need extra capacity to fulfill growing demands, you need to plan ahead.

Imagine you are running the Digby Company that has 900 units of capacity at the beginning of Round 2. You can produce up to 1800 units this year (Round 3), but estimate you will need at least 2,300 units in Round 4. If you run two shifts all year, you can double your capacity on the production line. Half of 2,300 (the capacity of two shifts) equal 1,150 units of capacity. You currently have 900 units of capacity so you need to order 250 additional units now, to be ready for 2014's production run. (1,150 – 900= 250).

The key message in planning capacity is *plan ahead.*

Exercise #7: Production Investment – Capacity & Automation

For your Foundation company to succeed, you will have to build quality products:

- That meet customer expectations (requiring effective marketing)
- At the lowest possible production cost (requiring efficient manufacturing)

Efficient manufacturing requires a concrete and specific understanding of two areas:

1. The costs of production, and
2. The investments that allow you to control those costs.

As Production Manager, your goal is to explore those relationships and build your understanding. We will soon learn how operating decisions are reflected on the income statement. The income statement can help you assess the effectiveness of your production decisions. We'll look at it in Module 4.

Production and Contribution Margin

Under Managerial Accounting, we talked about the Contribution Margin. The Contribution Margin is the amount of money left over from the sale of your product, after you have paid all the costs of producing that product. That money can "contribute" to the overall running of the business.

A contribution margin can be understood in two ways:

1. REVENUE – Total Variable Costs: A total over a period of time or,

2. PRICE PER UNIT – cost of making the UNIT (UNIT COST): A "per unit" measure.

Price X units sold	Revenue
Unit cost X units sold	–Total Variable Cost
Contribution margin (unit) X units sold	Contribution Margin

Because the number of units sold is a constant, the relationship between revenue, total variable cost, and contribution margin is the same as the relationship between price, unit cost, and contribution margin (unit).

The contribution margin is reported in your company's income statement.

Contribution margin is usually reported as a percentage of price (for a per unit contribution margin) or of revenue (for the total contribution margin). It doesn't matter which because the percentages are the same.

For example, consider the results for a company that sold 1,000 units at a price of $50 and a unit cost of $30

$50 X 1000		$50,000
-$30 X 1000		-$30,000
$20 X 1000		$20,000

Calculated on a per unit basis, the contribution margin is $20/$50 or 40%. Calculated on the totals, the contribution margin is $20,000/$50,000 or 40%. Notice that changing the number of units sold will change the size of the contribution margin on the income statement but it will not change the percentage. In the example, if 2,000 units had been sold the revenue would have been $100,000, total variable cost would have been $60,000, and the contribution margin would have been $40,000. The contribution margin as a percentage would still be 40%.

FOUNDATION.

Find Andrews' contribution margin for Round 1 in the FastTrack (Appendix 2). You will see it is reported as a percentage – per unit – on the front page of the report.

Now, find Andrews' contribution margin for Round 1 in the company's income statement. From your spreadsheet, click "reports" and then "annual report." You will see it is reported as a portion of overall revenue.

Contribution Margin as a Percentage Measures Operational Efficiency

To improve the efficiency of your operations (make more profit on every unit that you sell), you need to improve your contribution margin. The only way to improve your contribution margin is to increase your price or to reduce your unit cost. In Foundation, your unit cost consists of two components; material costs and labor costs.

From your experience as a Marketing Manager, you know that there are trade-offs associated with increasing your price and/or lowering your material costs.

All of the options for improving the contribution margin through marketing management, therefore, may result in lower sales volume.

The other option for improving the contribution margin, however, is to lower labor costs. Labor is calculated on a per-unit basis and is determined by two things: automation and overtime.

ACTION	RESULT
Increase your price	Lower monthly Customer Survey Scores Sell fewer units
Lower your material costs: • Make your product bigger • Make your product slower • Make your product less reliable	Lower monthly Customer Survey Scores Sell fewer units

Automation

Automation is a measure of how sophisticated the machinery used in the production process is. As automation increases, work processes change and human labor becomes more efficient because workers have more specialized machinery to work with. Another result is that highly automated machines need fewer people to operate them, so your staff is reduced.

There are three key points for using automation to help you meet your goals:

1. As automation goes up, labor costs go down.
2. As automation goes up, R&D project times increase.
3. Automation is expensive.

Automation and Labor Costs. You have access to some excellent information on labor costs. The base labor rate at the lowest level of automation (an automation rating of 1) has been calculated at $11.20 per unit for your company. The labor rate per unit is re-

duced by about 10% of that base number for each level of automation. The overtime rate – what you pay your workers on second shift – is time and a half, or 1.5 times the base rate.

It is going to be useful to calculate the labor costs at each level of automation. Fill out the remainder of Table 5, following the examples at automation levels 1, 2, and 3.

There is enormous potential for increased automation to reduce labor costs. At an automation level of 10, the base rate is $1.12 for first shift and $1.68 for second shift. Because your target is to manage your contribution margin, this relationship between automation and labor cost is important to you.

Assume you have developed a good product, with the size, performance, and reliability that best meet your customers' needs. You have set the price so it will generate the volume of sales required to be successful. In this situation, the higher your level of automation (the lower your labor cost per unit), the

Table 5- Labor Costs

Automation Level	Reduction in Labor Cost	Base Rate	2nd Shift Multiplier	2nd Shift Rate
1		$11.20	x1.5	$16.80
2	$-1.12	$10.08	x1.5	$15.12
3	$-1.12	$8.96	x1.5	$13.44
4	$-1.12		x1.5	
5	$-1.12		x1.5	
6	$-1.12		x1.5	
7	$-1.12		x1.5	
8	$-1.12		x1.5	
9	$-1.12		x1.5	
10	$-1.12		x1.5	

greater your contribution margin will be. That means you will make more profit on every unit you sell.

Let's calculate contribution margins, at different levels of automation, for your product. Your forecast shows you can sell 1,500(000) units at a price of $35.00 and you know your material cost per unit is $15.00.

Table 6 allows you to calculate the contribution margin (per unit), the contribution margin as a percentage of price, and the total contribution margin at the different levels of automation (assuming 0% overtime so you can use the base rate at that automation level).

There are three calculations to be done. Fill out the remainder of the table below to demonstrate the following at each of the automation levels listed:

1. Price - (material cost + labor cost) = Contribution Margin (unit)
2. Contribution Margin (unit) / Price = Contribution Margin (percentage)
3. Contribution Margin (unit) X number of units sold = Total Contribution Margin

Increasing the contribution margin by investing in higher automation (better machinery for your factory) is an investment in improved profitability. So if you raise your automation

Table 6- Contribution Margin

Price	Material Cost	Automation Level	Labor Cost	Contribution Margin (unit)	Contribution Margin %	Total Contribution Margin
$35.00	$15.00	1	$11.20	$8.80	25%	$13,200
$35.00	$15.00	3				
$35.00	$15.00	5				
$35.00	$15.00	7				
$35.00	$15.00	10	$1.12	$18.88	54%	$28,320

enough to lower your unit cost by $2.24 in round 2, you will make $2.24 more profit on every sensor that you sell in the future. However, there are trade-offs. Additional automation slows down product innovation so it takes longer to bring out new designs. It is also very expensive.

Automation and R&D Project Times. Section 4.3.3 in The Guide (online) demonstrates the relationship between automation levels and the length of R&D projects. Please refer to the graphic below.

Low Tech products should be repositioned every second year. These customers expect that each year their products will be .5 units smaller and .5 units faster. At automation ratings of 8 or above, the R&D project times get so long that repositioning might take more than one year. You can still manage your product at high levels of automation, but it requires careful planning with respect to timing.

High Tech customers are more demanding, with expectations that products will be .7 units smaller and .7 units faster each year. Therefore, you must reposition your product every year (to keep its age young and positioned on the "ideal spot") to meet the needs of High Tech customers. You can see from

the chart that if you have automation much above 3 or 4, High Tech repositioning takes too long to meet both goals of having the ideal spot and the youngest age.

Investing in Automation. Automation requires a big investment. It costs $4.00 per unit of capacity for every additional point of automation. So if you want to raise your automation by one level, say from automation level 3 to automation level 4, it will cost you $4.00 per unit of capacity. If you wanted to raise your automation two levels, from 3 to 5, it will cost you $8.00 per unit of capacity.

In this example at the end of Round 2, Able has a capacity of 900 units and an automation rating of 6.5. If you wanted to raise the automation rating one level (from 6.5 to 7.5), it would cost $3,600.

Figure 3

Physical Plant	
	Able
1st Shift Capacity	900
Buy/Sell Capacity	0
Automation Rating	6.5
New Autom. Rating	7.5
Investment ($000)	$3600

Automation is $4.00 per level of automation per unit of capacity. You are raising your automation one level (so $4 per unit of capacity) and you have 900 units of capacity. This project would require an investment of $4 x 900 or $3,600. Your simulation calculates this investment in the Production worksheet.

To test your understanding, you pose the following problem and answer the following questions.

Figure 2

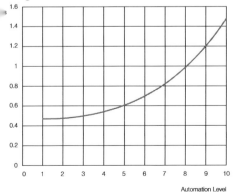

Automation Level

You are creating a new product AceX and want to build a very efficient factory to produce it. Since AceX will compete in the High Tech market, you think that an automation level of 4 would be the best. You want your factory to have a capacity of 800 units.

1. How much will you have to invest in the machinery for AceX's factory?
2. What will the labor cost per unit be if you are produce 800 units?
3. What will the labor cost per unit be if you produce 1,600 units?

Investment in Capacity

The other factor that influences labor cost is the capacity of your factory. The capacity of a factory is the number of units you can produce running one shift. How does capacity influence overtime? You can produce more than your first shift capacity, but every unit produced above your first shift capacity costs you one and a half times your base wage. This is standard across most businesses; overtime employees earn "time and a half." If your labor costs $10 per unit for the first shift, it will cost one and a half times that, or $15.00 per unit, for the second shift.

One way to avoid overtime is to have a large enough factory that you can produce all of the necessary units on the first shift. The major flaw with this strategy is that increasing capacity requires a significant investment. Expansion of capacity requires two major expenditures:

1. The basic production line, and,
2. The level of robotics (machinery) on that line.

Whether you are building a new factory or expanding an existing facility, the size of the investment is directly proportional to the number of units of capacity you want to add.

For example:

- The production line requires an investment of $6.00 for every unit of capacity you wish to add.

- If you want to add 200 units of capacity, it will require an investment of $6.00 times 200 or $1,200 for the "addition" onto your factory.

- If you are adding a new product and building a new production line that has a capacity of 800 units, you will need to invest $4,800.

Investing in the building gets you the basic machinery. To make the machinery more efficient, you have to improve its level of automation. You have already done the investment analysis for machinery when you did the automation analysis. How expensive is it to add machinery? It depends on what level of automation and how many units you want to be able to build. For every unit of capacity you want to add, machinery costs $4.00 per level of automation.

You currently have a factory with a capacity of 800 units at an automation level of 3. How big of an investment was required to create that factory? Since it is $6.00 per unit for the building and $4.00 per level of automation per unit for the machinery, you can calculate the investment by following these steps:

Table 7

Building	Machinery	Total
$6.00 x 800	($4.00 x 3) x 800	
$4,800	$9,600	$14,400

Notice that to add capacity, you enter the amount that you want to add. Because this is a new factory, you are going from 0 units to 800 units of capacity.

The Foundation spreadsheet allows you to click the "calculate" button to determine the cost of this in the Production worksheet.

You enter 800 in Buy/Sell Capacity. If you wanted to go from 800 to 1,000 in the next year, you would enter the amount of capacity you wished to add, or 200 units. The desired automation rating is what is entered. How do you account for this investment? It is recorded on the balance sheet under Fixed Assets as "Property Plant and Equipment."

You want to test your understanding a little more. Your current factory has a capacity of 700 units at an automation level of 4. What size investment would be required to bring the capacity to 1,100 at the same level of automation?

Selling Capacity. If you find that demand for one of your products has fallen, or you make a strategic decision to get out of a particular market, you can sell some or all of your production capacity. When you sell capacity, you will recover 65% of your original investment.

Figure 4

Physical Plant	
	Able
1st Shift Capacity	-
Buy/Sell Capacity	800
Automation Rating	-
New Autom. Rating	3.0
Investment ($000)	$14,400

In other words, you will get back $.65 on the dollar. To sell capacity, enter a negative num-ber (in Buy/Sell Capacity, the Foundation software calculates (and reports) how much money you will receive.

If you sell *all of the capacity* for your product, the simulation takes that as a liquidation order for that product. The product will disappear from the R&D worksheet in the next year. Any inventory that you have remaining in the warehouse is liquidated at one half the cost of production. "Liquidation" means that it is sold all at once, at half the unit cost. An advantage of this option is that you do not have to worry about your inventory - stocking out or having too much is no longer a consideration for this "liquidated" product.

If you *reduce capacity,* even if you downsize your factory so that you have only one unit of capacity remaining, the inventory in the warehouse is not liquidated. You can sell using whatever pricing strategy works in the market. This may be an advantage because you have the potential of making a contribution margin from the sale of these products. However, you are still responsible for managing your inventory with this choice. You may end up with too much inventory or you may stock out.

Figure 5

Physical Plant	
	Able
1st Shift Capacity	900
Buy/Sell Capacity	(899)
Automation Rating	6.5
New Autom. Rating	3.0
Investment ($000)	($18699)

To finalize your Production Manager rotation, please answer the following questions to ensure you have understood all of the issues involved:

Automation: Labor costs, contribution margins, and R&D project times

1. Assuming no overtime, if you raised your automation rate from 3 to 5, how much would your labor costs go down? *Remember: Each level of increased automation changes your labor cost by $1.12.*

2. If you raised your automation rating from 3 to 5, how much would that affect investment cost, assuming a capacity of 800(000) units?

3. Assuming no overtime, if you raised your automation rating from 4 to 7, how much would your contribution margin per unit go up? If you had set your price at $30, how much would your contribution margin as a percentage of sales go up?

Calculate the required investment in automation

4. You are creating a new product AceX to compete in the High Tech market, and you think that an automation level of 4 would be the best. You want your factory to have a capacity of 1,000(000) units. How much will you have to invest in the machinery for AceX's factory?

5. You have a production line for an existing product. The capacity is for 1,000 units with an automation level of 3. The per-unit cost of adding capacity is $6 for machinery and $4 per level of automation. If you increase the automation from 3 to 6 for the current capacity, what will that cost?

Calculate the required investment in capacity

6. Your current factory has a capacity of 700 units at an automation level of 4. What size investment would be required to bring the capacity to 1,100 at the same level of automation?

7. You are adding a new product and want the factory to have a capacity of 1,000 units at an automation level of 6. What size investment would be required to build this factory?

Determine the impact of reducing capacity and/or discontinuing a product

8. At the end of the year, you have 600 units of product ABYSS left in inventory. Each unit cost $20 to produce. Your gut reaction is that you need to discontinue this product. ABYSS's factory has a capacity of 500 units at an automation level of 6. If you decide to discontinue this product, how much money will you get for the factory? How much will you get for the inventory?

Margin Potential

Even more important than an understanding of contribution margins, labor costs, and automation ratings is the concept of potential margin gains or losses. This will allow you to assess whether you should dedicate time and resources to a product or customer segment. The higher the margin gains, the more attention you should give a product or customer segment.

So let's assume in a segment that the costs are as follows:

Table 8 - Material Positioning Component Costs.

	Trailing Edge Cost	Leading Edge Cost
Low Tech	$1.50	$8.00
High Tech	$4.00	$10.00

Note: These costs are for the beginning of Round 1. They are used solely to illustrate the Margin Potential concept

Now let's check the Buying Criteria on the Segment Analysis pages of the Foundation FastTrack for Round 0 to find the maximum permitted price and the minimum acceptable MTBF (Mean Time Before Failure) for each segment (lowering the MTBF decreases material cost).

The next step is to determine the minimum *Material Cost* per segment using the following equation:

MINIMUM MATERIAL COST = [(LOWEST ACCEPTABLE MTBF X 0.30) / 1000] + TRAILING EDGE POSITIONING COST
listed in Table 8

The same steps have to be taken to determine the minimum Labor Cost for each segment. Let's assume a base labor cost of $11.20 using the following equation:

MINIMUM LABOR COST = [$11.20 - (1.12 X AUTOMATION RATINGS BELOW)] + 1.12

- Low Tech Automation: 10.0
- High Tech Automation: 6.0

Now we can find the range of the contribution margin dollars and contribution margin percentage:

CONTRIBUTION MARGIN = PRICE - (MATERIAL COST + LABOR COST)

MARGIN PERCENTAGE = CONTRIBUTION MARGIN / PRICE

When we compare this to the maximum price customers are willing to pay, we have identified the margin potential for a particular product or segment.

Table 9 - Margin Potential

Segment	Maximum Price	Minimum Material Cost	Minimum Labor Cost	Contribution Margin	
				$	%
Low Tech					
High Tech					

Exercise #8: Research and Development

We learned as *Marketing Manager* how critical it is to understand our customers and what they want. But knowing what our customers want doesn't mean we can automatically provide it. Business involves many interactive decisions and every decision that you make has trade-offs. If you lower your price, you may make your cus-

tomers happy and sell more sensors. You may also make less money from each sale, however, and have less to invest in growing the business.

As *Production Manager,* you saw there were further trade-offs. You wanted to build plenty of products to satisfy customer demand, but needed to be careful about making too many products and building up inventory that might sit on the shelf, tying up cash.

Now as you move into the role of **Research and Development Manager,** you have an opportunity to design your company's products. Your current product, Able, is selling to both market segments but as buyers in each segment have different requirements, you are pretty sure Able isn't really satisfying anyone.

You have three options in R&D:

1. Revise an existing product,
2. Introduce a new product, or
3. Discontinue an existing product.

 Before we begin, view the Video on
Research & Development

Whenever you revise an existing product or design a new product, an R&D project begins. One of the most important things about an R&D project is how long it will take. Project length is important because it determines how much the project costs and when the new or improved product will be available. Here is a briefing on your R&D department and its operations:

- The bigger the change in the product, the longer the R&D project will take. This makes intuitive sense. If you are making a small change to an existing product, you know a lot about it already and it won't take long to revise. If you are offering a radically different product, there will be many more "unknowns" to consider and it will take longer to resolve.

- If you have more than one R&D project underway, each project will take longer. The R&D department is a limited resource.
- The higher the automation of the assembly line, the longer the R&D project will take. R&D projects not only change the product, but also the requirements for manufacturing the product. The more specialized the equipment used in the manufacturing process, the longer it is going to take to reconfigure it to produce the revised product.
- The longer the R&D project lasts, the more it is going to cost. R&D projects incur expense at a rate of about $1,000,000 per year. For example, a 6-month (1/2 year) project will have an R&D expense of $500,000, a 9-month project (3/4 year) will cost $750,000, and an 18-month project will cost $1,500,000.
- If a product is involved in one R&D project at the beginning of the year, you will not be able to schedule another project for that product for the rest of the year. Project scheduling is so important to success that schedules (and the resource commitments they require) can only be set once a year, in January. So if a product is in the process of development, you can't order your R&D staff to change it again until the current project is completed and the next scheduling cycle begins.
- The "time in market" is probably the most important consequence of R&D project length. R&D projects make products more attractive to customers. Because attractive products sell more, the sooner you improve your product, the sooner you can sell it. Conversely, the longer your project takes, the longer your less attractive product will be on the market. If your R&D project takes 18 months, it means that you are offering your less attractive product and will sell fewer products during those 18 months.

Managing Your Products

The Foundation spreadsheet provides a simple way to explore the trade-offs involved in R&D decisions. Here you can change one product characteristic at a time and see how long the project will take to complete by watching changes in the revision date. You will also be able to assess the change in material costs, and the change in the overall product attractiveness.

Trade-offs: MTBF

Table 10 - Revision and Demand Predictions

Change Able's MTBF to:	How long to revise?	R&D Cost to Revise	Material Cost to Revise	Predicted Demand
21,000			$16.04	1,122
20,000	15 Jan	$40K	$15.74	1,101
19,000	29 Jan	$80	$15.44	1006
18,000	13 Feb	$120	$15.14	913

Go to your Foundation spreadsheet to complete the following exercises.

Able currently has a MTBF of 21,000 hours. Change the MTBF in the R&D page (do not change any other specification) and record the Revision date and R&D cost (from the R&D worksheet), the Material Cost (from the Production worksheet), and the predicted demand (from the Marketing Worksheet) in Table 10.

Look for the relationships in Table 10.

1. How long does this revision take?
2. What is the R&D cost?
3. How does material cost change?
4. How much demand is likely to change?

Trade-offs: Position

Table 11 - Revision Costs

Position		How long to revise?	R&D Cost to Revise	Material Cost to Revise
Perf	Size			
5.4	14.6	25 September	$744	$12.54
5.9	14.1	3 May	$340	$14.54
6.4	13.6	- Able's Current Position -	0	$16.04
6.9	13.1	3 May	$340	$16.44
7.4	12.6	25 September	$744	$17.24

Able has a performance of 6.4, a size of 13.6, and a material cost of $16.04 (per unit). Based on that position, review the information in Table 11 and its impact on the length of time, R&D costs, and material costs.

In general, what are the implications for every .5 unit change in performance and .5 unit change in size?

1. How long does this revision take?
2. What is the R&D cost?
3. In what ways does the material cost change with every change in position?

Trade-offs: Age

Managing your product's age is very different than managing any other characteristic. There is not an "age" cell in the R&D worksheet. You can only change your product's perceived age by changing its position on the perceptual map – by changing its performance and size. Because age is an outcome of repositioning, managing age does not have any direct impact on the cost of the R&D project or any direct impact on material cost.

However, age does have a very big impact on the CSS and how attractive your product is to your customers. For both Low Tech and High Tech customers, age is the second most important characteristic and determines 29% of the Customer Survey Score. For Low Tech customers, position only contributes 9% of the CSS. Age is a much more important determinant of product "attractiveness." Each time you make a revision to a product's size or performance, you cut its perceived age in half.

Product Management: Low Tech - *Thinking Strategically*

There is an important implication here. As R&D manager, you do not want to revise a Low Tech product too often or it will be too "young" to attract Low Tech buyers.

If you reposition a Low Tech product when it is 4.0 years old, its "age at revision" will be 2.0. It will take another two years before the product is old enough to need repositioning again.

In the Low Tech market, the ideal spot drifts by .5 units smaller and .5 units faster every year. In two years, the ideal spot moves one unit smaller and one unit faster. Therefore, if you revise your Low Tech product every two

years by 1 unit – 1 unit smaller and 1 unit faster, you should be able to keep it near the ideal spot and cut its age in half to keep it within the customer's requirements.

You decide to test your idea using the Foundation decision tool. Selecting the R&D screen, you decide to position Able as a product for the Low Tech Market.

1. First, you change the MTBF to 20,000 which is the top of the range that Low Tech customers find most attractive, but also has relatively high production costs. By reducing MTBF, you will save $.30 on the cost of

materials used in production. With no change in demand, if you sell 1,000,000 units, lowering the MTBF will result in a $300,000 increase in profits.

2. Reposition Able to the ideal spot for Round 1 (the first year that you are running the company). In Exercise 2, you found the ideal spot to be a performance of 5.3 and size of 14.7.

3. With those changes, notice that the revision date is November 9th. Able will be available from January 1st to November 9th under its original specifications, with performance of 6.4, size of 13.6, and an MTBF of 21,000 (material cost of $16.04 per unit.) Able is 3.1 years old on January 1st and ages to 4.0 years old by November 8th. On November 9th, a new – improved - revised Able is introduced to the market. Able is "ideally" positioned for the Low Tech customer (performance of 5.3, size of 14.7, and an MTBF of 20,000). This new configuration has a material cost

of about $12.00. Its perceived age is 2.0 on November 9th and probably about 2.1 at the end of the year.

Note: The CSS (the demand for your product) in October will be based on Able's original specifications, while the CSS in November will be based the revised specifications. Therefore, the demand for Able at these two points in time will be very different.

4. In the second year (Round 2), you will not make any changes to Able – the MTBF is perfect and the age will go from 2.1 to 3.1 years old. However, in the third year (Round 3), Able will age from 3.1 to 4.1 years old, and it will be time to reposition again. In Round 3, the ideal spot is 1 unit faster (6.3) and 1 unit smaller (13.7) than it was in the first year. Those specifications would be the starting point for your repositioning because AGE is more important to manage than positioning. Hopefully, you can position it a little smaller and faster than the Round 3 ideal (so its CSS improves over time).

Product Management: High Tech - *Thinking strategically*

For High Tech customers, managing your products requires a different strategy. The two characteristics that are most important to High Tech buyers are positioning and age. You look at Able and decide that it would be difficult to make Able a good High Tech product because you can *either* reposition it to the ideal spot *or* try to keep the age as close to 0 as possible. But you can't do both.

The only way to have a great product for the High Tech market is to introduce a new product. To determine what product characteristics your sensor should have, you decide to review the information about the Customer

Survey Score and the expectations of the High Tech customers.

You start by deciding on a name. In your industry, all of the product names start with the same letter as the company name. Since you run Andrews, you choose "AceX."

You want to design a perfect product, so you go to the Customer Buying Criteria for the specifications. Reliability is easy; you choose an MTBF of 23,000. Position is a little bit harder. The ideal spot is changing month-to-month and year-to-year and you know

Name	Pfmn	Size	MTBF	Revision Date	Age Revision
Able	8.1	11.9	21000	17-Apr	2.2

If you wanted to manage Able's position for the High Tech market, putting it on the ideal spot (changing performance from 6.4 to 8.1 and size from 13.6 to 11.9) results in a revision date of April 19 of next year. The age profile doesn't change this year; Able ages from 3.1 to 4.1 year old. Next year, Able ages from 4.1 to 4.4 on April 18, and then the age is cut in half to 2.2. By the end of that year Able's age will be about 2.9 years. Not great; not even good.

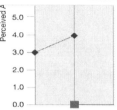

Name	Pfmn	Size	MTBF	Revision Date	Age Revision
Able	6.5	13.6	21000	17-Feb	1.6

If you wanted to manage Able's age for the High Tech market, making the smallest change possible (changing performance from 6.4 to 6.5) results in a revision date of February 17 at which point its AGE is cut in half from 3.2 to 1.6. By the end of the year, Able's age will be about 2.6 years. And, it is a long way from the ideal spot. Not great; not even good.

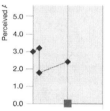

that it takes more than a year to invent a new product.

The ideal spot for Round 1 is performance 8.1 and size 11.9. If it takes a year, then AceX won't be available until Round 2. In Round 2, the ideal spot is .7 units faster (the ideal performance of 8.1 in Round 1 changes to 8.8 in Round 2) and .7 units smaller. (The ideal size of 11.9 changes to 11.2 in Round 2).

With the decisions you have entered into the model, you only have one product, Able, available for the first year. In the second year (Round 2), you will have only Able available from January 1 until August 16. From August 17 until December 31, you will have two products, Able and AceX. AceX will be a nearly perfect product on August 17. Its position is very near the ideal spot. At "0" years old, it is the perfect age. Throw in a MTBF of 23,000 hours, and AceX is all that a High Tech customer could want.

However, by December 31 the situation is starting to change. The ideal spot is drifting away from your current position and AceX is .4 years old. You are losing ground on the two most important product characteristics. It is clear that you will have to reposition a High Tech product every year in order to keep it on (or near) the ideal spot and to keep the age as young as possible. Since the ideal spot for the High Tech market becomes .7 units faster and .7 units smaller every year, that is how much you would change your product specifications.

Name	Pfmn	Size	MTBF	Revision Date	Age Revision	R&D Cost	Perceptual Map (at end of this year)
Able	6.4	13.6	21000			$0	
ACEX	8.8	11.2	23000	16-Aug-16	0.0	$1635	
NA	0.0	0.0	0			$0	
NA	0.0	0.0	0			$0	
NA	0.0	0.0	0			$0	
					Total	$1635	

*Note: Make a mental note that it also takes a year to build a production line to produce your new product AceX. Therefore, your production department needs to order construction of the line in 2016 so it will be ready in 2017, for example.

4 How do we keep track of the money?

Learning Objectives:

After reading this module and completing the associated exercises, you will be able to:

LO1: Describe the three categories of cash in a cash flow statement.

LO2: Discuss the types of activities that add or subtract cash flow from operating activities.

LO3: Define working capital and the working capital cycle.

LO4: Discuss the importance of managing the working capital cycle.

LO5: Differentiate between production cycle, accounts payable lags, and accounts receivable lags.

LO6: Calculate accounts receivable.

LO7: Discuss the importance of a credit policy for a company's cash flow.

LO8: Discuss the importance of managing inventory for a company's cash flow.

LO9: Calculate inventory turnover rates, inventory turnover days, and ideal inventory.

LO10: Describe the kind of information found on a company's income statement.

Key Terms To Look For

- *Assets*
- *Cash from operations*
- *COGS*
- *Contribution margin*
- *Depreciation*
- *EBIT*
- *GAAP*
- *Historical cost*

- *Liabilities*
- *Net change in cash position*
- *Net profit*
- *Net revenue*
- *Owner's equity*
- *Period costs*
- *SG&A*
- *Variable costs*

Cash is King: The Basics

We have discussed why we use accounting – to summarize and report on a company's financial position – and the difference between Managerial Accounting (to provide information for internal stakeholders) and Financial Accounting (to provide information for external stakeholders).

In practice, there are three key financial statements that provide financial accounting information about a company: Cash Flow Statements, Income Statements and Balance Sheets. Together they provide information managers use to make better decisions in all areas. Analyzing your competitors' financial statements will provide intelligence on their operation and the better you know your competition, the better prepared you are to compete. In this Module, we focus on cash flow statements and income statements. In Module 5, we turn to balance sheets.

We know that one goal of business is to make a profit – it's a critical point that has been made several times. Here is another critical point: **Profit does not equal cash.** Profit, as discussed in Module 1, is the difference between what it costs to make and sell a product and what the customer pays for it. Profit does not equal cash for several reasons.

First, cash is moving in and out of the business constantly and depends a lot on timing: When did you pay your suppliers? Have your customers paid you yet? When is the interest payment due on your loans? How much money is tied up in products you haven't sold yet?

Second, the numbers on the income statement (which is the accounting statement that shows whether or not you are making a profit) are entered according to standard accounting rules in order to maintain consistency, not necessarily to reflect the reality of where the cash in the business is tied up at any given point.

Third, as a consequence of the above, it is possible for a company to be showing a profit on its income statement but to become bankrupt because it has completely run out of cash to keep the operation running.

To really understand it all, we will start with the Cash Flow Statement because that's your go-to statement to ensure you have the cash to operate your business in every round of the simulation.

If cash is king, what happens when you spend it all? When a company is out of cash to continue its day-to-day operations, the company is bankrupt. In your Foundation Business Simulation – if you make a few poor decisions – you could find yourself bankrupt at some stage. In the spirit of "all experience is good experience", it's certainly better to learn the hard lessons of running out of cash in a simulation rather than in the real world! If we let you go bankrupt and drop out of the game, however, you lose the opportunity to learn a hundred other useful lessons about business.
So if you go bankrupt, we save you with our "lender of last resort", Big Al. If your company becomes insolvent, Big Al steps in with an emergency loan to allow you to continue your operations. That's the good news. The bad news is that Big Al charges a very high interest rate: 7.5% above your current short-term debt rate. So there will still be some pain, but you will be able to stay in the game and turn your company around.

The Cash Flow Statement

It is important to keep track of the cash moving through your business so you can be sure that you'll have enough to continue to run the company's operations. It is the **Cash Flow Statement** that identifies how much cash is actually available for use in a given period. Good business managers update their Cash Flow Statements regularly to keep a consistent eye on their available cash reserves.

The Cash Flow Statement records how your cash position has changed between the present and the last period you measured.

In Foundation, you can check out your Cash Flow Statement every time you make a decision if you like – you'll find it under "pro formas" in the simulation's menu.

In general, financial accounting reports strive for consistency, based on standards or guidelines. For example, the International Accounting Standards Committee works to unify accounting rules around the world, as many countries have their own accounting standards and associated agencies. In the United States, for example, it is the Finance and Accounting Standards Board, or FASB, which sets the GAAP rules.

Under FASB guidelines, there are three categories of cash in a Cash Flow Statement. The statement shows:

CASH FROM OPERATING ACTIVITIES: your day-to-day business activities.
CASH FROM INVESTING ACTIVITIES: selling or buying plant and equipment, for example.

CASH FROM FINANCING ACTIVITIES: from stock transactions, loan repayments etc.

Let's take each of these cash categories one at a time.

Cash from Operating Activities

Cash from Operating Activities traces money from the sale of a company's goods and services. To get a number for Cash from Operating Activities, you start with your **Net Profit** and then adjust it by eliminating everything that does not represent cash.

First you back out non-cash items like **Depreciation.** Put simply, Depreciation is a reduction in the value of an asset with the passage of time. Depreciation is a consistent way of expressing wear and tear on the things the company owns.

The next step in calculating Cash from Operating Activities is to look at changes (between reporting periods) in the **Assets and Liabilities** that impact cash flow, accounts such as **Inventory or Accounts Payable.** The up or down change in these accounts is recorded in the Cash Flow Statement as either a **use of cash** (which means your cash goes down), or a **source of cash** (in which case your cash goes up).

For example, if your last Cash Flow Statement identified $100,000 in inventory, and today you have $125,000 in inventory, that's an additional $25,000 in cash tied up in inventory. That change is what is recorded on the Cash Flow Statement – a minus $25,000 in cash, or a negative use of cash.

Underlying Principles in Accounting – Rules that Keep the Information Manageable

To understand the financial reports, we need to understand two of the basic principles that underpin the rules of accounting.

The reports you'll work with during your business simulation adhere to GAAP (Generally Accepted Accounting Principles). GAAP accounting is a set of rules used to generate financial reports. These rules look back at a time period, typically one year, and are used to produce reports based on the principles of Historical Cost Accrual Accounting. These principles have two key elements: Historical Cost, and the Matching Principle.

Historical Cost requires the company to record the original price paid for an asset, and then to write off part of the value of that asset each year according to a fixed schedule of *depreciation*. For example, if a company buys a laptop computer for $2,000, the company will list the laptop as an asset worth $2,000. The next year, the company reports a lower value for the same laptop. That's the way the financial records describe the fact that the laptop – like most assets the company owns – is getting older and wearing out.

If the depreciation schedule is a straight five years (i.e., 20% per year), a $2,000 laptop will be reported as worth $1,600 the following year, and $1,200 the year after that.

The *Matching Principle* says a business must match all revenue to the costs associated with generating that revenue, *at the same time*. At the time you sell a product, you put into your books the cost of the materials and labor required to produce it.

It does not matter if you bought the materials some time before the product was sold, or that you've already paid your workers for their labor. You can only report the cost of those inputs at the time you make the sale. This is important because it helps you to match up what you earn from a product, or from a service, with what you spent. That way, you can figure out if you are making a profit.

Accounting helps keep track of a business's finances but it doesn't represent exactly what is happening day-to-day. If the numbers tried to perfectly represent reality, they would be messy, unmanageable, and inconsistent. The accounting rules are simply the accepted, legal way of capturing all the action in a business in an orderly fashion.

Similarly, if your **Accounts Payable** last period was $100,000 and this period it is $125,000, that's $25,000 more in cash this period over last period. The Cash Flow Statement records a plus $25,000, or a positive use of cash.

So once your Net Profit is adjusted for non-cash items like Depreciation, and for changes in Assets and Liabilities in areas such as Inventory and Accounts Payable, you get **Net Cash from Operations.**

Cash from Investing Activities

The second category of cash is Cash Flow from Investing Activities. The Cash Flow Statement calculates the difference between what you spent or received due to investment activities that occurred between the last statement and this statement. Investments include things like the purchase or sale of land and buildings, or plant and equipment. Whether those investments provided cash or used up cash, the difference is totaled to give you **Net Cash from Investing Activities.**

Cash from Financing Activities

The third category tells you what cash came in and what went out on financing activities. That includes both short-term borrowing/lending such as loans from the bank or loans to other parties, as well as long-term investing such as stock transactions and the purchase or retirement of bonds.

The change in your overall cash position – based on the three categories of cash above

– gives your **Change in Cash** position, which can be either negative or positive.

In Foundation, your financial statements are updated for every decision you make. Therefore, if you want to know exactly how much cash is available for operating your business right now, take the Change in Cash Position from your Cash Flow Statement and add it to the Cash line on your Balance Sheet. For example, if your Balance Sheet showed $10 million in cash on December 31st last year, and your Cash Flow Statement shows a change in cash position of -$3 million today, you have $7 million left in cash at the end of the period.

Cash Flow Statement Example

Cash Flows from Operating Activities	2015	2014
Net Income (Loss)	$2,382	$2,485
Adjustment for non-cash items		
Depreciation	$960	$960
Extraordinary gains/losses/write-offs	$22	$0
Change in Current Assets and Liabilities		
Accounts Payable	$339	$855
Inventory	$2,353	($2,000)
Accounts Receivable	($902)	$3,647
Net cash from operations	$5,154	$5,593
Cash Flows from Investing Activities		
Plant Improvements	$0	$0
Cash Flows from Financing Activities		
Dividends Paid	$0	($1,000)
Sales of Common Stock	$2,000	$0
Purchase of Common Stock	$0	$0
Cash from long-term debt	$0	$0
Retirement of long-term debt	($1,000)	$0
Change in current debt (net)	$0	$0
Net cash from financing activities	$1,000	($1,000)
Net Change in Cash Position	$6,154	$4,593
Closing Cash Position	$11,394	$5,240

*Note: Negative cash flows are denoted by numbers in parentheses in this example. Negative values may also be represented with a negative sign in front of the number and/ or with the number shown in red.

The Cash Flow Statement above shows a negative figure for "Inventory" in the year 2014. A negative figure in inventory represents the value of the cash required for that expense of ($2,000) to build more inventory than you had in storage last period. This represents a *use of cash.* When that inventory is sold, it will generate cash. In the 2015 column, a positive figure of $2,353 indicates the company sold down their inventory from the previous year's inventory level to generate cash for the company. In other words, the company had less inventory in the most recent period compared to the period before and the sale of that inventory generated cash. This represents a *source of cash.*

Other observations for 2015 that can be made from reviewing the cash flow statement on the previous page include:

- Accounts Receivable were ($902) less than the year before - decreasing cash flow

- Net Cash from operations increased by $5,154 - indicating an increase in cash flow
- Common stock was sold to bring in $2,000 of cash to use within the company - a source of cash
- A long-term debt, such as a bond, was paid off (retired) for $1,000 - decreasing cash flow
- The combination of the cash from stock and retiring the bond ended up in a "Net cash from financing activities" of a positive $1,000 - increasing cash flow
- The "Net change in the Cash Position" indicates a positive $6,154 in cash flow
- The year ended with a "Closing Cash Position" of $11,394 in available cash, $6,154 more than you had last year.

The following table describes the cash flow activity and how each of these entries may result in cash coming into the business, or cash flowing out of the business.

Table 1 - Cash Flow Activity

	Cash Flow In Positive Cash Flow: Bringing cash in	Cash Flow Out Negative Cash Flow: Taking cash out
Cash Flows from Operating Activities		
Net Income (Loss)	Net income was higher than the previous period.	Net income was lower than the previous period.
Depreciation	Adds back to net income a deduction made in the income statement that was not a cash expense.	Does not apply.
Accounts Payable	Accounts payable was greater compared to the previous period.	Accounts payable was less compared to the previous period.
Inventory	Inventory levels were less than the previous period.	Inventory levels were greater than before.
Accounts Receivable	Accounts receivable was less compared to the previous period.	Accounts receivable was greater compared to the previous period.

Table 1 - Cash Flow Activity continued

	Cash Flow In *Positive Cash Flow:* *Bringing cash in*	Cash Flow Out *Negative Cash Flow:* *Taking cash out*
Cash Flows from Investing Activities		
Plant and Equipment	An investment in plant and equipment was sold.	An investment was made in plant and equipment.
Cash Flows from Financing Activities		
Dividends Paid	Does not apply.	Dividends were paid to stockholders.
Sale of Common Stock	Stock was sold (issued) to bring in cash.	Does not apply.
Purchase of Common Stock	Does not apply.	Stock was bought back (retired) by the company.
Retirement of Long-term Debt	Does not apply.	Long-term debt was paid off (retired) by the company.
Change in Current Debt	Short term debt increased.	Short-term debt was paid down.

Now that we have discussed the three categories of cash found on Cash Flow Statements and outlined the types of activities that add or subtract from a company's overall cash flow, let's take a closer look at factors that specifically influence Cash from Operating Activities. We will discuss the factors that influence Cash from Investing Activities and Cash from Financing Activities in Module 5.

Cash and the Working Capital Cycle

A company turns cash into products or services, and then turns these back into cash through sales. At any time, a company will have bills to pay (accounts payable) and customers who owe money (accounts receivable). And while the cash is flowing in and out of the business, managers have to ensure there is enough available cash at any time so the business can continue to operate and to meet its obligations. **Working capital** is the cash that is available to run day-to-day business operations.

Working capital management is concerned with day-to-day operations rather than with long-term business decisions. In general, long-term financing needs – such as buying a new plant – are best met through long-term sources of capital such as retained earnings, sale of stock, and the sale of long-term debt obligations (bonds). Working capital management policies address short-term problems and opportunities – "short term" meaning issues that generally occur within one year.

At its core, working capital management requires that business leaders effectively manage what is known as the "working capital cycle." The working capital cycle – also called the cash flow cycle – is a concept based on the time cash is tied up (in raw materials, for example) and therefore unavailable for other uses by the business.

Effectively managing working capital involves overseeing the working capital cycle to get the time lag between accounts payable and account receivable down to a minimum. This requires attention to a company's accounts receivable, inventories, accounts payable, and short-term bank loans. We will look at these one by one.

Working Capital Cycle: The Importance of Time (and Timing)

The working capital cycle includes all the activity that occurs between the time cash is spent producing a product and the time that payment is made on the product's sale. Therefore, the first step in the working capital cycle is when the company orders and receives the raw material, generating an "account payable". The final step is when you receive the money owed to you from the sale of the product on credit – when the "account receivable" is paid off.

The working capital cycle is *the length of time between the payment of the payables and the collection of receivables.* During the cycle, some of the company's funds are unavailable for other purposes. Short-term financing may be needed to sustain business activities during the cycle, and because there is always a cost to such financing – interest to be paid, for example – a goal of any business should be to minimize the cycle time.

To achieve that goal, three terms must be clearly understood:

1. PRODUCTION CYCLE refers to the length of time from the purchase of raw materials, through the production of the goods or service, and to the sale of the finished product.

2. ACCOUNTS PAYABLE (A/P) LAG is the time between the purchase of raw materials on credit and the cash payments made for the resulting accounts payable.

3. ACCOUNTS RECEIVABLE (A/R) LAG is the time between the sale of the final product on credit and collection of cash payments for the accounts receivable.

Let's look at examples with different payable and receivable time lags. In both examples, assume it takes 40 days after an order is received to process the raw material into finished product – this means the production cycle is 40 days.

30-DAY A/P LAG: In one example, the accounts payable lag is 30 days, and the receivables lag is 45 days. Your company receives the materials and starts to process them. Within 30 days after receiving the material, you have to pay your supplier (A/P lag); 40 days after receiving the material, you have inventory to sell. For 10 days, then, your cash is tied up in inventory that is not available for sale. If you deliver it to your customer on the 14th day of the production cycle, your customer has 45 more days to pay for it. On that day, your cash has been tied up in inventory for a total of 55 days (10 days before inventory was ready for sale and 45 days after).

45-DAY A/P LAG: A second example has the accounts payable lag at 45 days, and the receivables lag at 30 days. Your company receives the materials and starts to process them. Within 40 days after receiving the material, you have inventory to sell. Within 45 days after receiving the material, you have to pay your supplier (A/P lag), For 5 days, you have inventory available for sale with none of your own cash tied up. If you deliver it to your customer on the 40th day of the production cycle, your customer has 30 more days to pay for it. On that day, your cash has been tied up in inventory for only a total of 25 days. (You didn't have to pay your supplier for 5 of the 30 days after delivery).

To recap, the working capital cycle represents the time in which working capital is "tied up." If business managers can shorten the cycle, there will be less need for external financing, which means smaller interest payments and higher profits.

Managing Accounts Receivable and Accounts Payable

We have seen how A/P and A/R lags can affect cash flow and that there is a need for a policy that balances the company's need for readily available cash, the need to offer credit to customers, and the need to pay suppliers.

One way a business can attract customers and increase sales is to "sell on credit'" – to allow the customer to have the product before paying for it. However, there are costs to extending credit. Selling product without receiving cash generates an account receivable. You are "loaning" your customer the money to buy your product. Normally, a loan generates some value, usually an interest payment. An account receivable "loan" usually generates value through increased sales, not a cash interest payment. The total dollar amount of receivables is cash that is "tied up" and thus unavailable for other uses. This amount is determined by the volume of sales and the average length of time between a sale and receipt of the full cash payment:

ACCOUNTS RECEIVABLE = CREDIT SALES PER DAY X LENGTH OF COLLECTION PERIOD

For example, if a business has credit sales of $1,000 per day and allows 20 days for payment, it has a total of $1,000 x 20 or $20,000 invested in receivables at any given time. Any changes in the volume of sales or the length of the collection period will change the receivable position.

A *credit policy* refers to the decisions made about how to grant, monitor, and collect the cash for outstanding accounts receivable. Four factors must be considered in establishing an effective credit policy:

1. Creditworthiness standards – Can your customers pay you back?
2. Credit period – How long do they have to pay?
3. Collection policy – What will you do if they do not pay?
4. Early payment discount - Do you give them a discount if they pay early?

Purchasing equipment and raw materials represents a large portion of total operating expenses. A small manufacturing firm may spend in excess of 70% of total sales purchasing raw materials and converting them into finished goods (Cost Of Goods Sold or COGS is 70% of sales, and gross margin is 30%). In this type of business, accounts payable become an important source of financing in the short term. In essence, you are borrowing the use of the materials from your suppliers to create products. When you sell the products, you will have the required cash to pay back your suppliers.

As we covered earlier, however, the amount of time you can use the materials "on credit" is the A/P lag. As your A/P gets larger, your suppliers become reluctant to provide more materials and, if you don't have materials, you can't produce products. Managing prompt payments of accounts and keeping repayment cycles as short as possible make the company an attractive customer.

Managing Inventory

Because a company's profitability depends on its ability to sell its products, it must have enough inventory to meet demand. So the same important question we discussed in the marketing section (Module 2) remains – how much inventory is needed? The answer begins with the sales forecast, but because the sales forecast depends on many factors outside the control of a business, inventory management is challenging. Holding inventory levels at less than what is needed will cost the company in lost sales. Holding inventory in excess of what is needed will also cost the company because storage and insurance costs can be expensive. In addition, as we discussed earlier, holding inventory ties up cash so that it cannot be used for other purposes.

So we need sufficient inventory to cover our expected sales, but we may also want to prepare for potential sales increases by holding some level of "safety stock." The amount of safety stock is determined by comparing the cost of maintaining the additional inventory to the cost of potential sales losses due to not having adequate levels of inventory.

The following ratios are used to determine the optimal amount of each product to keep in inventory:

INVENTORY TURNOVER RATE = COST OF GOODS SOLD / INVENTORY

INVENTORY TURNOVER DAYS = NUMBER OF DAYS IN A PERIOD / INVENTORY TURNOVER RATE

IDEAL INVENTORY = COST OF GOODS SOLD / INDUSTRY AVERAGE TURNOVER RATE

For example, last year your business sold goods that cost $100,000, and your average inventory for the year was worth $10,000. The inventory turnover rate for last year was $100,000/$10,000, or 10 times. Furthermore, the company's inventory turnover days were 360 days/10, or 36 days. These numbers indicate that during the past year, your inventory turned over 10 times and, on average, it took 36 days to sell the entire inventory. When compared with industry averages, the relative strength of your business's inventory management can be revealed. A low inventory turnover rate could indicate overstocking, whereas high inventory turnover days can represent slow sales.

If the average industry turnover rate is 12 times, your business's ideal inventory levels for the year should have been:

$100,000 / 12 = $8,333

This figure may be used as a guideline for determining inventory levels during the current year.

The total costs associated with inventory include the time value of capital tied up in inventories, storage and handling expenses, and insurance, taxes, and costs relating to obsolete inventory. These costs are generally referred to as the *inventory carrying costs*. These carrying costs increase as inventory levels rise.

The Income Statement

The Income Statement records all the company's revenues and expenses, compares them, and calculates the difference between them. The difference between your revenues and expenses is your profit – or loss – for the period. If you want to know whether a business is making a profit on its goods and services, simply look at the Income Statement, also called a Profit and Loss Statement.

One way to think of the Income Statement is as a movie of what's happening in the business. It shows all the activities related to getting your products and services into your customers' hands – from the purchase of raw materials all the way through to delivery.

Here's how a traditional income statement is organized:

The first line is your total sales for the period, or net sales/revenue. It's net revenue because it reports how much the company has received – after discounts or other allowances you gave your customers have been deducted from the total (gross) sales number.

From that number, net revenue, we deduct the **Cost of Goods Sold** (COGS). The Cost of Goods Sold is just as it sounds – a tally of all the costs associated with the production of the goods and services you provide. That number gives us a Gross Profit, which is also called Gross Margin.

Gross Margin is simply the Net Sales minus all of the direct costs of making your products or services – costs that include materials and labor plus depreciation on the plant and equipment you use.

Moving down the Income Statement we get to *Selling and General Administration Expenses* or *SG&A*. That accounts for all the administrative costs of doing business such as marketing, salaries for your staff at headquarters, insurance policies, legal advice, and more.

The next line, *Non-Operating Items*, includes miscellaneous expenses that must be accounted for but are not part of the company's regular business activities. Let's say, for example, a computer company sells a building it doesn't need. The profit or loss from the sale is recorded in this section so it does not distort the picture we're building of the core operations of the business.

Once all of the expenses and Non-Operating Items have been accounted for, we get down to *Earnings Before Interest and Tax*, or *EBIT*.

What comes next is the Interest we paid our lenders on money borrowed, and the taxes we pay various governments for the privilege of doing business.

After those two final costs are deducted, we get to *Net Profit* (also called earnings).

Figure 1 - Example of Actual Income Statement - Actinium Pharmaceuticals, Inc. (ATNM)

Actinium Pharmaceuticals, Inc. (ATNM) - Other OTC

8.40 +0.07(0.84%) 3:55PM EDT

Get the big picture on all your investments.

Sync your Yahoo portfolio now

Income Statement

Get Income Statement for: [   ] GO

View: **Annual Data** | Quarterly Data

All numbers in thousands

Period Ending	Dec 31, 2013	Dec 31, 2012	Dec 31, 2011
Total Revenue	-	-	-
Cost of Revenue	-	-	-
Gross Profit	-	-	-
Operating Expenses			
Research Development	2,667	3,440	324
Selling General and Administrative	3,919	4,506	2,959
Non Recurring	-	-	-
Others	2	1	1
Total Operating Expenses	-	-	-
Operating Income or Loss	**(6,592)**	**(7,947)**	**(3,284)**
Income from Continuing Operations			
Total Other Income/Expenses Net	(4,184)	685	14
Earnings Before Interest And Taxes	(10,775)	(7,262)	(3,270)
Interest Expense	3	1,099	175
Income Before Tax	(10,778)	(8,361)	(3,445)
Income Tax Expense	-	-	-
Minority Interest	-	-	-
Net Income From Continuing Ops	(10,778)	(8,361)	(3,445)
Non-recurring Events			
Discontinued Operations	-	-	-
Extraordinary Items	-	-	-
Effect Of Accounting Changes	-	-	-
Other Items	-	-	-
Net Income	**(10,774)**	**(8,361)**	**(3,445)**
Preferred Stock And Other Adjustments	-	-	-
Net Income Applicable To Common Shares	**(10,774)**	**(8,361)**	**(3,445)**

Your Foundation Income Statement

In the Foundation Simulation, we use a variation of the traditional Income Statement that allows you to calculate a Contribution Margin rather than a Gross Margin. Often this is called also a "period and variable costs layout." It provides information about each product's Contribution Margin, which – as we discussed in Module 3 – represents the fraction of the sale price that contributes to offsetting the fixed costs of the business.

As explained earlier, a business has two classes of expenses – Period or Fixed costs, and Variable costs.

Variable costs vary with sales volume in the business – with the number of goods or services you sell. Take material costs, for exam-

Figure 2 - An example of a Foundation Business Simulation income statement.

2013 Income Statement

(Product Name:)	Able	NA	NA	NA	NA	NA	NA	NA	2013 Total	Common Size
Sales	$40,800	$0	$0	$0	$0	$0	$0	$0	$40,800	100.0%
Variable Costs:										
Direct Labor	$12,138	$0	$0	$0	$0	$0	$0	$0	$12,138	29.7%
Direct Material	$20,240	$0	$0	$0	$0	$0	$0	$0	$20,240	49.6%
Inventory Carry	$282	$0	$0	$0	$0	$0	$0	$0	$282	0.7%
Total Variable	$32,660	$0	$0	$0	$0	$0	$0	$0	$32,660	80.0%
Contribution Margin	$8,140	$0	$0	$0	$0	$0	$0	$0	$8,140	20.0%
Period Costs:										
Depreciation	$960	$0	$0	$0	$0	$0	$0	$0	$960	2.4%
SG&A: R&D	$0	$0	$0	$0	$0	$0	$0	$0	$0	0.0%
Promotions	$1,000	$0	$0	$0	$0	$0	$0	$0	$1,000	2.5%
Sales	$1,000	$0	$0	$0	$0	$0	$0	$0	$1,000	2.5%
Admin	$637	$0	$0	$0	$0	$0	$0	$0	$637	1.6%
Total Period	$3,597	$0	$0	$0	$0	$0	$0	$0	$3,597	8.8%
Net Margin	$4,543	$0	$0	$0	$0	$0	$0	$0	$4,543	11.1%

Definitions: **Sales**: Unit sales times list price. **Direct Labor**: Labor costs incurred to produce the product that was sold. **Inventory Carry Cost**: the cost to carry unsold goods in inventory. **Depreciation**: Calculated on straight-line 15-year depreciation of plant value. **R&D Costs**: R&D department expenditures for each product. **Admin**: Administration overhead is estimated at 1.5% of sales. **Promotions**: The promotion budget for each product. **Sales**: The sales force budget for each product. **Other**: Charges not included in other categories such as Fees, Write Offs, and TQM. The fees include money paid to investment bankers and brokerage firms to issue new stocks or bonds plus consulting fees your instructor might assess. Write-offs include the loss you might experience when you sell capacity or liquidate inventory as the result of eliminating a production line. If the amount appears as a negative amount, then you actually made money on the liquidation of capacity or inventory. **EBIT**: Earnings Before Interest and Taxes. **Short Term Interest**: Interest expense based on last year's current debt, including short term debt, long term notes that have become due, and emergency loans. **Long Term Interest**: Interest paid on outstanding bonds. **Taxes**: Income tax based upon a 35% tax rate. **Profit Sharing**: Profits shared with employees under the labor contract. **Net Profit**: EBIT minus interest, taxes, and profit sharing.

Other	$0	0.0%
EBIT	$4,543	11.1%
Short Term Interest	$0	0.0%
Long Term Interest	$641	1.6%
Taxes	$1,365	3.3%
Profit Sharing	$51	0.1%
Net Profit	$2,485	6.1%

Variable Margins
2013 Andrews F59135_001

ple. If you're selling more products, you are spending more on materials to make the products. Or look at labor. If you're making more products, you are spending more on labor either by increasing the size of your workforce or by paying your existing workers overtime.

Fixed costs, however, stay the same, within a fairly large range, no matter how much or how little operational activity takes place during the year. They are fixed for that period.

These are often called your "overhead." Fixed Costs include research and development, interest payments and depreciation, and office expenses like rent and electricity. Whether you sell one product or a thousand products, the fixed costs still have to be paid.

In a traditional Income Statement, remember, we deducted all of the Fixed and Variable Costs from the Net Revenue to give a Gross Margin.

In a Period and Variable Costs Income Statement, we first deduct just the Variable Costs to give a Contribution Margin, and then we deduct the Fixed Costs. By calculating the Contribution Margin, you discover how much income from each product line is left over, after production costs are taken out, to contribute to your fixed costs.

In your Foundation Income Statement, under each product name, the first line is net sales. Then we deduct the Variable Costs first

Income Statement	
Revenue	Funds that come into the company from the sale of goods or services. These can be sales that are in cash or on credit.
Variable Costs	Costs that vary with the level of activity - the more products you make, the greater the total cost.
Material costs	The cost of the materials (raw material and component parts) that were used in the products you sold.
Labor costs	The cost of the labor (human resources) used to produce the products sold.
Inventory carrying costs	The costs (warehousing, insurance, etc.) of having inventory available for sale but not yet sold.
Total Variable Costs Cost of Goods Sold (COGS)	This is the cost of making the products sold.
Contribution Margin	The difference between the revenue brought in by sales and the cost of making the products for sale. This difference is what is left over to cover fixed costs and, finally, to generate a profit.
Period Costs	Those costs that are fixed over a period of time. These do not vary with the level of activity.
Depreciation	This figure recognizes the amount of value that operating a business "uses up" in the plant (factory) and equipment.
Research and Development (R&D)	The investment the company makes in developing new products or improving existing ones.
Marketing expense	The investment the company makes in advertising, selling, and distributing products.
Administrative expense	The cost of running a business; legal expenses, accounting services, etc.
Total Period Costs	The costs of operating your business over a period of time
Earnings Before Interest and Taxes (EBIT), or Net Margin	Revenues minus variable costs (contribution margin) minus period costs.
Interest expense	The fee you pay to use other people's cash. This is the expense of your financing strategy.
Taxes	The revenue you pay to the government as a citizen of a society.
Net Income	Revenues minus variable costs minus period costs minus interest expenses and taxes. This is synonymous with profit, earnings, "return," and "bottom line." Creating net income for its owners is the reason a business exists.

– labor, materials, inventory carrying costs – which gives us the Contribution Margin.

Next we deduct the Fixed Costs – Depreciation and the Selling, General & Administration or SG&A costs – which gives us a Net Margin.

The benefit of separating Period and Variable Costs is that it helps us, as managers, to focus on the variable costs of production and to develop tactics to minimize them. The higher the Contribution Margin – the more money left from each sale to pay for overhead and go into profit – the better your bottom line will be.

The chart on the previous page will help you understand the various lines of the Income Statement.

Recognition of Transactions

As soon as an agreement is made between a company and its customers or suppliers, the transaction has to be recognized on the books. In other words, it is recorded when it occurs and not when the cash is exchanged. Often a company's income statement might show a company is profitable, but still the company runs out of cash. This may happen in a growth

Company snapshot: doing deals with accounting, a recipe for disaster

Groupon, the company that made a multi-billion dollar business out of offering cheap deals online, went from being the darling of online business investors to what venture capitalist and tech business expert Paul Kedrosky described as "a complete fiasco" in less than a year. Many of Groupon's problems stemmed from poor financial reporting.

Launched in 2008, Groupon immediately attracted strong investment, and launched an IPO in 2011. A few months before the offering, however, Groupon had to restate its financial reports, correcting errors in the way it reported its results. and reducing revenues from $713.4 million to $312.9 million. The problem was non-traditional accounting methods the *Wall Street Journal* called "financial voodoo". *Time Magazine* reported the culprit was "a funky financial metric it called Adjusted Consolidated Segment Operating Income (ACSOI)." ACSOI excluded marketing costs, which represented the majority of the company's expenses, making Groupon's financial results seem much better than they actually were. Groupon had flagrantly ignored the matching principle, which says expenses (the cost of the sale) must be reported at the time the revenue (money from the sale) is reported.

In April 2012, Groupon restated its earnings once again to reflect a larger quarterly loss after its auditor found what it described as "material weakness in internal controls." Scrutiny from the U.S. Securities and Exchange Commission followed, along with lawsuits from investors. Right up to the firing of Groupon's founder and CEO Andrew Mason in February 2013, Groupon's accounting practices were in the spotlight, with the company's audit committee and the competence of its accounting staff coming under severe criticism.

Groupon's business challenges are more diverse than accounting, however. Rapid growth, for example, (the company expanded to 45 countries and increased staff from a few people to 10,000 in less than five years) makes adequate internal control difficult to manage. Groupon also faces tough competition, with Amazon and Google setting up their own online deal programs.

The company, however, has diversified its services and begun to recover. Groupon's market capitalization, which was $16.6 billion at the IPO in November 2011 and dropped as low as $1.8 billion a year later, had crept back to $8.3 billion by the third quarter of 2013. Even Groupon's fired former CEO may be on his way back, releasing a rock/pop album of "motivational business music" called *Hardly Workin'* in July 2013.

phase when the company is investing in its growth, yet does not have the cash available to pay its debts because it has still products in development that are not ready for sale.

All of these occurrences are captured in the company's financial statements according to the rules that underpin accounting such as historical cost and the matching principle.

They key message from this module is that it is critical for a company to manage its cash flow *first*, and then to focus on managing its profitability over the long term. Run out of cash, and there *is no long term*.

Chapter Review Questions

Cash and The Cash Flow Statement

1. Describe the difference between profit and cash.

2. What are the differences between cash from operating activities, cash from investing activities, and cash from financing activities?

3. What is depreciation and what does it do to cash flow?

Cash and the Working Capital Cycle

4. Why is it important to understand working capital?

5. How does working capital relate to the Cash Flow Statement?

6. What is the working capital cycle and why does it matter?

7. What might be the ramifications, financially and from a marketing perspective, of increasing the accounts receivable lag time?

8. What are the tradeoffs of selling products on credit?

9. What is the Inventory Turnover Rate and how is it measured?

The Income Statement

10. What is the benefit of separating Period and Variable costs on the Income Statement?

11. What does a Contribution Margin represent?

12. What is the relationship between Revenue and Net Income on the Income Statement?

You – in the executive suite!

Accounting Manager

In Module 3, you completed your job rotation track as the **Production Manager** and **Research and Development Manager.**

You covered production scheduling, automation, new product development, product revisions, and all of the trade-offs and issues that have to be considered around timing and costing when you try to design and produce something – at a profit!

Now it's time to focus on the scorecard for your business – the financial reports. You are moving into the role of **Accounting Manager.**

Activities: Approximately 30 – 45 minutes to complete.	COMPLETED
A-1: Answer all **Chapter Review Questions** Your instructor will advise you on how to turn in your answers.	☐
A-2: In the **Summary Guide** at Appendix 1 read **Finance Decisions** 205.	☐
A-3: Read the following text through to the end of the module. **Answer** all of the questions on the Income Statement at the end.	☐

Exercise #9: Analyzing the Income Statement

Your orientation as Accounting Manager begins with a back-to-basics analysis of the Andrews Company's income statement. We are going to look at each element of the reports to ensure you have a thorough understanding of what they are telling you. Understanding these reports will be critical to your success in the simulation.

Please go to Appendix 2 for Andrews Financial Statements and refer to the Income Statement for the following exercises.

Andrews Income Statement

Last year, the Andrews company had total *revenues* of $44,049,000. This money came from the sale of 1,334,818 (rounding to 1,335,000) sensors at $33.00 each. There are a lot of decisions that affect how much revenue you can generate. Certainly the price matters. You can get more revenue for each sensor you sell if you raise the price. But if you raise the price, you might not sell as many sensors. The characteristics of your product will affect revenue (sales). In general, the smaller, faster, and more reliable your sensors; the more your customers will like them. The money you spend in your promotion and sales budgets will also increase revenue.

Variable costs are those costs that increase with the number of sensors you sell. Considered together, the total variable costs (plus depreciation) are sometimes called *"Cost of Goods Sold"* because they only recognize the material and labor costs that are incurred making the sensors that you sold that year; these numbers do NOT account for the sensors you made but didn't sell. Variable costs are tied to the costs of materials that go into the sensors and the cost of labor incurred in the production process. If you talk about the variable cost for each sensor (excluding depreciation), you usually call that *unit cost.*

Last year, you sold 1,335,000 sensors. For each of those sensors, the material cost was $17.28 and therefore, your total *cost of materials* for the 1.3 million sensors was $20,834,000. If you make your sensors smaller, faster, or more reliable, the cost of materials will increase.

For each sensor, the *cost of labor* was $10.35. To produce 1,300,000 sensors, the total cost of labor was $13,796,000. You can decrease your labor costs by investing in better equipment/machinery for the factory. "Better" means increasing the level of automation. Every level of automation you invest in lowers your labor cost by $1.12.

Inventory carrying costs are the additional expenses incurred when you have inventory in the factory. This is calculated at 12% of the cost of inventory left at the end of the year. You had no inventory left at the end of the year so there are no inventory carrying costs.

If you add all of the variable costs, you get $34,630,000. This is the cost of producing the goods that you sold. If you subtract your cost of goods sold (total variable cost) from the revenue you generated when you sold those goods, you get the contribution margin. You sold sensors and generated $44,049,000 of revenue. However, those sensors cost you $34,630,000 to produce. After you have paid for the cost of the goods you sold, you have $9,419,000 left over that will contribute to your profitability. This number is your *contribution margin.* These numbers are measures of how efficiently you are manufacturing the products you sell. For a manufacturing firm, these numbers are very important and are talked about in three ways:

1. *The total numbers:* $44,049 in revenue minus $34,630 variable costs provides a contribution margin of $9,419.

2. *The per unit numbers:* A price of $33 minus the variable cost per unit of about $27.63 ($17.28 [material] plus $10.35 [labor] plus $0 [carrying cost]) provides a contribution margin of $5.37 per unit.

3. *Percentages (expressed as a dollar of sales):* A total of 31.3% of your sales dollar goes to pay for labor, and 47.3% to pay for materials, for a total of 78.6% of your sales dollar going to cost of goods sold. This leaves 21.4% of the sales dollar to contribute to your overall profitability. In more common language, for every $1.00 of sales revenue, you are spending almost 32 cents on labor and almost 48 cents on materials. For every dollar of sales, you have a cost of goods sold of 80 cents; leaving you 20 cents towards being profitable. When you were hired, your Board of Directors made it clear that they expected a minimum 30% contribution margin.

You have your work cut out for you. To improve your contribution margin, you can:

- **Raise your price:** But fewer people will purchase at a higher price.
- **Lower your material costs:** Although you will need to check the production report to be sure, the only way is to make your produce less attractive - bigger, slower, less reliable. A strategy sure to lose sales!
- **Reduce your labor costs:** You can invest in greater production efficiency by increasing the automation for your equipment or greater capacity in order to lower overtime.

From your contribution margin, you subtract some of the costs of being in business for the year. Because these tend to be "fixed" over the course of the time period (in this case a year), they are referred to as period costs.

Depreciation is the recognition that you are "consuming" your investment in your factory every year. This $960,000 is the yearly recognition of "using up" the value of your fixed assets. This is a unique number on the income statement because it is not paid to anyone; it is a non-cash expense.

The next group of expenses is called SG&A, or Selling, General, and Administrative Expenses. **Research and development,** or **R&D** expenses are the expenses you incur when your engineers improve your product. Did your company spent appropriately ($919,000) on R&D last year? Could that have been too little or too much?

The **promotion expense** is what the company spends on advertising. Another way to think of this is money used to create awareness that your product exists. You can only sell products to people who are **aware** of your offerings. Last year, the company invested $1,100,000 in creating awareness of the product, so you wonder how much awareness (measured by what percentage of the market) that purchased?

The **sales expense** is what the company spends on getting your sales representatives to contact your customers. You can only sell products to people who have **access** to your sales representatives. Again, the company invested $1,100,000 last year to create access to your product, so you wonder how much access (what percentage of the market) was created? **Administrative expenses** are estimated at 1.5% of sales; this is simply administrative overhead.

You have total period costs of $5,011,000. This represents 11.4% of your total sales (or more than 11 cents of each dollar of sales). If you subtract this from your Contribution Margin ($9,419,000-$5,011,000), you get $4,408,000 for your Net Margin, or Earnings Before Interest and Taxes (EBIT). You started with sales revenue and subtracted the cost of making the goods sold (sensors), which left contribution margin. From the contribution margin, you subtracted the costs of being in business - the costs that are fixed for the year. You are left with your Earnings before you make your interest payments (cost of your financing decisions) and taxes (your burden as a citizen).

Interest payments are the rent you pay to use other peoples' money. Short-term loans tend to be to the bank (although you have heard rumors of your company having to take out short-term emergency loans from "Big Al," a reputed loan shark). Your predecessor must have paid off all of the short-term debt because the balance in the current debt account is $0, so the company didn't pay anything in interest on short-term loans last year.

Long-term interest payments are payments that you have to pay on your bonds (your long-term debt to finance the assets (e.g. property, plant, and equipment) required to operate the company). You currently have $7,200,000 of bonds outstanding (about 25.7% of your total assets is funded by bonds). Your company paid $841,000 in interest on bonds - a little less than 12% interest.

Other income statement observations include:

- The company pays a 35% income tax on its income, after interest has been subtracted. *EBIT* of $1,908,000 minus $841,000 is $1,067,000 in taxable income. 35% of that is $373,000. Ouch.

- A part of the employee contract is that your company has a *profit-sharing* program to share its profits with employees (after taxes have been paid). This year that profit-sharing pool is $14,000.

- Last year, the company's *net income* was $679,000. This is *profit*. Creating profit - creating wealth - is the major reason

the company was organized and why it does business.

- The company created $679,000 profit on $44,049,000 worth of sales. That is a *return on sales (ROS)* of 1.5%. This means around 1.5 cents of every $1 of sales is profit.

- The company created $679,000 profit using assets worth $26,377,000. That is a *return on assets (ROA)* of 2.6%; for every $1 of assets, the company made a little more than 2 cents profit.

- The company created $679,000 profit on owners' investments of $16,524,000. This is a *return on equity (ROE)* of 4.1%. This means that for every $1 the owners have invested, the company created 4.1 cents profit.

- The company created $679,000 profit for a corporation that has 2,269,049 shares of stock outstanding. This represents *earnings per share* of $.30. In other words, for every share of stock outstanding, the company created $.30 profit in this past year.

Now, it's your turn!

Now, let's look at several entirely different Income Statements - the statements from the Foundation Business Simulation. Work through the questions below to verify that you completely understand where to find all of the information, and what it is telling you.

Figure 3 - The Income Statement Survey: FastTrack Reports, Page 3

Income Statement Survey	Andrews	Baldwin	Chester	Digby	Erie	Ferris
Sales	$57,063	$68,647	$39,174	$72,090	$35,191	$43,645
Variable Costs (Labor, Material, Carry)	$33,831	$48,914	$28,052	$50,932	$24,537	$31,496
Depreciation	$1,920	$2,171	$1,820	$2,201	$1,703	$1,267
SG&A (R&D, Promo, Sales, Admin)	$5,882	$5,979	$4,032	$6,830	$3,962	$5,740
Other (Fees, Write Offs, TQM, Bonus)	$250	$354	$330	$325	$367	$195
EBIT	$15,180	$10,229	$4,940	$11,802	$4,622	$4,947
Interest (Short term, Long Term)	$958	$1,938	$1,938	$2,054	$1,892	$1,679
Taxes	$4,978	$2,902	$1,051	$3,412	$956	$1,144
Profit Sharing	$185	$108	$39	$127	$35	$42
Net Profit	$9,060	$5,281	$1,912	$6,210	$1,739	$2,082

1. Which company had the greatest amount of revenue in the reported year?

2. What is *Digby's* contribution margin?

3. If *Chester* had one product and charged $30, how many sensors did it sell last year?

4. How much did *Baldwin* spend to manufacture all of the sensors it produced last year?

5. How much did *Baldwin* spend to manufacture all of the sensors it sold last year?

6. What is the value of the machinery that *Ferris* used up making its products last year? (Did this decrease their cash? Did they have to pay anyone that money?)

7. How much did *Andrews* spend on product development, marketing, and administrative expenses last year?

8. How much did *Erie* pay in interest?

9. Which company had the greatest amount paid in interest?

10. How much did *Chester* pay in taxes?

11. How much profit did *Digby* earn?

12. Which company created the most wealth in the past year?

13. What percentage of *Andrews'* sales was profit?

14. What percentage of *Andrews'* sales was left over after you paid for making the product (material- labor- inventory carrying costs)?

5 How do we raise funds, reward shareholders, and manage our assets?

Learning Objectives:

After reading this module and completing the associated exercises, you will be able to:

LO1: Discuss the importance of a financing strategy to a company's performance.

LO2: Define the role of risk with regard to investment decisions.

LO3: Differentiate between the two types of transactions used to gain access to additional funds.

LO4: Describe the similarities and differences between loans and bonds.

LO5: Describe how the bond market impacts bond value.

LO6: Discuss how to evaluate the quality of bonds.

LO7: Differentiate between common stock and preferred stock.

LO8: Discuss why a company would choose to pay dividends.

LO9: Describe the purpose of the Balance Sheet.

LO10: Discuss the kinds of information found on the Balance Sheet.

LO11: Differentiate between assets and liabilities.

Key Terms To Look For:

- *Bonds*
- *Bond market*
- *Common stock*
- *Dividend*
- *Earnings Per Share*
- *Interest rate*
- *Loans*
- *Owner's equity*

- *Preferred stock*
- *Price Earnings Ratio*
- *Principal*
- *Speculative cash balances*
- *Stock market*
- *Transaction balance*
- *Yield*

Cash Does Not Equal Net Profit

In Module 4 we took a good look at money moving through the business, how we keep track of cash on a Cash Flow Statement, and how to keep an eye on profit with the Income Statement. We also looked at some of the accounting rules that businesses are required to follow when they report their results to external stakeholders.

A point that has been made several times is that cash does not equal profit. All the **Net Profit** number in the Income Statement shows is whether the "movie" of your business is going to have a happy ending or not. That is, if your products and services are making an overall profit.

All the decisions managers make in running a business either cost the company money or make the company money. If the company brings in more money than it pays out, then management is running a profitable business! It sounds simple, but as you already know, making money involves many individual decisions in different areas of the business, and all of these decisions need to be coordinated.

How much cash does a business need?

The important question for managers is: How much cash does the business need? Managers must be sure they have enough cash available to cover the company's day-to-day transactions, and that is called the **transaction balance.** However, they may want to keep some extra cash on hand to take advantage of special bargains (a supplier's clearance sale of raw materials, for example), or to take advantage of discounts offered by suppliers for early payment of your bills (accounts payable), or as a precaution against emergencies

FOUNDÂTION.
Financing your Foundation Company

In Foundation – just as in the real world – if you don't have enough cash or don't bring in enough revenue from the products or services you sell, or if you have too much money tied up in unsold inventory, or if you don't supplement your sales income with borrowing to cover your investments, you may become bankrupt.

The simulation ensures that a bankruptcy doesn't put you out of the game. Our lender of last resort, "Big Al" will keep your company solvent but, as you know, Big Al is a loan shark who charges interest at 7.5% above your current rate.

To ensure you don't run into Big Al, you need to do two things every round of the game: Manage your cash flow and decide how to fund your investments. In the previous Module we discussed managing your cash flow from operations. In this Module we turn our discussion to managing your cash from investment and financing activities.

Foundation gives you the opportunity to manage your investments and financing in a variety of ways. You will need to answer important questions. What's the best financing option for the investments you want to make? Short-term loans? Bonds? Do we increase or decrease stock holdings? Do we pay our shareholders a dividend this year?

The Finance screen in the simulation shows that you need to make decisions in five areas:

- *Accounts Payable and Accounts Receivable policies (which can also be set on the Marketing screen)*
- *Current debt (short-term loans – how much will you borrow?)*
- *Bonds (long-term loans – will you maintain them or pay them off?)*
- *Stock (should you issue more or buy some back?)*
- *Dividend policy (do you share profits with your owners this year?)*

(any unexpected expense). The cash held for such purposes is called the *speculative cash balance.*

There are many advantages to having enough cash on hand, and many problems when you don't have enough. Cash, however, does not work for you. Cash does not earn an explicit return. If you have too much cash on hand, you are not using your assets effectively and your cash is not being used in the most productive manner. Answering "how much is enough" is a critical management skill.

As an alternative to holding large cash balances, many companies hold part of their liquid funds in short-term marketable securities. These instruments earn interest and can be very easily converted to cash. In the United States, for example, there are several types of short-term marketable securities such as:

- TREASURY BILLS (T-BILLS), short-term loans secured by the US Government with a denomination of at least $10,000 and that mature in less than one year. Sold at a discount, the buyer pays an amount less than the face value of the T-Bill, but still receives the full amount when the bill matures.
- COMMERCIAL PAPER is an unsecured loan to a large corporation with good and well-established credit ratings. These loans usually mature between 15 and 45 days (but it can be anywhere from 1 to 270 days).
- CERTIFICATES OF DEPOSIT (CDs) are popular short-term instruments issued by commercial banks. CDs are issued in denominations up to $100,000 and may be traded in the secondary market. The Federal Deposit Insurance Corporation (FDIC) insures CDs.

Investment Financing: Getting Cash to Grow Your Business

Growing companies need money to fuel their growth. They need money to develop new products, to buy new equipment, to launch new promotion campaigns, and to take advantage of opportunities in the market as they emerge.

Individuals or organizations that might provide money to allow you to grow your business want something from you. It is an economic transaction that follows the rules of all economic transactions; people will only participate if they are made better off through the transaction.

There are basically two kinds of transactions that allow you to get access to additional funds: (1) taking on debt (loans or bonds); and (2) taking on new owners (stockholders). Both of these transactions have one thing in common: They provide cash to help the business thrive. In all other ways, however, they are quite different. Before we get into the details of these types of transactions, however, it is important to discuss the concept of "risk" because it underlies all investment and financing activities.

Risk

Put simply, *risk* is the possibility of losing some or all of an investment. In other words, risk represents the chance that an investment's actual return will be different than what is expected. For example, if you have money to invest, it represents wealth that you have created in the past and not yet consumed. You could use that wealth to buy tools that would allow you to create something of value that you could take to the market. This investment in yourself would give you a greater ability to create wealth in the future. However, if you are not going to use it yourself, you still want to put it to work. You want that money to work for you as hard as it can, 24 hours a day. One way to do that is let others use your money to create wealth that will come back to you in some form.

If you are a person who has money to invest, what do you want out of the transaction? You want the highest return you can get for your money, and you want to be sure that you do not lose your money. The degree of certainty (or uncertainty) that you will get your money back is the risk. In a market system, you have a lot of choices about how to put your money to work.

You might be attached to your money and only want it to work in a safe and secure environment. If that is what you want, you only "rent" your money to people who are going to use it conservatively. Maybe you rent it to the government, which can guarantee its safe return. The problem is that everything else being equal (which it isn't) there are a lot of people willing to put their money out for a safe use. When there is a lot of money competing to be put to safe use, it is easy for those "safe users" (for example, electric utilities or governments) to get the use of that money cheaply. For the person investing the money, therefore, the "return" is expected to be low.

The hope and the risk of new cancer treatments

 An example of one of many biotech firms seeking funds from investors in 2013 was Actinium Pharmaceuticals, which went public in January that year. Actinium is testing – with initial success – treatments using "alpha particle therapy" to target and kill cancer cells. Clinical trials have focused on therapies for types of Leukemia and Non-Hodgkin's Lymphoma.

When the company launched its IPO, the President and CEO said: "As we are expanding our ongoing clinical trials and adding new ones, it is very important to have access to public markets and provide liquidity for our investors who helped us reach this stage in the clinical development of our drug candidates." And while the company had reached a market capitalization of $81 million by October 2013, with its stock price increasing from $1 to $7.75, the CEO himself said the company was trialing "drug candidates" and was still some distance from having a drug ready to launch in the oncology market.

The company has many supporters – a report from investment bankers Laidlaw & Company says "We believe the company's technology platform ... produces novel drugs that will ultimately become viable oncology treatments." The report assesses the potential international market for the company's products at between $800 million and $1 billion. There is strong potential upside, although the company had not yet been profitable nor generated any cash flow from operating activities from its inception to the end of 2013.

But, as Genetic Engineering and Biotechnology News site genengnews.com says, "clinical trial failures can kill biopharma companies." And they might just have similar consequences for the patients! "Just look at TeGenero," genengnews says, "a company that filed for insolvency in 2006 after its disastrous Phase I clinical trial of TGN1412 nearly killed its first human subjects."

Large and established drug companies may be able to absorb drug test failures but clinical trials cost many millions of dollars, and the risk of failure – and the loss of those funds if the tests go badly – is the risk borne by investors in companies such as Actinium.

On the other hand, you might be willing to risk your money in the hope of high returns by giving it to someone who will use it in a venture that just might not work out economically, but, if it does, will provide a very high return. That's your risk. For instance, you might put your money to work in a biotech firm. They always need more money to create useful mutant biological stuff. The problem is that at this point, a low percentage of biotech projects work out. The ones that do work out, however, can make huge amounts of money. To rent your money or attract your interest, they have to offer you a high return on those funds. The common rule is:

The higher the risk, the greater the expected return.

Now that we have discussed the concept of risk and introduced the broad ways a company can gain access to cash (taking on debt and/or new owners), let's turn our attention to the accounting instrument used to record a company's financing activities – the Balance Sheet.

The Balance Sheet: Documenting Assets & Liabilities

In Module 4 we called the Income Statement a financial "movie" that shows how money moves through the business over time. The Balance Sheet, in contrast, is a financial snapshot of a business' assets and liabilities at any one point in time. It's a "freeze frame," giving you the exact financial position of a company's assets and liabilities at a certain point in its history. Keep in mind that the difference between all assets minus all liabilities is the value of the company that is retained for its shareholders: ***the equity.***

The Balance Sheet shows not only how much cash you have in the bank at that time, but also the value of your inventory, how much your creditors owe you in accounts receivable, the value of your assets, and a lot of other information. However, most importantly, the Balance Sheet will tell you if you have any equity left in your company, which would be left over after you sold all the assets and repaid all the liabilities.

Financial Snapshot

A Balance Sheet snapshot of a business can be produced at any time, for shareholders or for potential buyers for example, but is ***always*** produced for shareholders at the close of the financial year. The financial (or fiscal) year for most companies in the United States ends December 31st but in other parts of the world, the financial year may end on June 30th. It really does not matter when a financial year starts or ends, as long it is always equal to 12 months.

A business, of course, is dynamic and thus changes not just day-to-day but in many cases hour-by-hour. Because of this, it is important to remember that a Balance Sheet represents just one point in time and, like the other financial statements, is a way of presenting a company's financial information in a uniform way.

There are three parts to a Balance Sheet. On one side are the company's ***Assets*** (what you own). On the other side are ***Liabilities*** (what you owe) plus the owners' *Equity* in the business. Owners' Equity is known by several names such as Stockholders' Equity, Shareholders' Equity, and Net Worth.

Whatever you call it, Owners' Equity means the same thing – it is what is left over after you deduct what you owe (your liabilities) from what you own (your assets). Put the opposite way, if you add your Owners' Equity to your Liabilities on one side of the Balance Sheet, you'll get a figure equal to the value of your Assets on the other side, because the *Balance Sheet always balances.*

There are two categories of assets on the Asset side of the Balance Sheet and they are *Current Assets* and *Long-Term Assets.*

Current Assets are things that can be converted into cash in less than a year such as cash itself, accounts receivable, and inventory.

Long-Term or Fixed Assets are things in which your company has a long-term investment such as land and buildings, or plant and equipment.

On the other side, Liabilities are also divided into two categories, *Current Liabilities* and *Long-Term Liabilities.*

Current liabilities are debts you have to pay within a year such as accounts payable, accrued expenses – that's expenses you owe but have not yet paid – and short-term debt – such as a loan you took out to cover your working expenses.

Long-term debt is debt that you have more than one year to pay, such as mortgages or bonds.

Owners' Equity also has two major accounts – *Common Stock* and *Retained Earnings.* Common stock is the value of the company stock owned by shareholders. Retained earnings represent the profits the company chooses to reinvest, rather than pay out as a dividend.

Balance Sheet "Infrastructure"

Sometimes you'll hear people talk about the "infrastructure" on a company's balance sheet. That refers to how the Assets of the business are supported – whether they are funded more by Liabilities or debt, or more by Owner's Equity.

If the Liabilities portion of the Balance Sheet is really high, that means most of your Assets are financed through debt. In that case, the Owners' Equity portion will be quite low.

In this case, the company would find its investors and debt holders asking serious questions about why the management of the company is getting so deeply into debt. If debt gets too high, it threatens the company's viability and hence the owners' investment. It is important that managers work to build up the equity in the business so the business can grow.

On the other hand, if the Assets are financed mostly by Owners' Equity, then the company's debt will be proportionally very low. In this case investors are equally concerned but asking a different question. Now they want to know why the managers are using their Equity, rather than third-party borrowing, to fund the Assets.

Getting the "infrastructure" on the Balance Sheet right – so that it satisfies investors and the day-to-day needs of the business at the same time - is a constant management challenge.

The only way a business can grow – the only way you can have a bigger company this year than you had last year – is if the Owners' Equity portion of the Balance Sheet is growing over time. The chart on page 121 summarized the lines on a Balance Sheet.

Now that you understand Risk and the Balance Sheet, let's discuss some specific types of transactions that can be used to secure additional funds to run your company.

Figure 1 - Example of Actual Balance Statement - Actinium Pharmaceuticals, Inc. (ATNM)

Period Ending	Dec 31, 2013	Dec 31, 2012	Dec 31, 2011
Assets			
Current Assets			
Cash And Cash Equivalents	5,533	5,619	5,704
Short Term Investments	-	-	-
Net Receivables	-	-	-
Inventory	-	-	-
Other Current Assets	218	167	258
Total Current Assets	**5,752**	**5,786**	**6,199**
Long Term Investments	-	-	-
Property Plant and Equipment	14	3	1
Goodwill	-	-	-
Intangible Assets	-	-	-
Accumulated Amortization	-	-	-
Other Assets	-	-	-
Deferred Long Term Asset Charges	-	-	-
Total Assets	**5,766**	**5,789**	**6,200**
Liabilities			
Current Liabilities			
Accounts Payable	460	928	645
Short/Current Long Term Debt	6,865	3,715	4,564
Other Current Liabilities	-	-	-
Total Current Liabilities	**7,325**	**4,643**	**5,208**
Long Term Debt	-	-	-
Other Liabilities	-	-	-
Deferred Long Term Liability Charges	-	-	-
Minority Interest	-	-	-
Negative Goodwill	-	-	-
Total Liabilities	**7,325**	**4,643**	**5,208**
Stockholders' Equity			
Misc Stocks Options Warrants	-	-	-
Redeemable Preferred Stock	-	-	-
Preferred Stock	-	-	-
Common Stock	25	21	137
Retained Stock	(66,517)	(55,743)	(47,382)
Treasury Stock	-	-	-
Capital Surplus	64,933	56,868	48,238
Other Stockholder Equity	-	-	-
Total Stockholder Equity	**(1,560)**	**1,146**	**992**
Net Tangible Assets	**(1,560)**	**1,146**	**992**

Loans

A loan is a form of a rental agreement. When you borrow money from someone, you are renting the use of that person's money. The amount borrowed is the *principal* of the loan. The lender gives you the money for a certain period (term of the loan) and you pay them a fee called *interest* for the use of that money. In almost all business situations, the fee for using other people's wealth is a *percentage* of the money you are renting and is called the *interest rate.*

In business, every company experiences risk. The level of risk might be a function of the industry you are in, your strategy for competing in that industry, and your experience in serving the market. Your financing strategy, or the way you go about getting the money you need to grow your business, also influences your risk. The more debt you have, the more risk you are exposed to. Debt involves a contract whose terms you must meet. If you do not meet your obligation (make your payment), the contract usually specifies a remedy. This may include that your creditor can force you to sell your assets until you can meet your contractual obligations. When this happens, you are in the process of going out of business. The greater the percentage of assets you acquire by debt, the greater the possibility that you could be forced to sell key assets to meet your obligations.

Borrowing money increases the total value of your company and infuses cash into the business, *but this money is not income.* The transaction involves increasing the balance of your cash account <u>and</u> increasing the value of the appropriate liability account. Paying back the loan reduces the balance in your cash account (and the value of your company) and the balance in the appropriate liability account.

It is important to point out that paying down the principal of a loan is not an expense. However, the interest that you pay to use or "rent" the money is a legitimate business expense. Interest expenses reduce the balance in your cash account and the balance in your retained earnings account. Because interest payments come out of retained earnings, they are part of (and expensed on) the income statement and reduce your net profits. The more you borrow, the higher the interest rate and the higher the interest payment. Additional payments against the principal reduce both the principal amount due and the interest payments.

FOUNDATION®

*All companies in **Foundation** face the same level and type of market risk. Therefore, the proportion of your assets that is financed by debt determines your risk level.*

Your company's risk is measured by the debt-to-assets ratio. We will look closely at the many ratios you can use to measure different elements of your company's results in Module 6. The debt-to-assets ratio, however, measures a company's financial risk by determining what proportion of the company's assets has been financed by debt. It is calculated by adding the company's short-term and long-term debt and dividing it by total assets.

When your debt-to-assets ratio approaches 80%, banks will not lend you additional funds, and they will charge you the highest interest rate possible. Keeping your debt-to-assets ratio at an acceptable level - below 80% in this case - will allow you to have access to more-affordable capital that you can use to operate and expand your business.

$$\text{Total Debt To Total Assets} = \frac{\text{Short Term Debt} + \text{Long Term Debt}}{\text{Total Assets}}$$

Balance Sheet

Assets	This includes the "stuff" or economic resources that the company has use of and from which it can expect to derive future economic benefit.
Current Assets	Assets that can (will be) converted to cash within the year
Cash	Currency readily available to the business.
Accounts receivable	The amount your customers owe because they purchased from you on credit.
Inventory	The value of the products (merchandise) that have been acquired for sale to customers and are still on hand.
Total current assets	These are the assets used to operate your business–an important part of working capital.
Fixed Assets	Assets that have a long-term use or value, including land, building, and equipment.
Property, plant and equipment	The purchase price that you paid for the land, buildings, and equipment that you use to create your products or services.
Accumulated depreciation	How much of the value of your plant and equipment you have used up while operating your business over time.
Total fixed assets	The net value of your property, plant, and equipment.
Total Assets	The value of all of the assets (stuff) of your business.
Liabilities	These are "loans," or debt contracts.
Current Liabilities	The loans that have to be paid back within a year.
Accounts Payable	The amount that you owe your suppliers for materials (inventory) that you purchased on credit.
Current debt	The loan payments (part of a long-term loan) to be made this year.
Total current liabilities	The debt that you have to pay back within one year.
Long-term liabilities	The loans (or debt contracts) that have to be paid back at some point in the future (in more than a year's time).
Total liabilities	The amount of other people's wealth you are renting the use of, as if you were using their money on contract.
Owners' Equity	The value of the owners' investments in the company.
Common Stock (paid-in capital)	The value of what the owners "paid in" as a direct investment in the company. (n a corporation, the sale of stock)
Retained earnings	The portion of owners' profits that they choose to reinvest in the company.
Total owners' equity	This is the owners' claim against the assets of the business - or the value of owning the business.
Total Liabilities and Owners' Equity	This will always equal Total Assets - as liabilities and owners' equity account for where the money came from to acquire the assets.

Short-Term Bank Loans

Short-term loans are loans that need to be paid back within a year. Banks will lend funds to a business over the short term if they feel the business has a reasonable risk profile. Whether it is a savings bank or a commercial bank, the most important point to keep in mind when dealing with a bank is that bankers seek to avoid risk. Their primary concern is always the safety of their funds. Therefore, the company will not only need to fill out an application, but provide documentation of financial history (past balance sheets and income statements) and submit a business plan to assess future potential financial success. This information allows the bank to assess risk.

Bonds and the Bond Market

A bond is a form of long-term financing. When you borrow money from a bank, you sign a debt contract to use the bank's money for a certain period of time and to pay a specific rate of interest. You might have to pledge specific assets as security, or collateral, for the loan. If you miss payments, the bank can force you to sell those assets and use that money to retire the loan.

Companies and government entities can develop a similar debt contract, but instead of borrowing money from a bank, they can borrow money directly from investors. These debt contracts are called bonds. Bonds are referred to as *securities* because they represent secured (or asset-based) claims for the investors. Stocks are another type of security. These are secured or asset-based claims against the company. Both stocks and bonds are traded in *securities markets.*

The debt contract is called an "indenture" and contains the critical information of a loan including answers to these questions:

- Who is borrowing the money?
- How much money is being borrowed?
- For what period of time?
- At what rate of interest?
- How and when is the loan going to be paid off?
- How will the loan amount be secured?

When you borrow money from a bank, you provide information in the loan application that helps the bank determine how likely you are to meet the terms of the contract. The bank uses this assessment to determine whether or not to loan you the money and how high an interest rate they should charge. The higher the risk of non-payment, the higher the interest rate you have to pay.

It is impractical for every investor who might want to buy a bond (loan some money) to assess the risk of the company (or government entity) that is issuing the bond. Instead, a few well-established companies, such as Moody's and Standard & Poor's, will assess the company and the bond issue and assign it a risk rating. The ratings range from AAA, which is excellent, to D, which indicates the organization presents an exceptionally high level of risk.

Bond ratings progress from a rating of "excellent" to "very poor" in the order indicated in Table 1 below.

The lower the bond rating, the higher the interest rate the issuing company will have to pay in order to attract investors. Companies get very concerned when their bond rating is degraded. It communicates a negative message to the financial community and to the market in general.

In the U.S., a company that wants to issue a new bond has to get permission from the Securities and Exchange Commission. The company then typically goes through an **investment bank.** An investment bank is a financial institution that specializes in issuing and reselling new securities such as stocks and bonds.

Table 1

Excellent	Low Risk
AAA AA A	
BBB BB B	
CCC CC C	
DDD DD D	
Very Poor	High Risk

The company's financial managers and the investment bankers evaluate the reasons for the bond issue (what the money will be used for), the length of the loan, how much money they want, and how much interest they expect to pay.

The investment bank then works to market the new bond issue. They contact big investors - such as banks, insurance companies, and pension funds - to determine the willingness of the market to buy the bonds and to create a distribution network for the bond issue. The investment bank also **underwrites** (buys) a significant portion of the bond issue. This first sale of the newly issued security takes place in the **primary securities market.**

FOUNDÂTION.

When you sell new bond issues in Foundation, the interest rate you have to pay is 1.4% higher than your short-term rate. You would choose to do this if you might have to borrow more money in the future. The more you borrow, the higher your risk and the higher the interest payment. It does not take very long before your short-term rate will be above the 1.4% premium, making the earlier decision to "lock in" an interest rate for the term of the bond a better decision. When you issue new bonds, there is a commission that you have to pay to the investment bankers to help you issue the new bonds. The year your bonds mature, they are transferred from long-term debt to short-term debt and automatically paid off. The amount you pay is the value of the bond issue as shown in the third column of the table above. Your bond price goes up and down depending on the interest rate. If you want to retire bonds, or buy back your bonds before they come to maturity, you have to pay the closing price.

Because bonds are a secured claim, investors who own them can buy and sell them to other investors. These transactions occur in the **secondary securities markets (or exchanges)** or the "bond market." In the bond market, the bond (debt contract) can trade above or below the face value of the bond. In general, bond prices move in the opposite direction of interest rates - as interest rates fall, bond prices go up, and as interest rates rise, bond prices drop.

A bond is an investment whose return is specified in the debt contract. Consider a very simple example: A $1,000 bond that pays 10% interest per year for 5 years.

As an investor, you view investments as shown in Table 2

Table 2

YEARS	"Bond A"
Year 1	$100
Year 2	$100
Year 3	$100
Year 4	$100
Year 5	$100 + $1,000
TOTAL	$1,500

Because this is a contract, the return on your investment does not vary at all. Suppose as an investor, you had the opportunity to choose between buying the 5-year, 10% bond or a new, 5-year, 15% bond (assume equal risk or bond rating). If the two investments involving $1,000 looked like this, which would you choose?

Table 3

YEARS	"Bond A"	"Bond B"
Year 1	$100	$150
Year 2	$100	$150
Year 3	$100	$150
Year 4	$100	$150
Year 5	$100 + $1,000	$150 + $1,000
TOTAL	$1,500	$1,750

The rational investor would pick the investment with the higher return: "Bond B" paying 15% interest. However, if the investor who owned "Bond "A" was motivated, she might offer to sell it at $980. If she attracted no buyers, she might offer it at $960, then $940, and then at some lower price. The potential buyer would then be as well off buying "Bond A" as "Bond B." As the return on the alternative investment (interest rate of the other bond) goes up, the trading price of existing bonds goes down.

Consider the same scenario, but the alternative bond offers a 5-year, 5% return as shown in Table 4.

Table 4

YEARS	"Bond A"	"Bond B"
Year 1	$100	$50
Year 2	$100	$50
Year 3	$100	$50
Year 4	$100	$50
Year 5	$100 + $1,000	$50 + $1,000
TOTAL	$1,500	$1,250

The rational investor would want to buy "Bond A". The current owner of "Bond A" faces a situation in which motivated buyers are competing to buy his investment. The owner would then bid the price of a 10% bond higher than the face value ($1,000) because the return is better than any alternatives. At some price, say $1,120 for discussion purposes, the two investments would be equally attractive and would generate buyers. A $1,120 price for a bond that pays $1,500 would be about as attractive as a $1,000 price for a bond that pays $1,250.

Bonds are bought and sold every day on the bond market. At the end of a trading day, the information about the outstanding bonds, the value of their issue, their trading prices, yield, and the bond ratings of the companies are published in the financial press. In the Foundation FastTrack report the information looks like that in Table 5.

Table 5

Company	Issue	Value	Yield	Close	S&P
Digby	10.8S2015	$4,347,878	10.3%	105.16	AA
	13.2S2016	$23 MIL	11.4%	115.48	AA

In this instance, the Digby Company has two different issues of bonds outstanding.

The first bond "10.8S2015" is:

- An issue that pays 10.8% each year until the bond matures in 2015.
- One that provided Digby $4,347,878 when the series was issued.
- Currently trading at 105.16% of its face value.
- Showing a face value of $1,000, so it would currently cost you $1,051.60 to purchase one of these bonds.
- One with a 10.8% return on a price of $1,051.60, so its real return, or yield, is 10.3%.

- The company has an AA bond rating based on its current financial status

The second bond "13.2S2016" is:

- An issue that pays 13.2% each year until the bond matures in 2016.
- A significant issue, raising $23 million.
- Currently trading at $1,154.80 for a $1,000 face-value bond.
- Showing a purchase price of $1,154.80 on a 13.2% bond and providing a real yield of 11.4%.
- The company has an AA bond rating based on its current financial status.

Stocks and Dividends

When you sell shares of stock, you are selling ownership rights to a corporation. Owners, or stockholders, never have to be paid back, and you do not have to pay them interest on the money that they are investing in the company. However, owners have a claim against the company's assets and the wealth that is created in the form of net income, earnings, and profit by the company, plus they have a say in the management of the company. The stockholders' ownership claim *never ends* as long as they hold the stock.

Stock Market

When you own a stock, you are actually a part-owner of a corporation. As a shareholder, you have a "say" in how the company operates, although your voice may be just one among thousands of other shareholders and the strength of your voice is usually affected tby the percentage of shares you own.

Companies initially issue stock to raise capital to run their businesses, often motivated by the fact that they need more money. A corporation sells shares to investors in an organized fashion called a public offering, the first of which is its *Initial Public Offering*, or *IPO*. After the company's IPO, investors are free to sell their shares and buy more, but not from the company directly. Instead, shares are traded on organized stock markets like the New York, London, or Hong Kong Stock Exchanges.

A company can issue common stock or preferred stock. *Common stock* represents a simple share of ownership and each common stock share has one vote to cast when electing the corporation's board of directors.

If the company were to go bankrupt, the corporation would have no financial liability to common shareholders, and those shares may become worthless.

Preferred stock, a form of stock that is traded at a far lower volume than common stock, does have privileges. Preferred shareholders, often those having some kind of history or relationship within the company, may receive higher dividends and have a first claim to assets if a company should go bankrupt.

Shares of stock are traditionally represented by a piece of paper called a stock certificate. Since shares of stock trade electronically, you may never actually see a physical certificate for the share that you own. The brokerage holds the shares on your behalf in what is known as a "street name" which is nothing more than a method of bookkeeping and has no effect on your ownership of the stock.

FOUNDĀTION.

Dividends should be paid from the profits of the business. When you are managing your Foundation company, it is generally not a good idea to pay dividends in a year in which you are borrowing money. Owners and the market for potential owners interpret this as borrowing money to pay the dividend. Owners give the managers of the company their money to grow their wealth, not for the managers to take out loans in their name. Owners do not like managers to hold "excessive" cash balances. It is the owners' money, and they expect those funds to create more wealth. Cash does not earn significant return. Owners think that if you do not have a productive use for their cash, you should give it back to them by paying a dividend. A "productive use" is to invest it in new products, make facility improvements, or take other actions that will put that cash to work for the business.

Owning shares in street name is much more efficient and convenient, especially when it is time to sell the stock.

Like a bond, stocks are secured investments. They have a claim against the assets of the company. The company sells new shares of stock to potential owners through the **primary securities market** in a process similar to the way new bond issues are sold. The company meets with an investment banker who reviews the business strategy and specific plans for the money that is to be raised. The investment bank underwrites, or buys, markets, and distributes the new shares. Underwriters charge commission and make money by holding some shares until the price per share rises. Again, once stock has been issued, owners can buy from and sell to others on the **secondary securities markets (exchanges)** or stock markets around the world. The company itself receives no cash for shares that are sold in the secondary markets, and every corporation wants to see its stock price increase for the benefit of its shareholders and the financial reputation of the corporation.

If you are a potential investor in a company (someone who is thinking about purchasing shares of stock in a company), you have choices about which company's shares you might want to purchase. You want to invest your money in a company that is going to create as much wealth for you as possible.

There are two ways in which owning stock increases your wealth:

1. When the value of your shares increases as the stock price goes up
2. When the company distributes to owners some of the profits it has created in the form of cash payments called dividends.

Paying Dividends

When a company creates profit, the profit belongs to the owners. There are only two things that can happen with that profit:

1. It can be kept in the company as retained earnings

2. It can be distributed to the owners in the form of a cash disbursement or payment. If it is paid out to the owners, it reduces the amount of cash on hand.

Value and Stock Claims

Interactions between buyers and sellers determine stock price. A potential buyer might consider three things in determining how much to pay for stock in a particular company:

1. The value of the stock's claim against the assets of the company

2. How much profit the company makes per share of stock

3. How much of that profit is distributed to owners (as a dividend)

The value of this claim is determined by dividing the total owners' equity from the balance sheet by the number of shares outstanding. For instance, if the value of the owners' claim is $100 million and there are 2 million shares of stock issued and outstanding, then each

share has a claim against the assets of the company worth $50. This is called the **book value** of the stock.

There are two ways to increase book value:

1. Increase the value of total owners' equity

2. Reduce the number of shares outstanding (buy back stock)

The easiest way to increase owners' equity is to make a profit to reinvest, or retain it, in the company, which increases the value of the "retained earnings" account. If you sell more shares to increase the value of the common stock account, you have increased the value of total owners' equity, but you have also increased the number of shares you have to divide it by in order to get book value. In general, current owners would prefer that you borrow money to grow the company, if you can afford the interest payments, rather than dilute the value of their claim.

Stock Reports

Large volumes of stock are traded every day. At the end of the day, the transactions in the market are summarized so investors can make informed decisions about future purchases. Here's how the stock report looks in the Foundation FastTrack:

Table 6

Company	Close	Change	Shares	Dividend	Yield	P/E	EPS
Andrews	$51.29	$22.48	2,000,000	$2.00	3.9%	5.8	$8.88
Baldwin	$69.86	$21.09	2,157,790	$0.50	0.7%	5.6	$12.49
Chester	$41.26	$6.75	2,045,860	$1.00	2.4%	6.8	$6.04
Digby	$37.40	$10.60	4,096,380	$2.00	5.3%	8.1	$4.61
Erie	$15.82	($0.47)	3,209,871	$0.00	0.0%	18.0	$0.88
Ferris	$65.20	$24.76	2,339,022	$3.00	4.6%	6.0	$10.84

In the above table, the trading of six companies' stocks is summarized. Let's use the first one, Andrews, as an example:

CLOSE

At the end of the trading day, buyers in the stock market determined that Andrews' stock was worth $51.29 per share.

CHANGE

Because this is $22.48 higher than the close at the end of the last trading period, the last closing price was $28.81: $28.81 + $22.48 = $51.29

SHARES

Andrews has 2 million shares of stock outstanding. The share price at the last trading period was $51.29. Therefore the total market capitalization of Andrew is $100,258,000 ($51.29 x 2 million)

DIVIDEND

The company decided to share all or part of the profits with the owners of the company. The dividend that was "declared" by those managing the company was $2.00 and each shareholder received that amount for each share they own. Issuing these dividends reduces their cash by $4 million: ($2 x 2 million).

YIELD

A yield of 3.9% is a comparison of the dividend amount to the closing price of the stock. The $2.00 dividend payment represents a 3.9% return (yield) on the $51.29 stock price: $2.00 / $51.29 = .0389 or approximately 3.9%

PRICE EARNINGS RATIO – P/E

The Price/Earnings ratio, or the PE, measures how many times you would have to multiply the earnings to get a number close to the stock price. Andrews' stock is trading at 5.8 times as much as it earned in this one year.

EARNINGS PER SHARE – EPS

Each share of Andrews' outstanding stock (2 million) has earned $8.88 of net income (Earnings per Share). This indicates their total net income must have been $17.76 million (2 million x $8.88).

Recap: Cash Flows, Financials, and Company Performance

Now is a good time for a quick recap of what we have covered. In Module 4, we introduced the three types of financial reports that are typically used to summarize a company's financial standing and spent quite a bit of time talking about the Cash Flow Statement and the Income Statement. In this Module we reviewed the ways a company can gain access to additional cash to run its operations and to grow its business. We also introduced and discussed the information found on a company's Balance Sheet. All three financial statements provide important information for your decision making as a manager.

- The Cash Flow Statement helps keep track of cash and ensure you always have enough on hand to keep business operations running smoothly.

- The Income Statement shows where you are (or are not) making a profit and, therefore, which parts of the business require more attention.

- The Balance Sheet demonstrates the way you – as managers of a business – are working the owners' investment in the business.

In Module 6, we'll consider the way we measure performance (financial ratios) in our business, because this also has an impact on our financial decision making as well as on our operations. We will also discuss other ways to assess a company's performance and the importance of aligning a company's strategy to the types of decisions that are made about how to run the business.

FOUNDATION

Cash Flow from Investing & Financing Activities in Foundation

In Module 4 we looked in detail at the first category of cash on the Cash Flow Statement, cash flows from operating activities including depreciation, accounts payable and receivable, and inventory. The two other categories of cash – from investing and financing – are linked to the issues we have discussed above.

The second category of cash, cash flow from investing activities, includes the changes in plant and equipment we discussed in Module 3 – such as adding capacity and increasing automation levels, or selling off your unused production capacity.

The third category tells you what cash came in and what went out on financing activities. That includes both short-term borrowing such as loans, and long-term investing such as share transactions and the purchase or retirement of bonds.

Your Foundation simulation updates your financial statements every time you make a decision. Now that you understand the Balance Sheet, you can use it plus the Cash Flow Statement to discover exactly how much cash is available for operating your business right now. Just take the Change in Cash Position from your Cash Flow Statement and add it to the cash line on your Balance Sheet.

Here's an example. If your balance sheet showed $10 million in cash on December 31st last year, and your cash flow statement shows a change in cash position of -$3 million today, you have $7 million left in cash to run the business today.

Chapter Review Questions

Investment Financing

1. How does a company's financing strategy impact its operations and performance?

2. What is risk and how does it affect decisions about investment?

The Balance Sheet

3. What is the primary difference between financing through loans versus stock?

4. What is a loan and how do interest rates affect a company that takes out a loan?

5. In what ways are bonds different than loans?

Loans, Stocks, and Dividends

6. How can we tell the difference in the quality of different bonds?

7. How are common stocks different from preferred stocks? Why would a company offer preferred stocks?

8. Why would a company choose to pay dividends?

9. What is the purpose of the Balance Sheet?

10. What is the difference between assets and liabilities?

11. What are the accounts that make up Shareholder's Equity on the Balance Sheet?

You – in the executive suite!

Finance and Accounting Manager

In Module 4, you started in your job rotation track as **Accounting Manager**. Now let's expand your role and make you the **Finance & Accounting Manager**.

Remember that every business needs to "make its numbers" in order to remain sustainable and meet all of its obligations including paying staff, paying vendors and suppliers, and - of course - billing customers.

Activities: Approximately 120 – 150 minutes to complete.

COMPLETED

A-1: Answer all **Chapter Review Questions**
Your instructor will advise you on how to turn in your answers.

A-2: Before you begin the exercises, view the **Video on the Finance Department**.

A-3: Read the following text through to the end of the module. **Answer** all of the questions on the Balance Sheet, Stocks, and Bonds at the end.

Exercise #10: Analyzing the Balance Sheet

In Module 4 we had a thorough look at the Income Statement – the "movie" of the business that shows us whether or not the company is making a profit.

Now we will take a thorough look at Andrews Company's Balance Sheet, the snapshot of the finances of the business taken on December 31st.

Please go to Appendix 2 for Andrews Financial Statements and refer to the Balance Sheet for the following exercise.

On December 31st, Andrews Company has $14,117,000 in *cash*. With Total Assets worth $26,377,000, that represents 53.5% of your assets in cash. That seems like too much cash. There is so much more that cash could be doing than just sitting in the bank – it could be turned into more sensors to sell, more promotions to help sell them, or used to upgrade your factory by increasing the capacity of the production line or by adding automation.

You also have $3,620,000 in *accounts receivable.* Accounts receivable is the account that keeps track of sensors that you sold last year, but haven't yet been paid for. Your customers owe you this money. Your receivables policy gives your customers 30 days to pay for the sensors they buy from you. Last year, you sold 1,335,000 sensors at a price of $33 each. The current balance in your accounts receivable, or A/R, represents 109,697,000 sensors at $33 each that you haven't received the cash for yet. This makes sense as it is about 1/12, or one month, of the total.

You have a balance of $0 in the *inventory* account. The inventory account keeps track of sensors that you are either in the process of making or that you have made but not yet sold. Last year, therefore, you sold everything you made.

You currently have one factory, your *Plant and Equipment,* and its value is $14,400,000. The factory can produce 800,000 units a year (with no overtime) with an automation level of 3.

Accumulated depreciation is how the financial statements recognize that the factory wears out over time. Andrews Company uses a 15-year straight line depreciation method. That means that every year the depreciation expense on your income statement is 1/15 of the value of your investment in your factory. One fifteenth (1/15) of $14,400,000 is a depreciation expense of $960,000 a year. The accumulated depreciation of $5,760,000 represents about 40% of the initial investment in the factory, suggesting the factory has been in use about six years.

The current accounting value of your factory *(total fixed assets)* of $8,640,000 represents the $14,400,000 initial investment minus the depreciation for six years of use ($5,760,000).

In total, Andrews' management has control over $26,377,000 worth of assets. This is the company's *Total Assets.*

Where did that money come from?

The money to operate and grow your company can only come from two places: debt and owners' investments. On the Balance Sheet, the *liability accounts* represent different kinds of debt. *Owners' Equity* accounts are the investments made by the owners of the corporation.

The *accounts payable* are a type of short-term "loan" from your suppliers – those companies from whom you buy the component parts used in the production of your sensors. You will have to pay your suppliers

$2,653,000 within the next 30 days for materials already received.

The *current debt* account keeps track of loans that have to be paid back in the coming year. This is also known as current liabilities. It can include loans from the bank or the infamous "Big Al", or the face value of any bonds that mature in the coming year. You have no current debt at this moment.

The *long-term debt* (or long-term liabilities) keeps track of money borrowed by issuing bonds. You currently have four bond issues ($866,667; $1,733,333; $2,600,00 and $2,000,000) for a total of $7,200,000. All bonds are 10-year contracts.

There are two owners' equity accounts: *common stock* and *retained earnings*. The common stock account keeps track of the money the corporation's owners paid "out of pocket" to purchase the stock. Your stockholders paid $5,323,000 to purchase 2,269,049 shares. The average price for a new share was about $2.35. What a bargain! Those shares trade now trade at $11.17.

The *retained earnings* account keeps track of profit that has been retained for use in the company. All the profit created by the company belongs to the owners of the company - in Andrews' case, the stockholders. Their profit can be paid out to them in the form of a dividend payment, or it can be retained in the company and used to grow the business. Owners give the company money for one reason - so that the company's managers will increase profit and make them "better off."

If you retain earnings (profits) for use in the company, you have to use them to make your owners wealthier. In the past six years, the company has made $11,201,000 in profits that the board has chosen to retain for use.

So, for a quick summary in round numbers: Management has control over $26.4 million worth of assets. You subtract the $9.8 million the company has borrowed which leaves the owners value at more than $16.6 million. If you split that equally among the 2,269,049 shareholders, each share has a "book value" of $7.28. The total value of the owners claim *(total owners' equity)* is $16,524,000. Another look at the Balance Sheet shows that 37.4% of your assets are currently funded by debt and 62.6% of the company is funded through owners' investments.

The *Balance Sheet* shows what resources you have and where the money came from to pay for those resources. The *Income Statement* describes how you used the resources last year to create wealth (make a profit).

Now, it's your turn again!

The Balance Sheet Survey: FastTrack Reports, Page 3

Balance Sheet Survey	Andrews	Baldwin	Chester	Digby	Erie	Ferris
Cash	$9,812	$12,070	$8,715	$13,236	$8,978	$7,313
Accounts Receivable	$4,690	$5,642	$3,220	$5,925	$2,892	$3,587
Inventory	$0	$3,216	$2,591	$4,016	$1,883	$5,639
Total Current Assets	$14,502	$20,928	$14,526	$23,177	$13,754	$16540
Plant and equipment	$37,440	$32,569	$32,692	$33,015	$32,070	$25,300
Accumulated Depreciation	($8,142)	($8,036)	($8,047)	($8,021)	($7,930)	($7,200)
Total Fixed Assets	$29,298	$24,533	$24,645	$24,994	$24,140	$18,100
Total Assets	$43,800	$45,461	$39,171	$48,171	$37,894	$34,640
Accounts Payable	$2,523	$4,060	$1,841	$4,236	$1,415	$2,770
Current Debt	$1,867	$6,134	$6,364	$7,880	$5,679	$7,936
Long Term Debt	$7,333	$11,858	$11,755	$11,488	$11,828	$7,751
Total Liabilities	$11,723	$22,053	$19,960	$23,604	$18,922	$18,456
Common Stock	$8,323	$5,212	$4,436	$4,376	$5,109	$3,224
Retained Earnings	$23,754	$18,196	$14,775	$20,191	$13,863	$12,960
Total Equity	$32,077	$23,408	$19,211	$24,567	$18,972	$16,184
Total Liabilities & Owners' Equity	$43,800	$45,461	$39,171	$48,171	$37,894	$34,640

Once again, let's look at several entirely different Balance Sheets to check your understanding. Please answer the following questions:

1. How much does **Chester** own? (in dollars)

2. How could you tell from the Balance Sheet if a company had taken an emergency loan?

3. What is the value of the sales that **Digby** has made but hasn't been paid for yet?

4. What is the value of sensors Ferris has in stock?

5. Which company "stocked out" (had no units of their product left in the warehouse) this year?

6. How much did **Erie** spend to buy the factory and machinery?

7. How much is **Erie's** factory and machinery worth today?

8. How much money has **Baldwin** borrowed that has to be paid back in the next year?

9. What is the total value that company **Baldwin** has in long-term debt?

10. Which company has the greatest amount of debt?

11. How much money has **Ferris** accepted as cash investment from owners?

12. If **Digby** has disbursed a total of $6,000 in dividends since the start of the company, how much total net income have they generated (cumulative profit)?

13. What is the value of the net income that has been re-invested (kept) in **Erie**?

14. How much money has **Chester** borrowed that doesn't have to be paid back this year?

15. What would be the net wealth of the owners of **Chester** after they had met all their obligations?

16. What is the dollar amount of assets under your control that was financed by loans?

17. How much – in dollars - of the assets under your control is financed by owners' investments?

Exercise #11: Financing Your Foundation Company

You know that you will need financial resources (capital) to operate your company effectively. You also know that over the next couple of years, you are going to need large amounts of money to reach your goal of creating a larger, more competitive company. There are only two sources of capital, as you know: You can borrow it or get additional investment from your owners. Both have advantages and disadvantages, and limits.

Under what conditions should you borrow and under what conditions should you seek owners' investments? You already know that there is no simple answer. Instead, you look to answer these two questions:

1. What limits the availability of funds?

2. How do my decisions affect my performance?

Debt

In your own life you strive to eliminate debt. However, you cannot manage a company in the same way as you manage your personal finances. In your personal life, debt buys assets that don't produce income. The interest payments on your loans consume your income and wealth. But in business, you borrow money to acquire income-producing assets. Without debt, your company's asset base (which defines your capacity to compete in the market) will not be as large as it would be if you used debt. When the cash from debt is used effectively within the company, it can be a valuable resource. Conceivably, a competitor could have identical levels of owners' investment but could have assets worth two to three times as much as yours.

If you can borrow money at 10% and make 20%, you should borrow all that you need. The relevant questions are:

- Can you find investments that generate a higher return than the cost of the borrowing?

- What is the risk that our investments will not produce the expected return?

However, you also know that the riskiness of your loans is a function of how much debt you have. The more debt you have; the higher the risk. The higher the risk, the higher the interest rate you have to pay. When you have a lot of debt, you are paying a high interest rate on a lot of money. The interest you pay is an expense that reduces your profit.

For bonds, you are limited because bondholders will lend you up to 80% of the current accounting value of your Plant and Equipment (80% of your Total Fixed Assets). Therefore, if the depreciated value of Plant and Equipment totaled $50M; you could issue no more than a total of $40M in bonds.

Assume from the Round 2 FastTrack reports that you have Total Fixed Assets worth $29,298 ($37,440 in Plant and Equipment that has been depreciated by $8,142). 80% of that value would be $23,438; the limit on your total amount of money you can borrow using bonds.

You currently have outstanding bonds worth $7,333. If you subtract that from the limit, you get the maximum you can issue this year, $16,105. ($23,438 - $7,333 = $16,105). The Finance worksheet in Foundation calculates and reports this limit for you.

Figure 2

Long Term Debt		
Retire Long Term Debt ($000) ⓘ	$	0
Issue Long Term Debt ($000) ⓘ	$	0
Long Term Interest Rate ⓘ		9.1%
Maximum Issue This Year ⓘ		$16,105

Equity

You can raise money by issuing shares of stock. Investors give you cash in exchange for ownership rights in the company. They freely enter into this exchange because they believe that you will make them better off. They are "better off" to the extent that the value of their shares of stock (the price at which it trades) increases over time. Stock price is the measure of how much wealth you have created for your owners.

MARKET CAPITALIZATION: Market Capitalization is the value that the stock market places on the firm - stock price multiplied by shares outstanding. One can argue that Market Capitalization is a better measure than stock price for evaluating the wealth created because if two firms have the same stock price but one firm has issued twice as many shares, then they would have created twice as much wealth.

What drives stock price? Stock price is a function of three things:

1. BOOK VALUE: Book value is defined as total owners' equity divided by the number of shares outstanding. Owners' equity is the value of the owners' claims against the company's assets.

2. EARNINGS PER SHARE (EPS): EPS is a measure of how much profit is created for each share of stock. It is calculated by dividing profits by the number of shares outstanding.

3. DIVIDENDS: Dividends are a cash disbursement (payment) of profits to the owners and are declared on a "per share" bases (e.g., $2.00 per share).

Of course, stock prices are influenced by many other factors. Your goal is a simple understanding of stock price that gives you the ability to manage it.

Stock price is a measure of the market value of the company, and that value is expressed on a per share basis. To understand what drives stock price, think about what would influence the price you would be willing to pay to buy a business.

Perhaps the first thing would be the value of the assets the company owns. If you wanted to buy a restaurant that had land and building worth $450,000 and another $200,000 in equipment and fixtures, which information would influence how much you would be willing to pay?

It is not the value of the assets (the building and equipment) that's important, but how much of those assets that the current owners own. So you would need to subtract how much they owe (Total Liabilities) from the value of the assets to get an accurate measure.

If the current owners owed $350,000, the value of the owners' claim against the restaurant would be $300,000 ($650,000 - $350,000).

TOTAL ASSETS = TOTAL LIABILITIES + OWNERS' EQUITY

The Owners' Equity is the value of the owners' claims against the assets of the company. If you divide that number by the number of "owners" you get the Book Value. In the case of a corporation, instead of dividing by the number of owners, you divide by the number of shares and get a "per share" measure of asset value owned free and clear.

The value of a business is much more than the value of its assets, however. It is in the new wealth (profit) that can be created by employing those assets. How much profit did the company create last year? How much profit the year before? More importantly, how much profit can the company create next year? In 5 years? In 10 years? You would be willing to pay a lot more for a company that generated $1,000,000 in profit every year than a company that generated $200,000. Earnings Per Share is the amount of profit generated expressed on a "per share" basis.

Dividends reflect past performance. Your owners expect you to generate a profit every year. Within reason, they expect you to make more profit every year. What do they expect you to do with the profit? If your company is growing (bigger factories, new products, better machinery), the owners will let you use past profits to finance that growth. The owners let you do this with the expectation that you are developing an increased capacity to make them wealthier.

If the company has cash in excess of what it needs to operate and grow, the owners expect you to give them their money back. These are the profits you have earned in their name.

One of the reasons that dividend policy is going to be important to you is that your Board of Directors has limited your investment options. You have no freedom to invest outside the company. As you make profits, you have no investment options beyond the business you are in, so you have to pursue an aggressive dividend policy. How do stockholders evaluate your dividend policy? First, dividends are averaged over the past two years. Second, dividend amounts above the current EPS (or above the two-year average EPS if dividends are falling) are ignored. This makes sense to you. If you pay out more per share (dividend per share) than you earn per share (EPS), then the payment is not out of profits. You must be reducing your retained earnings; you must be reducing your book value. That is not a sustainable practice.

The best way to increase your stock price is to increase profits every year and give the profits to the owners if you don't have any other way to make them wealthier.

From the Finance screen in Foundation, you can set your dividend policy. If you enter $1.00 as the dividend per share, your cash position would decrease by $1.00 for each of the 2,475(000) shares, or $2,475,000.

A dividend of $2.00 would reduce cash by $4,950,000 ($2 x 2,475).

You are limited as to how much new stock you can issue. New stock issues are limited to 20% of your company's outstanding shares. With 2,475(000) shares of stock outstanding, 20% of that is 495(000). That is the maximum number of new shares your company can offer (issue) in the coming year. Because your shares are currently trading for $27.48 each, if you issued 495(000) of them, you would raise $13,602,600. That is the amount of the stock limit reported.

Figure 3

Common Stock		
Shares Outstanding (000) ⓘ		2,475
Price Per Share ⓘ		$27.48
Earnings Per Share ⓘ		$3.21
Max Stock Issue ($000) ⓘ		$13,603
Issue Stock ($000) ⓘ	$	0
Max Stock Retire ($000) ⓘ		$3,401
Retire Stock ($000) ⓘ	$	0
Dividend Per Share ⓘ	$	0.00

Emergency Loans

If a normal business runs out of cash, it is in big trouble. It has to sell some of its assets, reducing its ability to compete. In the worst case, it goes bankrupt.

If you run out of cash in Foundation, you will immediately get a loan from "Big Al". As this only happens in emergencies, you should start thinking about it as an emergency loan

Foundation provides you with an accurate model of your company and the outcomes of your decisions. It uses "Your Sales Forecast" to determine *projected* outcomes. These projections establish the information in the pro forma statements. Whatever you enter, the program will show you how successful you *should* be in the market if you sell what you forecast.

If your forecast is inaccurate - too high or too low - the information provided in the pro forma statements may be meaningless or even deceptive.

As soon as you schedule production for a certain number of units, your inventory management targets (a least 1 but not more than 60 days of inventory) are established. If you were to enter the number of units from the top of that range, the profit and cash available at the end of the year reported in Foundation is going to be the best possible outcome.

You complete your sales forecast and decide to make 1,800 units of Able available for sale at $35.00 each. You make your marketing decisions. You set your production schedule so that 1,800 units are available. You make a $20,000 investment in increased capacity and automation. A total of 1,800 units is entered in the "your sales forecast" cell in the Marketing worksheet. You check and your pro forma Income Statement shows $9,765

profit. You started the year with $9,812 in cash and end with $1,206. You have financed a $20,000 investment out of operations; no loans, no increased owners' investments.

But that is *only* if you sell 1,800 units.

Figure 4 - Cash position forecast with a sales forecast of 1,800 units.

Cash Positions

December 31, 2016 ⓘ	$9,812
December 31, 2017 ⓘ	$1,206

If you have 1,800 units available for sale, you want at least one unit but not more than 60 days of inventory in the warehouse at the end of the year. Sixty days of inventory is 300 units. If you had 1,800 units available and had 300 left at the end of the year, you must have sold 1,500.

How good is your performance if you only sell 1,500 units? You enter 1,500 into "your sales forecast" and check. You are still profitable but your profit has fallen to $6,184. You started the year with $9,812 in cash but ended with a shortfall of $6,878 (because you still have the $20,000 investment in capacity).

You are definitely going to need to raise some additional capital. If you do not, you will run out of cash and have to take an emergency loan from "Big Al."

Figure 5 - Cash position forecast with a sales forecast of 1,500 units.

Cash Positions	
December 31, 2016 ⓘ	$9,812
December 31, 2017 ⓘ	($6,878)

This exercise suggests a workflow – always make all of your operating and investment decisions first. After that, you can calculate your inventory management range and enter the bottom of that range to give you your "worst case" for the sales forecast. With all of that information, you can make your financing decisions.

And yes, it's your turn again!

Please look at the stock market and bond market summaries and answer the questions below.

Figure 6 - Stock Table

Company	Close	Change	Shares	MarketCap ($M)	Book Value	EPS	Dividend	Yield	P/E
Andrews	$27.48	$10.28	2,474,994	$68	$12.96	$3.66	$0.00	0.0%	7.5
Baldwin	$19.48	$5.79	2,220,036	$44	$10.54	$2.38	$0.00	0.0%	8.4
Chester	$13.68	($0.26)	2,160,748	$30	$8.89	$0.88	$0.00	0.0%	15.6
Digby	$23.60	$7.31	2,137,845	$50	$11.49	$2.90	$0.00	0.0%	8.1
Erie	$12.43	($0.22)	2,226,267	$28	$8.52	$0.78	$0.00	0.0%	15.9
Ferris	$16.05	($0.44)	2,054,656	$33	$7.88	$1.01	$0.00	0.0%	15.8

Stock Market Summary

1. Which company's owners had the greatest increase in wealth last year?

2. Which company has sold the most shares of stock?

3. How is market capitalization calculated?

4. Which company has created the most wealth for its owners?

5. How is book value calculated?

6. Looking only at the stock table, what is value of **Digby's** Total Owners' Equity (from the Balance Sheet)?

7. Who created the most profit per shareholder?

8. How is "EPS" of the stock table calculated?

9. Looking only at the stock table, how much profit did **Digby** create last year?

10. If company **Andrews** had declared a dividend of $2 per share, how much would their cash position have decreased?

11. How is the "yield" of the stock table calculated?

12. How is "P/E" of the stock table calculated?

Figure 7 - Bond Table

Bond Market Summary					
Company	Series	Face	Yield	Close$	Rating
Andrews					
	12.0S2013	$1,733,333	11.4%	$105.28	AA
	13.0S2015	$2,600,000	11.5%	$112.96	AA
	9.0S2021	$3,000.000	9.0%	$100.00	AA
Baldwin					
	12.0S2013	$1,733,333	11.8%	$101.54	B
	13.0S2015	$2,600,000	12.3%	$105.88	B
	10.0S2020	$2,480,000	10.6%	$93.93	B
	11.0S2021	$5,044,916	11.1%	$99.41	B
Chester					
	12.0S2013	$1,733,333	11.9%	$101.02	B
	13.0S2015	$2,600,000	12.4%	$104.92	B
	10.0S2020	$2,366,478	10.8%	$92.37	B
	10.9S2021	$5,055,277	11.2%	$97.10	B
Digby					
	12.0S2013	$1,733,333	11.8%	$101.37	B
	13.0S2015	$2,600,000	12.3%	$105.56	B
	10.0S2020	$2,291,811	10.7%	$92.89	B
	11.0S2021	$5,128,211	11.2%	$98.28	B
Erie					
	12.0S2013	$1,733,333	11.9%	$101.19	B
	13.0S2015	$2,600,000	12.4%	$105.24	B
	10.0S2020	$2,366,478	10.8%	$92.89	B
	11.0S2021	$5,128,211	11.2%	$98.26	B
Ferris					
	12.0S2013	$1,733,333	11.9%	$100.68	CCC
	13.0S2015	$2,600,000	12.5%	$104.29	CCC
	10.0S2020	$425,144	10.9%	$91.34	CCC
	11.0S2021	$2,992,039	11.4%	$96.55	CCC

1. What is **Digby's** long-term debt?
2. Which company has the greatest long-term debt?
3. What interest rate is **Erie** paying on the bond that is due in 2021?
4. In 2015, how much will **Chester** have to pay to retire the bonds that mature that year?
5. If I wanted to buy one of **Baldwin's** series 13.0S2015 bonds (face value $1,000) on the secondary market, how much would I have to pay?
6. Which is the most risky company to loan money to?
7. How is yield calculated on the bond table?

6 How Does It All Work Together?

Learning Objectives:

After reading this module and completing the associated exercises, you will be able to:

LO1: Discuss the factors that influence strategic choices.

LO2: Describe the components of a SWOT analysis and the common questions that are asked in each component.

LO3: Explain how a SWOT analysis informs business strategy.

LO4: Describe the linkages between goals and strategy.

LO5: Discuss the five characteristics of effective goals.

LO6: Compare and contrast the three groups of customers that are important to growing and sustaining a business.

LO7: Compare and contrast operational effectiveness and strategic positioning.

LO8: Define competitive advantage and the kinds of business resources that create it.

LO9: Describe the "five forces" that drive competition in an industry.

LO10: Compare and contrast the two generic strategies of cost leadership and differentiation.

LO11: Discuss ways a company can pursue a cost leadership strategy.

LO12: Discuss ways a company can pursue a differentiation strategy.

LO13: Describe the four quadrants of the Balanced Scorecard.

Key Terms To Look For:

- *Balance scorecard*
- *Business model*
- *Competitive advantage*
- *Cost leadership*
- *Differentiation*
- *Generic strategies*
- *Goals*
- *Industry*

- *Mission*
- *Operational effectiveness*
- *Success measurements*
- *Strategic analysis*
- *Strategic choices*
- *Strategic intent*
- *Vision*

Alignment, Coordination, and Evaluation – Critical Factors

Sporting analogies are common in business because – just like team sports – business is competitive and requires the efforts of people with different expertise all working together.

Former sports coaches have built lucrative second careers teaching leadership to business people, our business-speak is peppered with sporting analogies from "don't drop the ball" to "it's a marathon, not a sprint," and any sales team securing a big contract may well whoop as loud (and celebrate as hard) as a team winning a championship!

There are two key areas in which team sports and business are alike: Both require the coordinated efforts of people with different skills, and their success is measurable on a scoreboard. We'll cover both of these issues in this module.

The comparison to sports, however, may stop there. In all other areas, according to Octavius Black, CEO of Mind Gym - a performance training consultancy - sports and business have very little in common.

> "Athletic sport is primarily about completing a single task to an exceptionally high standard. Business is invariably a multi-task, multi-layered affair. The single-mindedness of the brilliant fly half would be catastrophic for the corporate high flyer. They would be marked down for lack of big picture thinking and sent to back office processing.

> "Sport is all about beating someone else. There are no win-win solutions, you can't increase the size of the mar

ket in victories and you don't need to watch out for new entrants who play by different rules." (The Sunday Telegraph, July 15, 2012)

In the world of business, things are not as clear-cut as in sports. There is no simple rule-book and the competition can, and at times does, change the game entirely. In this complex environment, therefore, how do we coordinate and align our efforts, stay ahead of our competitors, and measure our success?

Managing Resources under Pressure

Irrespective of up or down economic cycles, today's business environment is more competitive and fluid than at any other time in recent history. To a certain extent, a company can reengineer, restructure, and cut costs, but ongoing success requires the ability to grow revenue and margins. Therefore, management must align and coordinate its resources consistently in order to nurture growth. Creating the process of aligning and coordinating resources, however, can prove to be as tough and ruthless as surviving a reality-based television show.

The process becomes more and more challenging when management has to make its decisions in a competitive environment. Competitors in an industry scrutinize any realignment of resources by another player in context of the choices now available to them. For example, in our Foundation simulation if Andrews realigns its market offering, the management teams of Baldwin, Chester, Digby, Erie, and Ferris will attempt to identify and understand Andrews' actions and attempt to initiate counter measures.

Searching for Alternatives

As we discussed in Module 2, because of resource constraints, it is virtually impossible for any firm to excel in all functional aspects of business all at once. Management, therefore, needs a clear understanding of customers' needs to find ways to satisfy them within their firm's capabilities.

While evaluating various possible competitive alternatives, managers typically refrain from implementing "revolutionary" changes in their market offerings; instead, they engage in "evolutionary," or incremental, market moves. This is understandable, because the underlying problem in predicting future market shifts is that customers often make purchasing decisions based on many different criteria simultaneously, including brand, quality, performance, price, and service.

It is frequently easier to modify the "core engine" of a product or service offering by adding one or several "engine variants" rather than introducing "the new thing" that might capture new customers and market segments, but, at the same time, potentially risk the firm's market position and profitability. The choice is even more challenging in an environment where a competitor can make similar moves, or simply copy your every step. Think about Samsung and the way it copied Apple's playbook until it was stopped by legal action in various courts around the world. Whenever we make decisions that have multi-year, lasting impacts on a firm's operations, they should be well planned. We refer to these critical firm-level decisions as strategic choices.

Making Strategic Choices: Where are we now?

In order to make strategic choices, a company must understand the challenges, opportunities, and future trends, both inside and outside its chosen industry and markets. This requires a company to clearly define the industry and markets in which it exists as well as how it would like to operate within this context. The clear understanding that comes from defining the industry and markets is necessary for making choices about where to direct and use human and financial resources.

At the same time, a company has to be always ready and able to respond to industry and market changes. These changes can be triggered by shifts in the external environment, such as a recession or labor strikes, or can be caused by the internal environment, such as not meeting customer requirements for product features, quality, or price. A company's competitors can also force changes within the broader marketplace, or even force the company to exit particular markets. For example, think about the way Apple's smartphone grabbed most of the mobile phone market share of Blackberry, Motorola, and Nokia.

In order to develop a systematic understanding of the important issues a company faces, we have to look to the pros and cons of all potential forces that might impact our chosen strategy. As a starting point for this discussion, many organizations use a SWOT analysis – **S**trengths, **W**eaknesses, **O**pportunities, and **T**hreats. A **SWOT** analysis focuses on both internal and external factors:

INTERNAL FACTORS: Strengths (Pros) and Weaknesses (Cons)

EXTERNAL FACTORS: Opportunities (Pros) and Threats (Cons).

Questions asked in a SWOT analysis include:

Figure 1

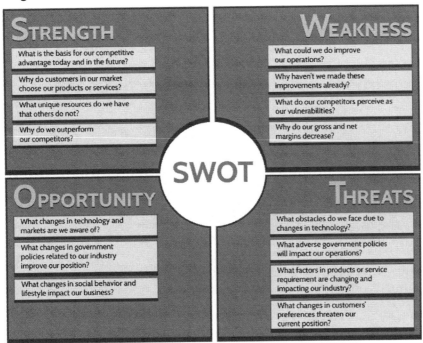

STRENGTH	WEAKNESS
What is the basis for our competitive advantage today and in the future?	What could we do improve our operations?
Why do customers in our market choose our products or services?	Why haven't we made these improvements already?
What unique resources do we have that others do not?	What do our competitors perceive as our vulnerabilities?
Why do we outperform our competitors?	Why do our gross and net margins decrease?

SWOT

OPPORTUNITY	THREATS
What changes in technology and markets are we aware of?	What obstacles do we face due to changes in technology?
What changes in government policies related to our industry improve our position?	What adverse government policies will impact our operations?
What changes in social behavior and lifestyle impact our business?	What factors in products or service requirement are changing and impacting our industry?
	What changes in customers' preferences threaten our current position?

Setting Goals: How do we get there?

After a thorough SWOT analysis, senior executives can summarize the company's top-level goals and create a concise description of their focus. The next step is to determine how to align skills and capabilities the company has, or needs to acquire, to achieve success.

The company's *vision* is an aspirational description of what the leaders of the company want to accomplish. It outlines core activities, but is typically far broader than the available resources and competencies the company possesses. If well understood and executed, it will allow the company to reach the desired market leader position. The vision underpins the company's *mission*, which reflects the corporate values and fundamental beliefs a company has adopted. In communicating the company mission to employees, customers and other stakeholders, a company clearly defines its corporate responsibilities.

Once an organization has set a strategic direction and outlined how it intends to operate in its chosen industry and markets, the next step is to determine how to marshal its resources to reach its goals. Put simply, the company needs to move from understanding and defining its strategy to determining the kinds of actions that will facilitate successful implementation. In addition, these actions must be continuously monitored to ensure that they are effectively moving the company towards its strategic goals.

A company needs firm goals so it can monitor the success of the tactics it chooses to implement its strategy. This is typically, but not always, done on a yearly basis as a company sets annual goals, monitors progress toward those goals, and then at the end of the year evaluates whether or not the goals have been met. For any goal to be most effective and useful it should have the following "SMART" characteristics:

S–Specific (clearly described and detailed)

M–Measurable (includes aspects that can be assessed)

A–Achievable (challenging, but attainable)

R–Relevant (important to the chosen strategy)

T–Time-bound (linked to a certain deadline and milestones)

Whenever a company develops its annual plan for its operations, including the various SMART goals tied to operations, it is also important to consider how these goals link to the company's management systems and structures. To ensure success - or to assess failure - a company must put in place the organizational structures, management tools, procedures, and policies necessary to facili-tate the implementation of its goals. Questions that need to be addressed include:

- What has to be accomplished to meet our goals?
- What resources are required to meet our goals?
- Who will be responsible for each goal?
- What does goal success look like?
- How will we adjust to slower than expected progress toward our goals?

Growing the Business: How do we sustain the momentum?

In theory, growth is quite simple: Increase both "topline" (revenue) and "bottomline" (profit) performance by choosing a strategy that seems right, and learn everything you can about what is necessary to make it work.

Experience suggests, however, that it can't be that simple. If it were, stories of failed companies would be extremely rare. Think about the following questions:

Figure 2

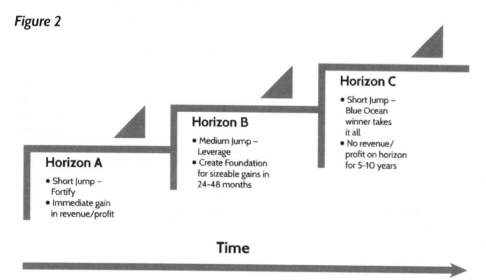

Horizon A
- Short Jump – Fortify
- Immediate gain in revenue/profit

Horizon B
- Medium Jump – Leverage
- Create Foundation for sizeable gains in 24-48 months

Horizon C
- Short Jump – Blue Ocean winner takes it all
- No revenue/ profit on horizon for 5-10 years

Time

- Why did Sony miss the chance to invent a product like the iPod?
- Why doesn't AT&T own the Internet?
- Why was Sotheby's, the world's premier auction house, upstaged by eBay?
- Why didn't the Encyclopedia Britannica organization start Google?

Even very successful companies get it wrong. If business were simple, there would not be over 20,000 books on corporate and business growth and more than 35 million Internet search results on the topic. Clearly, growing a business is difficult and challenging. Nevertheless, when you analyze the literature on business growth and sustainability, common themes emerge.

First, a company can bring better or cheaper products to *existing customers.* Here, a company typically introduces products or services at the low end (i.e., for customers who earn low wages, or companies that have major budget constraints) of the market. This tactic often disrupts the strategies of its competitors. Perhaps companies such as Dollar General, Wal-Mart, Costco, Tesco, and Target illustrate this approach by selling cheaper, but still with quality, products, and services that are acceptable to the marketplace, thereby challenging established department stores (e.g. JCPenney, Bloomingdale's, Neiman Marcus) and general grocery stores.

Alternatively, a company can offer products to the *"overserved"* customers, which includes customers who see a given product as "good enough" and/or tend not to fully use or care about new product features. Here, companies might reduce investments in additional product improvements and extra features. Discount airlines are an example of companies that offer services to these kinds of overserved customers. Apparel companies such as ZARA or H&M use the same approach in the fashion industry, offering fashionable clothing at substantially lower prices than established brands such as Chanel or Prada.

The ultimate, strategic move that disrupts a marketplace is to reach out to *"non-customers"* with relatively simple, convenient, and customizable products and services. For example, companies like Facebook, LinkedIn, and Twitter appeal to all segments of the market with easy-to-use, customizable social network services.

Overall, fostering a growth-oriented organization in practice is often more difficult than simply focusing on existing and new customer relationships. One of the biggest challenges, beyond managing internal and external resources and opportunities, is the timing of a strategic move. Being in the right place at the right time matters. What this means is that it is critical to develop your growth strategy and consider all of the potential tactics you may choose within the designated "time horizon." Time horizons in business typically fall into three categories:

When thinking about how to best formulate, implement, and time the execution of a strategy, keep in mind a simple adage: *The best strategy badly implemented is like having the worst strategy brilliantly executed.* In the early 1990's Apple launched the Newton, a product that was essentially an early version of the iPad or iPhone. It completely bombed in the marketplace. Today, the iPad and iPhone dominate the marketplace and have disrupted entire industries. It took the company some time to align strategy, implementation, and timing but eventually it had a good strategy, implemented well.

Operational Effectiveness versus Strategic Positioning

Whenever companies search for an advantage in the marketplace, we commonly refer to it as "competitive advantage." However, when planning for competitive advantage it is important to distinguish between operational effectiveness and strategic positioning.

Operational Effectiveness means performing similar activities better than your rivals. *Strategic Positioning* means performing different or similar activities from your competitors in different ways.

From an operational-effectiveness standpoint, a challenger will benchmark and attempt to outperform the dominant company following a similar value proposition (i.e., an appeal to the marketplace). On the other hand, strategic positioning by a company will deliver a unique value mix. This unique offering will be in tune with the company's own resources and competencies, making it more difficult for a competitor to respond.

However, keep in mind that identifying the best strategic position in the market is irrelevant if you fail to execute it operationally within your company. Of course, the opposite is also true. Companies that encounter such "asymmetry" between operational effectiveness and strategic positioning are doomed to fail in the long run – even Big Al or government interventions cannot save them. Look, for example, at Blackberry and Nokia who both dominated the mobile phone market for almost two decades, but missed the importance of smartphones and the opportunities offered by the millions of user applications humankind could develop. All in all, a company must offer greater value to a customer to attain competitive advantage over its rivals.

The Art of the General: See that Rock? Is it an important rock? Do we need to go there?

Opportunities and options, constraints and choices - these are the forces that affect business strategy. And no matter what course of action we choose, there will be trade-offs – costs and benefits that result from our choices.

As an analogy, think about a general who is tasked with deciding how best to position resources and personnel. In the distance, there appears a potentially important location to secure in order to ensure victory, so the question becomes "should we take that the rock?" Immediately, the general starts looking for additional clues, prepares to alter course, or just simply assumes that perhaps this could be the "wrong rock." Yet, even when these issues are addressed, there remains the need to coordinate and align the decision that is made with the resources and personnel that must be brought together to accomplish the mission.

It is important to recognize that coordination and alignment are interdependent. In other words, to realize success, strategic choices and resource allocation must work in tandem. Of course, coordination and alignment can be a complex process when we don't clearly see the direction we are moving. However, as long as you pay attention to details, understand your capabilities, and effectively execute the choices you make, you will be able to successfully compete in your industry and targeted markets.

Just one more thought: The more people involved in making coordination and alignment decisions, the more difficult it will be to reach a consensus quickly and to choose the best path forward. Think how long it takes to reach a consensus on a venue for dinner when your entire family is in town. Usually, someone has to take the lead and make the decision for everyone when no agreement can be reached.

The same happens in a business. Typically the company's board of directors appoints the "Commander" or the Chief Executive Officer (CEO). Though we often hear only about the stellar compensation and golden parachutes that CEOs receive, every day CEOs have to make complex, difficult, and far-reaching decisions in order to maintain a continuously growing, profitable, and sustainable company. Let's take a look to the basic four buckets of a CEO's responsibilities:

PLANNING PROCESS: A CEO is required to understand the interrelationship of all business functions such as marketing, product development, production, finance, and human resources, and how they affect the value chain of the company.

BUSINESS MODELS: It is critical to an organization that its CEO understands all the attributes of the business that affect revenue streams. In other words, the attributes of the organization that influence the internal cost structure, the customer value proposition, business performance, and how innovation can shape its business environment. Remember, when we refer to revenue streams, we are talking about "top-line", versus the "bottom-line" which is the profitability of the business.

COMPETITIVE ADVANTAGE: Before a CEO commits a company to a specific path, it is crucial that the management team identifies the available resources and assesses how different market factors in its industry will impact business performance. The better the company's capabilities and the bigger the gap between its own and its competitors' capabilities, the better the chances the company will succeed in implementing its mission.

STRATEGIC CHOICE: This is actually the best part of being CEO. Once the CEO has analyzed the topics and issues from the three buckets outlined above, the company is ready to take action. In other words, the CEO chooses the direction and sets the operating agenda. Jim Collins, a renowned management guru, makes the point: *It's not doing many things well, but instead doing one thing better than anyone else in the world.*

Creating Competitive Advantage

Up to this point, we have discussed the planning process, different business models, and strategic choices. It is now time to focus on the ultimate outcome of any business strategy: creating sustainable competitive advantage. Put simply, a sustainable *competitive advantage* occurs when a company uses its resources in a way that allows it to gain a better, often more profitable, long-term position in the markets in which it offers products and services.

There are many different ways to look for competitive advantage. It is almost like arguing if a glass of water is half-empty or half-full. To identify a competitive advantage, it is helpful to ask some simple questions:

- What are we best at today and in the future?

- What can our organization do better than any other organization today and in the future?

- How do we reach our customers today and in the future?

- What skills or capabilities make our organization unique today and in the future?
- Where do our profit margins come from today and what about in the future?

Typically, the search for competitive advantage begins with gaining a deeper understanding of potential customers, products, production and delivery processes, as well as geography – all of which are factors discussed in previous chapters. When examining these factors it is useful to focus on the field of companies that share the primary business activities of your company (manufacturing sensors, for example). This field is commonly referred to as an industry. Industries can be further broken down into industry sectors (motion sensor or pressure sensor sectors, for example). The reason for doing all this work is to analyze a cluster of similar companies that are one's "competitors." This allows you to understand the strengths and limitations that a company might have in terms of its successes (profits) and failures (losses), current market position, and of course, the resulting competitive advantage.

Sustainable competitive advantage ultimately comes from how one coordinates and aligns the business's resources. These resources include the company's financial, technological, and human resources. Generally speaking, the extent to which any of these resources can result in competitive advantage will differ depending on three characteristics. Simply put, is the resource:

RARE? Meaning that it is unique in the marketplace; you have it and no other companies (or very few) do.
NOT EASILY IMITATED? Meaning that it is not easily copied or replicated by others.
NON-SUBSTITUTABLE? Meaning that something else cannot be used or substituted in its place; e.g., machines sub-

stituting for people, or an outsourced company providing manufacturing capacity.

The Driving Forces of Competition

In his groundbreaking work in the 1980s, Michael Porter developed a framework for how we understand the driving forces of competition within an industry. In his analysis Porter identified five factors that naturally act together:

1. Threat of new entrants to a market
2. Bargaining power of suppliers
3. Bargaining power of customers
4. Threat of substitute products
5. Degree of competitive rivalry

Depending on the characteristics of the industry, each of the factors might be more or less important.

Figure 3

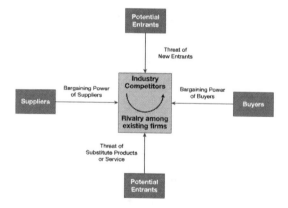

To illustrate this model, let's consider the companies in the Foundation Simulation. As you know, there will never be more than six competitors, so no new competitor (a seventh company) will ever enter the industry. It is often helpful to first look to the "center of gravity" of the five forces, the *degree of*

competitive rivalry. In particular, we need to determine the nature of the rivalry, which reflects the intensity of competition in the industry. This allows us to choose the most effective strategy. Rivalry depends on many factors, but the following seven issues are critical:

Table 1

Issue	Impact
Number of competitors	Competitive rivalry will be higher the more competitors are in the market.
Market size and future growth	Competition will be most intense when markets decline or stagnate.
Product differentiation and customer loyalty	The greater the customer loyalty and/or the higher the product differentiation the less intense the competition.
Availability of substitutes	If customers can choose among substitutes or similar alternatives the intensity of competition will increase.
Capacity utilization	Any existence of excess capacity will increase the intensity of competition
Cost structure	Intensity of rivalry will increase if companies' fixed costs are a relatively high percentage of their total costs because profits will depend primarily on manufacturing output.
Exit barriers	If there are no purchasers for companies that attempt to exit the industry or it is difficult to sell their assets, intensity of competition will stay at least constant.

Even though in the Foundation Simulation there cannot be more than six companies, it is still important to understand how a *barrier to entry for a potential entrant* can affect your strategy. In Foundation, new entrants can appear in a sub-segment of the market. For example, a competitor may begin to fo-cus on either the low or high end of the market. In addition, any new product offerings or entry by a competitor into a market segment can increase the level of rivalry among the competitors. Finally, companies that are already in an industry or sub-segment of the market hold stronger positions if the barriers to entry are higher and vice versa.

The remaining two forces, the power of suppliers and customers and the possibility of substituting products and services, can still threaten the strategic position a company has obtained within an industry. Although these forces are not really a threat in the Foundation Simulation, we will briefly discuss them because they certainly influence the "real world" of business.

A *substitute product or services* can be more easily realized if one is able to provide an alternative service or product that satisfies the same need. For example, the need for news can be met with printed media content like newspapers and magazines or with online sources such as websites, blogs, and social media. The more credible a substitute to a company's offering, the more it will limit the price that can be charged. This reduces the company's profit margins and subsequently lowers the potential profit pool of the entire industry.

The *power of suppliers* and the *power of customers* operate in a similar manner because suppliers and customers are basically operating from the opposite marketplace perspectives (one group is selling, the other group is purchasing). The level of power these groups have follows some general rules. First, both groups are typically more powerful when there are only a few of them around. Second, their power further increases when supply is limited or when a single customer purchases a significant portion of an industry's output.

Table 2 - Examples of Barriers to Consider in Foundation

Barrier	Potential Consequence
Financial investment	High capital requirements might mean that only companies with sufficient financial resources can compete. *For example, if your Foundation company does not have the financial resources to invest in automation or capacity, you will have a competitive disadvantage in relation to your competitors in the long run.*
Economies of scale	The higher the quantities you produce, the lower the unit costs will eventually be, thus making it difficult for your competitors to break into the market and compete effectively. *For example, a Foundation company that produces a million sensors will have lower per-unit manufacturing costs than a company that manufactures 10,000 sensors. The higher the production level, the more likely the company will develop process experience and utilize technology more efficiently so it can offer lower prices.*
Differentiation	Whenever a company can create a strong relationship (i.e. loyalty) to its products, and/or make them more easily available, and/or offer a unique customer value proposition, it makes the market more difficult for competitors to sustain or gain share in the long run. *For example, in your Foundation company you can make investments in R&D to create products with different value-driver extensions, or focus more heavily on accessibility and awareness compared to your competitors.*
Access to suppliers and distribution channels	A lack of access to suppliers (e.g. materials, equipment) and/or distributors (e.g. sales organizations) will make it difficult for competitors to enter the market. *For example, in your Foundation company it would be difficult to develop new products if your Research & Development department did not exist because you would not have access to this expertise even outside your company.*
Price-based competition	Just the threat of a potential "price war" can discourage your competitors from entering a market. Though predatory pricing is not legally permitted in many regions of the world, often companies find ways to circumvent it. *For example, in your Foundation company you cannot lower your price below a certain price level.*
Regulatory constraints	Though this will not be a problem in your Foundation company, patents often act as a barrier to enter an industry.

Third, power is high when customers and suppliers are reluctant to switch to a competitor. This is typically the case, for example, when customers have a high degree of loyalty, often established through brand, availability, and accessibility.

All in all, the various forces a company faces in an industry will always encourage management to add as much value as possible to the products and services a customer is willing to pay for. Thus, most companies have developed sophisticated tools to help understand where potential value can be added to their core processes and support activities (the *value chain*), in order to differentiate themselves from competitors on expertise and ultimately on cost.

Generic Strategies

You may have noticed two concepts threading throughout this module. Companies often focus their strategic efforts: (1) on providing their products and services based on a low cost approach and/or (2) on differentiating their products and services from competitors in order to manage their costs by setting different prices.

Though there are many shades of gray to the low cost and differentiation approaches, both concepts apply to any company and to any industry. Thus, we often refer to them as "generic strategies." We briefly describe these generic strategies below.

Cost Leadership

A company embracing a cost leadership generic strategy maintains a market presence in a well-defined "niche" (a specific market segment) or operates broadly across all segments of the market. Such a company gains competitive advantage by keeping R&D, production, material, and labor costs to a minimum. Lower costs enable the company to compete on the basis of price and volume. Consequently, the prices of their products and services will typically be below the industry average.

When well executed, a company focusing on cost leadership will cycle its products through an entire "lifecycle" in order to maximize profitability. For example, the electronics industry (e.g. smartphones, television panels, Blu-ray players, etc.) begins with product offerings at the high end of the market and then trickles them down over time to all other customer segments (customers with very limited budgets, for example). This product lifecycle continues until the product matures and has saturated the market (i.e., only a limited amount of potential costumers exists).

Another low-cost approach is for companies to go in the opposite direction and begin in the low end of the market. This approach is generally less frequent. Volkswagen is a good example. The company started out with a very affordable car (the "Beetle") intended to be widely available. In fact, the name "Volkswagen" means the "people's car." Today, Volkswagen manufactures many higher-end cars such as Audi, Porsche, Bentley, Lamborghini, Bugatti, and many others.

As in the real world of business, you have the opportunity to drive down manufacturing costs in your Foundation company. In addition, you are able to increase the automation levels of production, which can also improve margins and offset costs such as overtime for employees on second shift.

Differentiation

With this generic strategy, companies seek to provide customers a very different, and often extremely unique, experience in order to differentiate their products or services. Sometimes the experience is considered a luxury in and of itself. Other times the unique experience could be derived from technology. Of course, a combination of both can be used as well. For example, think about a car. A car in its simplest form is just a mode of transportation to get you from point A to B. However, the experience that a Rolls-Royce seeks to provide is much different than a Ferrari, or a Volkswagen, or a Ford for that matter.

Closing the gap on the cheap seats

EasyJet – the British low-cost airline that launched in the mid-90's with the slogan 'flights as cheap as a pair of jeans' – announced record profits of US$641million in 2013, more than 50% over its results in 2012. Southwest Airlines, the US low-cost airline that started it all in the 1970's – with hostesses in orange hot pants and white go-go boots – also finished 2013 with record profits, and its 41st consecutive year-end profit.

The low-cost carrier (LCC) market has matured, but as analysts point out, the gap between LCC and legacy airlines services has narrowed significantly in latter years. As the legacy airlines saw their markets erode, they cut costs and services in an attempt to meet the competition. As the no-frills airlines became successful, they had more money to introduce a few small ruffles.

EasyJet, for example, now markets to business travellers and has introduced allocated seating. Ryanair, its major European competitor based in Ireland, has followed suit. The sector is also growing aggressively in new markets. According to the Center for Asia Pacific Aviation, the penetration of LCCs in Southeast Asia is now 50% – up from less than 5% in 2003. Malaysian-based AsiaAir, the leading Asian LCC, will launch in the Indian market this year, taking on local competitors such as SpiceJet, IndiGo and GoAir.

Low-cost carriers developed a new profit model for air travel. They cut costs in myriad ways. They cut fleet costs by hedging gas price contracts to smooth fuel costs and using one type of aircraft with minimal additions (Ryanair's seats, for example, did not recline or have seat back pockets, in order to reduce weight and maintenance costs). They cut labor costs by hiring less experienced staff at lower pay grades. They cut passenger amenities to the bone, offering no in-flight entertainment and charging for each service, including food, beverage, luggage, pillows, blankets – even debating the merits of charging for bathroom use. They cut airport fees by ensuring planes spent minimum time on the ground, using secondary airports instead of major hubs and avoiding jetways that attract high usage fees. The result was an ability to cut prices – sometimes to as low as zero (excluding taxes and charges) – with simple fare structures such as one-way fares priced at half return fares and seat prices that increase as flights fill.

According to the *Economist*, however, *"the cost gap between traditional and budget airlines has fallen by an average of 30% in six years, partly because legacy airlines have abandoned old differentiators like free baggage and in-flight catering on short-haul flights. "The service being offered by low-cost and legacy carriers is now more or less the same," says one analyst."*

The result may be the end of zero-plus-fees airfares. *"In America, where Continental, Northwest, Midwest and AirTran have all merged with other carriers, average fares have risen by 13% since 2009. The days of cheap flights are over and, as usual, passengers will foot the bill."*

A company gains competitive advantage through differentiation by distinguishing its products with excellent designs, high awareness, easy accessibility to customers, and new products offered regularly. Consequently, such companies seek to develop a highly skilled R&D function that keeps designs fresh and exciting. Products will keep pace with market changes by offering improved features, such as size and performance (e.g., smaller, faster smartphones). Even when costs are managed very well, companies pursuing differentiation with product design will often end up with a price above industry average and thus need to closely link production capacity to a higher market demand.

Instead of focusing on new designs of a given product in a particular market segment, another differentiation strategy can be accomplished by maintaining a presence in *every* segment of the market. For example, the French luxury goods manufacturer LVMH provides champagne and wine as well as fashion products to the market. The Italian fashion design conglomerate, Armani, offers furniture and hotel services. Some companies execute such strategies by focusing on broader product categories across market segments, like Nike (shoes and apparel) or Sony (electronics). Certainly, companies will strive to run their product and service offerings across their product lifecycles as we already discussed in the Cost Leadership section. However, doing so using a differentiation strategy is very challenging to implement.

In summary, competitive advantage can be achieved by either focusing on cost leadership or on differentiation. The activities used to implement these generic strategies can be narrowly focused or broadly scoped, but they will always focus on reducing cost or increasing differentiation in order to achieve a competitive advantage.

Puttin' on the Ritz

 A barman at the Ritz-Carlton in Marina del Ray, California was told the young couple he was serving had cancelled their honeymoon in Hawaii because the groom had been diagnosed with cancer. A little while later, the night manager appeared with two tropical drinks, a cheery "Aloha" and escorted the couple back to their suite where *"orchids carpeted the floor, Japanese lamps glowed, and seashells and sand were scattered across the room. Pictures of the happy couple in "Hawaii" were presented as a memento of their stay."*

This is one of many in a montage of Ritz-Carlton moments collected on the company's website, where it promotes its above-and-beyond-the-call-of-duty style of service. There is the wheelchair-bound gentleman heard to bemoan the fact he couldn't go down to the beach with his wife, who the next morning discovered a timber ramp built from his room to the beach. The businesswoman whose birthday breakfast tray included a webcam bringing her husband and daughter into her hotel room. The guest whose luggage combination lock mysteriously stopped working until the hotel staff called the bag's manufacturer in Germany for help.

The Ritz-Carlton, part of the luxury sector of the Marriott hotel group, is a top-tier hotel management company that manages individually owned hotel properties for their private owners.

Its motto is *"we are ladies and gentlemen serving ladies and gentlemen,"* and its many service success stories are shared at the daily 15-minute lineup meetings most of its 38,000 employees attend.

In its manifesto "I am Proud to be Ritz-Carlton," the first of its "service values" is "I build strong relationships and create Ritz-Carlton guests for life." That repeat business is fostered by ensuring all employees are given responsibility for solving problems on behalf of guests, with a budget of up to $2,000 per incident (for everything from Japanese lamps and seashells to custom built ramps!)

Simon Cooper, then President and COO told Forbes in 2009 that Ritz-Carlton hired just 2% of the people who apply for jobs. Those who succeed receive more than 100 hours of training. *"Training is really important, because it nurtures the careers of our ladies and gentlemen."*

Mr. Cooper said the company did not think of itself as a hotel chain. *"A breakthrough in our thinking was understanding that we are not a hotel brand but a lifestyle brand,"* he said.

"More than 3,000 people have bought in for several million dollars each, and to me those people are brand devotees for life. Of course, all strategies are sensitive to significant market turns, but from the long-term perspective of growing a customer base that is absolutely married to the brand, it has worked out extremely well."

Figure 4

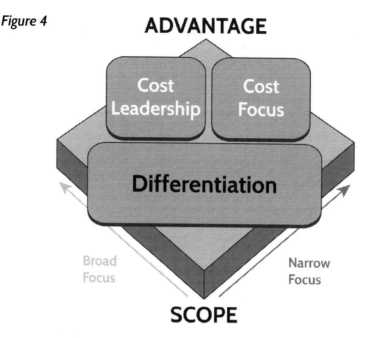

Recall that we discussed that choosing a strategy always results in making tough choices about who a company wants to be, who it wants to serve, and how this will be accomplished. This also means there will be trade-offs, advantages, and disadvantages in any strategy. Given that companies focus only on one of the quadrants shown in the figure above, any chosen strategy that seeks to build competitive advantage through cost leadership or through differentiation bears the risk that:

- Competitors imitate another company's business activities
- Differentiation becomes less important to customers and buyers
- Demand disappears
- Customers choose only companies that provide a broad portfolio
- Technology changes over time
- New customer segments emerge requiring completely different value drivers than currently offered

Measuring Success: The Importance of a "Balanced" Approach

Measuring success in business is critical, but long before that we need to know what success *means* for your particular business. This flows from your company's mission and its strategy – whether it is to provide the most exclusive handmade chocolates, deliver the best pizza in town, or build the world's most luxurious supersonic jet.

Alignment and coordination are all enhanced, as we have discussed, when a business has a clear strategy. Measuring how well the company is achieving its strategy also depends on the strategy itself because that determines what is important to measure.

A company's strategy points to the benchmarks used to indicate a company's success. For example, a discount retailer like Wal-Mart doesn't measure its success using the same benchmarks as a luxury retailer like Chanel. They are in the same industry (retailing), but are very different businesses using very different business strategies.

In Foundation there are several options for measuring your success. There is the Rubric Report which helps you to track your progress throughout the simulation and to diagnose where there are management problems for your company. The TeamMATE reports, which you will learn about in this module's exercises, also help you to diagnose your team process and how it is progressing.

However, to provide the big picture about whether or not your company is meeting its targets, Foundation uses the **Balanced Scorecard.** We will take a closer look at the Balanced Scorecard and later investigate

some of the common financial ratios that measure business success. These are ratios you will come across both in your simulation, and throughout your business career.

The Balanced Scorecard

The Balanced Scorecard is more than a grouping of financial measures; it is a strategic assessment tool that can accurately portray a business's, or a business unit's overall strategic progress.

The Balanced Scorecard asks managers to consider their business from four different perspectives. *The critical point is that all four perspectives are equally important in measuring success - the scorecard is "balanced."* For instance, only one perspective focuses on the financial metrics. The implication? Focusing only on financial assessments of performance is not enough to improve an organization.

Figure 5

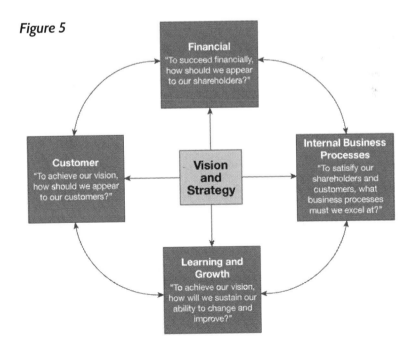

The four perspectives (or "quadrants" of the scorecard) are:

1. The Customer
2. Internal Business Processes
3. Learning & Growth
4. Financial

Customer Perspective. The customer perspective asks the question: *"how well are we satisfying our customers' needs?"* Robert Kaplan, one of the originators of the Balanced Scorecard, says customers' concerns can generally be broken down into four areas:

- Quality
- Time
- Performance
- Service

Within each of these areas there are a number of sub-elements. Take the area of "time," for example. A customer might be concerned with the amount of time a manufacturer takes to introduce new designs, or how quickly the manufacturer can deliver a product (the production cycle). One of the goals in this perspective is to be perceived as the most innovative supplier to the industry. Clearly then, new product introduction cycle time is a vital statistic, as is the portion of revenues generated by products or services that are less than two years old. Innovators would not want the additional perception of a low-cost leader, for example, because low cost is inconsistent with innovator's goals.

In Foundation, your score in this quadrant measures a wide range of customer-focused parameters including awareness, accessibility, December Customer Survey, and market share.

Internal Business Perspective. The internal business perspective asks the question: *"What do we need to correct within our own business to ensure we deliver the value propositions the market needs and expects?"*

For example, a manufacturer that sets its strategy to be the low price leader in the marketplace needs to focus very carefully on driving down all internal costs for making and selling its products. It takes strict discipline. To meet this goal, the manufacturer would need lower labor and material costs than its competitors. Even marketing costs would have to be reduced. Questions about the internal business perspective need to be uncompromising. What do we want to be best in the world at, and what do we have to do to get there?

In Foundation, your score in this quadrant includes measures such as your contribution margin, plant utilization levels, and days of working capital.

Learning and Growth Perspective. Nothing in business is static; the innovation and learning perspective asks, *"How do we develop and grow in order to continue to create value?"* In 1903 the economist Joseph Schumpeter said companies needed to engage in "the creative destruction of capital" to succeed. He was referring to the need for corporations to be willing to pull apart their existing processes and systems, reconfigure them, and then move forward with new, different, and more highly developed value propositions as the markets in which they operate change. The more rapidly markets change, the more important this reinvention is, and businesses that cannot "creatively destroy" will inevitably give way to businesses that can.

To achieve a management culture that embraces change and allows "creative destruction," manufacturers like your Foundation company turn to initiatives that improve their innovation and promote a "learning culture" inside their organizations. Redesigning the manufacturing processes, sales and market-ing, and administrative efficiencies are also essential to this perspective.

In Foundation, your score in this quadrant in-cludes employee productivity and some el-ements of the human resources and TQM/sustainability modules, if they are activated.

Financial Perspective. In this perspective, the question is: *"How is our strategy and tactical execution translating into profitability and economic viability?"* Some might feel there is no need to review financial measures, be-cause by carefully watching the other mea-sures of the Balanced Scorecard, financial success will naturally follow. This may be true in some cases, but it is not always true. For example, low cost companies might watch

their cash position all but evaporate if there are not enough buyers for their products--no matter how efficiently they are produced. Therefore, the financial perspective asks two distinct questions:

1. Are we making a profit in the activ-ities in which we are engaged and therefore growing the company/in-creasing shareholder value?

2. Do we have the appropriate levels of cash to operate both in the short term and the long term?"

We will return this perspective in more detail in the exercises for this module as we discuss and define the types of financial measures that are frequently used in this Balanced Scorecard quadrant.

A Final Note: How it all works together...

From the relatively simple building blocks of ideas, people, and capital with which we be-gan our discussion in Module 1, we have seen over the course of this journey that business-es can develop in very different ways and that they have quite complex interactions with internal and external stakeholders. All of these interactions matter to the success and sustainability of a business.

As we discussed in this module, it is vital that every business, in whatever market it oper-ates, sets a very clear strategy and keeps a

close eye on the operational execution of its chosen strategy. Critical to this process is how success is measured and monitored relative to the firm's strategy and the perfor-mance of its competitors. In the next module we are going to broaden our horizon to the community and culture in which the business operates and think about how good business decision making needs to be underpinned by sound ethical principles.

Chapter Review Questions

Making Strategic Choices

1. What factors influence the strategic choices a company will face?

2. What does S.W.O.T. stand for and how does a SWOT analysis matter to business strategy?

3. What are the common questions that are asked in each of the components of a SWOT analysis?

Setting Goals

4. What is the importance of goal setting to business strategy?

5. What are the characteristics of effective goals?

Growing the Business

6. What are the differences between the existing, overserved, and non-customer categories?

7. How does one grow or sustain a business in relation to each of these categories?

Operational Effectiveness vs. Strategic Positioning

8. What is operational effectiveness?

9. What is strategic positioning?

10. What four basic decisions are generally the responsibility of the CEO?

Chapter Review Questions

Creating Competitive Advantage

11. What is competitive advantage and what kinds of question can we ask to help identify sources of it?

12. What are the characteristics of business resources that promote competitive advantage?

13. What are the "five forces" that drive competition in an industry?

14. What are some ways to create "barriers" in the Foundation Simulation?

Generic Strategies

15. What are the differences between the two generic strategies of cost leadership and differentiation? What are the goals and actions that are associated with each?

Measuring Success

16. What makes the Balanced Scorecard "balanced"?

17. What are the four quadrants of the Balanced Scorecard? What is the central question that is asked in each perspective of the Balanced Scorecard?

You – in the executive suite!

General Manager

In Module 5, you completed your job rotation track as *Finance and Accounting Manager.*

Now it is time to move to a general management role. *General Managers* sometimes have a broad mix of responsibilities. In our case, we are just going to look at specific aspects of the two critical elements we introduced with this module: Coordination and Evaluation. Coordination is necessary to achieve your strategic goals, and evaluation is critical to measuring your progress. towards your goals.

Under Evaluation we will look more closely at the financial ratios used in the Balanced Scorecard – and in business everywhere – to measure various elements of performance. Any General Manager needs to understand these ratios. In Coordination we will give you the opportunity to pay close attention to your skills as a member of a business team.

Activities: Approximately 60 minutes to complete.

COMPLETED

A-1: Answer all **Chapter Review Questions**
Your instructor will advise you on how to turn in your answers. ☐

A-2: Read the following text through to the end of the module.

The section on financial ratios is to improve your understanding of this quadrant of the Balanced Scorecard. ☐

A-3 The section on team dynamics refers to the online self-directed learning module TeamMATE, and may or may not involve team effectiveness questionnaires, depending on your instructor's requirements. ☐

Exercise #12: Evaluation – Financial Ratios and Market Measures

One way to measure whether you are operating a sustainable and profitable company is to keep a close eye on measures called financial ratios. These are terms you have often heard during discussions about business and include:

- ROE (return on equity)
- ROA (return on assets)
- ROS (return on sales)
- Asset Turnover

The above ratios are all "profitability ratios" because they compare various numbers (for example sales or assets) with the profit the company is generating. However, you can also measure success using "market ratios" such as overall Market Share or Market Capitalization that demonstrate how well the company is performing in the marketplace, compared with its competitors.

Profitability Ratios

We know that a business exists to make a profit – so profit is a very clear measure of success – but we also know that how much profit is a "good" result and how much a "bad" result is a function of the type of business you are in. We balance other elements – such as sales or assets – against the profit number to give more information about the *quality* of the result for the business we are measuring.

In accounting, the word "return" means the company's profit **compared with** another element of the company's financial results. Below are the key profitability ratios and how to read them.

Return on Sales

$$\frac{\text{PROFITS}}{\text{SALES}}$$

Return on Sales (ROS) compares profit with sales. ROS looks at the revenue or the sales dollars we've generated from our products and services to see what percentage of that goes all the way to the bottom line, into net profit.

Think of ROS as an efficiency measure. It answers this question: Of every dollar that comes into the business, how many cents does the business get to keep? What percentage of your sales ends up in Net Profit?

For example, if the total sales for a business are $2 million and the profit $200,000, we divide $200,000 into $2 million for an ROS of 10%, meaning 10 cents in every dollar is profit.

Is 10% ROS a good result or a poor result? That all depends on the type of industry and the type of company we are looking at. In a commodity business – like a supermarket, for example – ROS will be low because only a few cents from each item makes it into profit. These businesses focus on large volume sales, not profits on individual items to drive their profits. A 4% ROS for a supermarket, then, would be excellent. However, for a company in high tech electronics where volumes are low but the company makes a high margin on every sale, 4% would be a dismal ROS.

Asset Turnover

$$\frac{\text{SALES}}{\text{ASSETS}}$$

Asset Turnover compares sales with the company's assets. Asset Turnover doesn't look directly at profit but it implies something about profit. It is a measure of how effectively we've used our assets in generating revenue.

Asset Turnover is calculated by taking sales for a given period divided by the asset base on the Balance Sheet. How often can your sales match the value of your assets in that period? How often can you make your assets earn their keep or how often have you "turned over" the value of your assets?

If, for example, you have assets of $1 million and your sales during the year are $1.5 million, then your asset turnover is 1.5, $1.5 million divided by $1 million.

Return on Assets

$$\frac{\text{PROFITS}}{\text{ASSETS}}$$ Return on Assets, or ROA, gives us a different perspective on a company's returns in relation to its assets. ROA is a way of looking at the stewardship of a company. It compares profit with the total assets of the business. We have a value for our assets - that's how much we have tied up in the business. ROA tells us how much profit the managers of the business – the stewards of those assets – are able to make on those assets.

We calculate ROA by taking net profit and dividing it by the assets on the balance sheet. ROA is a vital measure for assessing the health of asset-heavy businesses with lots of money tied up in plant and equipment, raw materials, and inventory.

ROA is an excellent measure of both the effectiveness and efficiency of the operations side of the business. A high ratio indicates good utilization of company resources.

Return on Equity

$$\frac{\text{PROFITS}}{\text{EQUITY}}$$ Return on Equity (ROE) compares the equity that the owners of the business have tied up in the business with the business's profit.

You'll remember from the Balance Sheet that Owners' Equity or Net Worth is common stock plus retained earnings - the accumulation of net profits over the years that were not paid back to the owners in dividends. To assess the return on that equity, we take net profit for the year and divide it by shareholders' equity to get Return On Equity.

Market Ratios

Market ratios assess a company's health according to its stock price and other relationships in the stock market. These ratios, of course, are only relevant for publicly traded corporations, such as your Foundation company.

Earnings Per Share

Let's start with Earnings Per Share. EPS is reported for a publicly traded corporation every quarter, and is viewed as a critical number in terms of assessing the value of stocks.

EPS is calculated by taking net profit for the quarter or year in question, and dividing it by the number of shares outstanding – or the number of shares held in the marketplace. Predictions over whether EPS will be up or down – higher or lower than estimated – have a great deal of immediate impact on stock price.

In some ways, that impact is misleading. Over the long term, it is more than the profitability of a business that drives its success, as we learned with the Balanced Scorecard. Net Profit, as we have also discussed, is not cash flow. Companies that show a profit can still become bankrupt if they don't manage their cash flow – and EPS ignores how much cash a company has, or does not have, to run its operations.

As a qualifier, then, analysts and business people will often discuss the "quality of earnings" to suggest their confidence that those profits reflected in the EPS will turn into cash. In this way they are high quality rather than virtual or imagined profits created by accounting tricks.

Price to Earnings

The next market ratio is the Price to Earnings ratio. P to E is calculated by taking the stock price at a given point in time and dividing it by Earnings Per Share. This usually results in a large positive number. For example, the stock price might be 10 times the earnings per share or 20 times the earnings per share. This number is often referred to as the "multiple" instead of the Price to Earnings ratio – simply because it's a multiple of EPS.

Managers often discuss the relative size of their P to E ratio, at times bemoaning the fact that it's too low: "Our stock price should be worth more than 10 times our earnings per share!" While that may be the manager's assessment, it's not the market's assessment.

On the other hand, sometimes analysts say that the P to E multiple is too high, suggesting over-valuation of stock on the market. A correction usually follows.

Dividend Yield

When a company pays a dividend, that dividend is often compared to the trading value of the stock price in the stock market in a ratio called the Dividend Yield.

Dividend Yield is calculated as the Dividend divided by the stock price.

The Dividend Yield is the percentage of returns we are generating compared with the stock price. This is similar to the interest on your bank account. When you assess that interest, you compare it with the capital tied up in the account. The Dividend Yield tells you what your "interest" is on the money you have tied up in a stock.

Exercise #13: Coordination – Team Effectiveness Training

On our job rotation track we have looked at various managerial responsibilities and functions such as accounting, production, marketing, etc. It is possible to run a business in which each area of management focuses on its own area of expertise, but just as a sporting team can't achieve its best results without working together as a team, a business in which each discipline works within its own silo will never achieve the best result.

One of the benefits of a business simulation is the opportunity to see, experience, and analyze all the various managerial roles and how they interact and can be coordinated around a strategy to achieve success. Another key benefit – if you are running your simulated business in a team – is the opportunity to practice team-based decision making. Even if you are running your simulated company individually, however, this module can help you become a better team player.

Teamwork – a Managerial Core Competency

Team-based decision making is a reality of management in every type of industry. For an aspiring manager, the ability to work effectively in a team is a core competency.

While there is no single, universally accepted model for the ideal team process, there have been decades of research into how individual team processes can be improved and what destroys effective team-based decision making.

Business teams can be conceptualized by an "input-process-output" model. Of the three components, the most difficult to measure is process. Yet it is the process – the *way* in which inputs (people, resources, and ideas) are transformed into outputs (business results) – that is the key factor in determining the quality of the results.

Taskwork and Teamwork

In business, teams have to accomplish operational or technical tasks every day, such as keeping the machines running, the books balanced or the product up to date, and this necessary work can be labeled "taskwork." To get the best result in line with business goals, however, teams have to be able to coordinate, cooperate, and adapt their tactics to changing circumstances – and that's "teamwork".

In your business simulation, the taskwork includes designing products in R&D, setting the price for products and the sales budgets in marketing, deciding on capacity and automation in production – all are important elements of the taskwork that must be done to run your business. If you are working as part of a team, however, you may have discovered that the simulation environment includes competition, stress, resource challenges, compromises – in fact all of the elements that impose themselves on team decision making in the real business world every day.

The simulation is an ideal environment to train people in *teamwork* and the interpersonal behaviors that facilitate it.

Substantial literature has been published in the past 30 years on the essential dimensions of team process that underpin effective team functioning and performance. In your Foundation business you can access a self-directed learning module based on this research and designed to build team effectiveness. The tool, called TeamMATE, includes a Teamwork Toolkit that will be valuable throughout your career to help guide you towards effective team skills.

TeamMATE allows you to:

Monitor
Analyze
Train, and
Evaluate

your team process in real time during the simulation.

The imperative of balancing the needs of the company and marketplace with the diverse capabilities and personalities of team members ensures the simulation closely mirrors real world management experience.

You will access TeamMATE and the Teamwork Toolkit from your company welcome page. Simply select the TeamMATE icon from the tool bar and begin.

7 Doing it Right: Social Responsibility and Ethical Decision Making

Learning Objectives:

After reading this module and completing the associated exercises, you will be able to:

LO1: Define what represents an ethical issue.

LO2: Describe the ethical decision-making process.

LO3: Define social responsibility.

LO4: Compare and contrast concepts such as triple bottom line and corporate philanthropy.

LO5: Discuss the four steps of the ethical decision-making process.

LO6: Describe the five major approaches (theories) of business ethics.

LO7: Differentiate between primary and secondary stakeholders.

LO8: Apply the ethical decision-making process to business situations.

Key Terms to Look For:

- *Business ethics*
- *Common good*
- *Ethical decision making*
- *Fairness*
- *Individual rights*

- *Primary stakeholders*
- *Social responsibility*
- *Triple bottom line*
- *Utilitarian*
- *Virtue*

The Broader Context of Business

Business, by its very nature, cannot operate in a vacuum. Instead business requires constant interaction with a wide range of stakeholders, and each of these stakeholders is impacted by the actions a business takes. As we discussed in Module 1, business stakeholders are both internal (e.g., owners and employees) and external (e.g., suppliers, bankers, customers, etc.).

And every day, while businesses are operating within their commercial, physical, and community environments, their activities are constrained by laws, regulations, and in some cases culture. Within that web of interactions and restrictions, however, there are gray areas – areas where human behaviors, lack of clarity, and conflicting rules and expectations can lead to problems that need to be solved not by financial or managerial logic, but by ethical reasoning. This is the domain of business ethics.

An awareness of ethical principles in general helps to determine the standards of behavior that guide us in our daily life. These principles shape our relationships at home, at work, and within our chosen profession, our communi ty and society at large. Such considerations are at the heart of how we structure our organizations: our schools, our businesses, our community and non-profit groups, our places of worship as well as our governments, the laws we enact, and the systems we provide to our citizens such as health care, energy, transportation, and taxation.

We make ethical decisions every day, often without thinking about them: whether to slide through a stop sign when we don't notice any traffic; whether to cheat (just a little) on expense reports or taxes; whether to download music we didn't pay for; or even how we deal with a coworker or classmate who doesn't contribute their share of the work.

Ethical principles also come into play in nearly every decision we make when running a business. The difficult part, however, is being able to first recognize the "ethics" in a given decision and then to follow a thought process that more fully informs the decisions we ultimately make. The main goal of this module is to help paint a clearer picture of business ethics, why they matter, and what we can do to improve our ethical decision-making skills.

Business Ethics Basics

To understand the broad implications of business ethics, we should start by defining a few terms. Put simply, an *ethical issue* is one where a person's actions, when freely performed, may either harm or benefit others – or both. Therefore, *ethical decision making* is the process through which you determine what course of actions you will take. This process necessarily involves making choices while considering the possible consequences of those choices for the business and its stakeholders.

Typically, a decision is deemed "ethical" when it is both legal and morally acceptable to the larger community and is based upon careful consideration of the facts. Sometimes what is legally acceptable in a business context may not be considered "morally acceptable" to the broader community. In these and many other circumstances the application of ethical decision making is critical to avoid adverse consequences either to stakeholders or to the business itself. We will return to a discussion of the ethical decision making process later in this module.

Ethical practice relies on rational thought to inform us how we "ought to act" in such matters as fulfilling our obligations and duties, being compassionate and fair, respecting the rights of others, and contributing to the greater good of society. It is important to point out that simply believing that you are "an ethical person" is no guarantee that others will view you this way. In fact, it is the actions we take (our behaviors) that are most often what is ultimately judged to be "ethical" or "unethical."

Business is essential for a prosperous society, and we rely on businesses to act ethically by not putting their own interests above those of the society at large. In other words, we need those who lead businesses to consider the impact of their activities on the rest of us. Business ethics, however, aren't just relevant to chief executives who make major decisions. Ethical issues come up at every level of business. Start work in any type of business at all and you are likely to encounter job-related ethical conflict.

Ethics and Social Responsibility

Business ethics operate on two levels. At the individual level, decisions with ethical considerations need to be made in all areas of business. The company as a whole, however, also bears a social responsibility. After all, it is society at large that makes the operations of *any* business possible.

The pressures on organizations to act in responsible and ethical ways come from a variety of stakeholders, including a firm's

Legally correct – but what about the ethics?

Walmart In 2000, Wal-Mart employee Deborah Shank was driving her minivan when it collided with a semi-trailer. The accident left her with permanent brain damage, confined to a wheel chair and living in a nursing home. Deborah's husband and family were awarded a $700,000 settlement for damages from the trucking company which, after legal costs and expenses, left $417,000 to be put into a trust for Deborah's ongoing care.

Six years later Wal-Mart, which provided Deborah's health insurance, sued her for the $470,000 the insurer had paid for her medical expenses. The legal action was entirely valid because there was a clause in Deborah's health insurance contract that said any money won in damages by an employee could be recouped by Wal-Mart. The court, therefore, ruled in Wal-Mart's favor.

Over the following years, her husband had to rely on Medicaid and social security payments for her care, her 18-year-old son was killed in Iraq while fighting in the U.S. army and the Supreme Court declined to hear her appeal to the earlier court ruling. It took a news story by CNN in 2008, followed by a public outcry and calls for a boycott of Wal-Mart's stores, for the company to reverse its decision.

Most importantly Wal-Mart – the world's largest retailer with revenues of $469 billion in 2013 – changed the clause in its health care plan to allow for "more discretion" in individual cases where damages are awarded following accidents. *"Occasionally, others help us step back and look at a situation in a different way. This is one of those times,"* Wal-Mart Executive Vice President Pat Curran said in a letter.

Everyday life - but no one's going to notice...

Ethical breaches can lead to blatantly illegal activities that destroy businesses, families, fortunes ... but the seeds of unethical behavior can seem insignificant, even acceptable because "everybody does it" or "no one will even notice." Some examples are sneaking food out from the restaurant you work for, a boss promising an employee a day off to reward them for additional work then not following through, someone taking credit for someone else's work, doing a fake online review of a friend's business, calling in sick to go to the beach, sliding a personal purchase into a business expense account, copying a piece of software from work onto your home computer. How many more examples can you list, from your imagination or your experience?

customers, employees, industry groups, etc. Laws and regulations also frame the types of actions seen as "acceptable" in a given soci-

ety. However, as we have said, compliance with the law is often not the same thing as acting in a responsible or ethical manner. One way to view business ethics is as a part of the *"pyramid of social responsibility."*

Social responsibility is an ethical or ideological theory that holds that an organization or individual has an obligation to society at large. Sometimes this is referred to as the "social contract" between business and society, and includes the informal expectations that the public holds for business practices.

In its simplest form, social responsibility in business involves four steps that begin at the base on the pyramid below:

1. Be profitable (required)
2. Obey the law (required)
3. Be ethical (expected)
4. Be a good corporate citizen (desired)

Figure 1

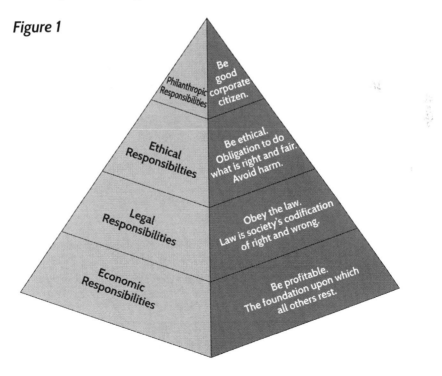

TBL measuring and driving business development

The concept of the triple bottom line has been embraced by private, publicly listed, and publicly owned corporations. Michigan-based Cascade Engineering, for example, is one of many private firms that have integrated the concept of the triple bottom line into management and reporting systems:

"We think of the concept of sustainability as the three interconnected gears in motion. Each category is an interdependent, innovation-enabling mechanism. The three gears (Social, Environmental and Financial) cannot exist independently; each in turn, provides momentum and innovative thought to the next. To drive one forward is to drive all three forward; the result is a sustainable system where innovation begets innovation."

General Electric – one of the world's largest technology companies – also focuses on the principles of TBL through its annual "citizenship report", summarizing the company's commitments *"to finding sustainable solutions to benefit the planet, its people and the economy."*

Many public enterprises are using TBL to plan and monitor economic development projects including industrial parks, cultural precincts, and rural economic networks.

Triple Bottom Line

Pressure to act in a more socially responsible way has led many businesses to focus on more than just profits and to adopt a broader view of business success. This viewpoint has been called the *"triple bottom line" (TBL)* and involves businesses evaluating success in terms of financial, environmental, and social performance – sometimes referred to as a focus on "people, planet, and profits."

Corporate Philanthropy

Efforts to increase social responsibility also can be found in corporate philanthropic activities, as companies seek to improve the communities and societies in which they reside and operate.

A recent report from the Committee Encouraging Corporate Philanthropy in New York, an international forum of CEOs and Chairpersons, said 84% of corporate executives believe *"that society now expects businesses to take a much more active role in environment, social and political issues"* than ever before.

The report, based on research by McKinsey and Company, notes:

"Successful philanthropy today is not simply writing checks to the local charity. Philanthropic pursuits are becoming an important way for most corporations to communicate with stakeholders, gauge their interests, and satisfy their elevated expectations. By choosing the right philanthropic programs - those that yield social benefits and address stakeholder interests - companies can build a good corporate reputation. And a good reputation is both a source of tangible value and a reservoir of good will to be tapped if a company runs into trouble."

The report concludes that the most successful philanthropic programs are those that are operated using the principles of sound management applied elsewhere in the company: a clear strategy, good teamwork (harnessing the talents and capacities of a variety of people), and constant, ongoing measurement against goals or standards.

"By treating giving as a business unit," the CECP report says, *"the philanthropy team is empowered to contribute to the wealth of the company just as the rest of the business does."*

Not Just a "Few Bad Apples"

Of course, we more often hear about organizations that fail to act ethically and responsibly. These tend to be the situations that make the news headlines and rightly so, considering the costly consequences of many ethical breaches. Engineers at Thiokol had safety concerns about the cold weather performance of a space shuttle part – the O-ring – but did not ensure that this information was communicated to key officials. The Space Shuttle Challenger exploded on launch on a cold morning in 1986, killing all seven crew members.

BP's Deepwater Horizon oil rig continued drilling even though its blowout preventer was defective, faulty software was causing rig systems to crash, emergency alarms were disabled, and a relatively inexpensive acoustic trigger (which could have shut down a damaged well), was not installed. Eleven BP employees were killed, 17 more were injured, and nearly 5 million barrels of oil leaked into the Gulf of Mexico.

News Corp. executives were caught in a phone hacking scandal that was thought to involve eavesdropping on politicians, celebrities, and members of the Royal Family but was later discovered to include private citizens - including crime victims and the relatives of soldiers killed in action. The scandal, including accusations of police bribery and improper influence, led to the closure of the *News of the World* newspaper after 168 years.

The failure of American International Group in 2008, due to under-collateralizing one of its credit products, had a devastating effect on the world economy, precipitating a global

It seemed like a good idea at the time.....

When the Duchess of Cambridge was hospitalized during her early pregnancy in 2012, hosts of the *Hot30 Countdown* radio program in Sydney, Australia, were able to get private information about the Duchess's condition by calling the hospital pretending to be the Queen of England and the Prince of Wales.

The call was made around 5:30 a.m. London time and – with no switchboard operator on duty at the private hospital – the nurse answering the phone, Jacintha Saldanha, transferred the call directly to the nurse treating the Duchess, who gave details of her condition. The goal of the hoax was to get the Duchess on air and had been cleared by the radio station's lawyers. It appeared to be a very successful stunt, until – three days later - Jacintha Saldanha was found dead in the nurses' quarters. She had hanged herself and left several suicide notes, one blaming the radio presenters.

The consequences of the "hoax" were far reaching. Advertisers boycotted the radio station, which then donated $500,000 to a memorial fund in support of the victim's family. A street demonstration was held in front of the British High Commission in New Delhi and there were calls for further protection for Indians working abroad (Saldanha was a native of India). The radio program was canceled and the pranksters lost their jobs. Legal action followed in Britain and Australia, but the British Crown Prosecution Service eventually determined no laws had been broken because: *"however misguided, the telephone call was intended as a harmless prank."* What difference do you think ethical decision making, using the guidelines discussed next, could have made to the outcome?

financial crisis. These and other sensational business stories involved unethical business behavior that eventually affected thousands.

The examples above certainly point out that the consequences for acting unethically or irresponsibly can be severe and long-lasting for organizations. Yet organizations don't make decisions, people do. It was *individuals* in these organizations who decided on the particular courses of action that ultimately led to negative outcomes.

To be clear, this does *not* mean that poor decisions are the result of one or two "unethical" employees (so-called "bad apples"), which is the common explanation that is given in these situations. Nor does this mean that corporate work environments have little influence on ethical decision making. To the contrary, an organization's culture – the social aspects of its work environment – can have an effect on the way people think and act, especially in regard to ethics and social responsibility.

For example, the seeds of an ethical crisis often go unrecognized. A series of small, even unrelated, decisions can culminate in "the perfect storm." A person who is normally honest and virtuous in their personal life may justify unethical behavior at work as "just business" or "that is the way things are done around here." Perhaps that person put personal success and the financial security of his or her family before his or her responsibility to society at large, or felt compelled to act against his or her better judgment due to pressure from an authority figure, a corrupt organizational culture, or an organizational culture that offered no clear expectations about how to act.

What doesn't make the news, but is more common, is this type of scenario: A mid-level advertising executive pressures a new hire to "fudge" a routine advertising spending report provided to their client, a brand manager of skin care products with a large pharmaceutical company. The executive suggests, "it's just the way it's done around here." Against better judgment, the new hire complies and numbers are massaged to misrepresent the agency's spending of client funds. The client's brand manager detects the fraud and notifies the entire corporate chain of command, sparking a crisis of confidence between the client and the advertising agency.

When the situation is reviewed at the agency's senior level, whose job and career will be on the line in an effort to appease the client and save the business relationship? The account supervisor with years of experience in the skin care market, or the most recent addition to the account team?

Certainly developing an ethical consciousness might have helped the young recruit in the example above. However - and this is part of the paradox of business ethics - it might not have had any impact on the outcome for the individual. Acting ethically and refusing to fudge the numbers may have led to the same result. The new recruit might have lost his job for not being a good "fit" for the position. The client might have fired the agency for poor results. The only *guaranteed* reward for the ethical actions is the knowledge that everyone had acted ethically.

With some understanding of basic ethical principles and training in how to approach ethical problems, however, we can be less vulnerable to undue or untoward pressure in the workplace and better able to help shape a company's ability to be a good corporate citizen on the world stage. Understanding how to use ethical decision-making tools, therefore, may be as important to understanding business as understanding the disciplines of marketing, finance, and operations.

The Ethical Decision Making Process

Trying to engage in an ethical decision making process presents several challenges. The first challenge with being an ethical decision maker is that many problems do not scream, "Look at me! I'm an ethical issue!" That is, ethical dilemmas are not always clear-cut cases of "right versus wrong." In fact, many ethical dilemmas involve situations that are "right versus right," where choices entail deciding on truth versus loyalty, short-term versus long-term effects, or individual versus community. A second challenge is that ethical decision making requires effort, perhaps even more effort than we typically give toward other decisions. A third challenge is that ethical decision making requires that we avoid our natural tendency to make snap judgments or use quick solutions.

To help meet these challenges, it is important to follow a deliberate and systematic process. Generally speaking, there are four steps to the ethical decision-making process:

1. Investigate the ethical issues
2. Identify the primary stakeholders
3. Increase the number of alternative courses of action
4. Inspect the consequences of the alternatives

While proceeding through the steps above may take more time and effort, there are several benefits. A multi-step process encourages discussion with others and may uncover additional viewpoints as well as revealing how these viewpoints are similar or different. It allows fair evaluation of conflicting perspectives, each of which may involve what appear to be "good" or "right" reasons. By considering multiple courses of action, decision makers may reject a proposed ac

tion as inappropriate, even if it was originally widely supported. A multi-faceted evaluation can highlight which option may be the best choice, and can build consensus regarding that decision, particularly as key decision makers consider public reaction to their choice. Finally, a multi-step process provides a structure to use to evaluate the decision after action has been taken, and to determine what practical knowledge the situation provided.

Now, let's walk through each of these steps in more detail.

Step 1: Investigate the Ethical Issues

The first step in the ethical decision-making process is to gather relevant information about the situation and to use that information to identify the ethical issues involved. This means you need to collect the facts and define the ethical dilemma or problem that you face.

Information that is "relevant" can be revealed by asking questions such as:

- What are the potential legal issues? What laws or regulations are related to the situation?
- Has the organization faced this situation before? If so, what actions were taken previously and why?
- Who has the final authority to make a decision?
- Are there organizational rules, policies, or regulations that govern the decision?

Once you've gathered all the relevant facts, it is time to use those facts to define the ethical issues involved in the situation. At the broadest level, there are several categories of ethical problems that help identify ethical issues. For example, does the situation present a case of bribery, an abuse of resources, a conflict of interest, or a form of discrimination? These ethical problems can occur in any function of business.

A useful tactic for exploring the ethics of a situation is to apply different ethical theories or perspectives. The value of applying different perspectives is that it forces you to see the problem from multiple viewpoints, which is *absolutely essential* to the ethical deci-

sion-making process. Doing this helps reveal aspects of the problem that you might not have considered, and can often suggest the best way to carry out a decision.

There are many specific ethical theories or perspectives that can be applied. However, the majority of these fall into five general approaches. These are briefly discussed next.

Utilitarian. This approach assesses a possible action in terms of its consequences or outcomes. For a company that is the net benefits and costs to all individual stakeholders. The goal of this approach is to achieve the

Table 1 - Some examples of ethical breaches common to business functions

Accounting and Finance	Compensation issues, such as excessive payments made to senior executives.
	"Creative" accounting, misleading financial analysis or reporting.
	Bribery, kickbacks, and facilitation payments, which, while perhaps beneficial for the short-term interests of a company, can be anti-competitive or offensive to societal values.
Marketing and Sales	Price fixing, price discrimination, and price skimming.
	Attack ads, subliminal messages, sex in advertising, and products regarded as immoral or harmful.
	Specific marketing strategies such as green washing, bait-and-switch, shill, viral marketing, spam, pyramid schemes, and planned obsolescence.
	Unethical marketing to children, such as marketing in schools.
Production and Operations	Defective, addictive, and inherently dangerous products such as tobacco, alcohol, weapons, motor vehicles, chemicals and drugs.
	New technologies and their potential impacts on health (e.g., genetically modified food, mobile phone radiation, etc.).
	Impact of production processes on the natural environment.
	Product testing ethics: animal rights and animal testing, or use of economically disadvantaged groups (such as students) as test participants.
Human Resources	Discrimination on the basis of age, gender, race, religion, disabilities, weight, or attractiveness.
	Issues affecting employee privacy such as workplace surveillance and drug testing.
	Occupational safety and health.

greatest good for the greatest number while creating the least amount of harm or preventing the greatest amount of suffering. In a business context, a utilitarian approach might rely on a statistical analysis of probable outcomes, a classic costs/benefits assessment, or consideration of the marginal utility (the added value) of a consequence for various stakeholders in the group.

Individual Rights. This approach focuses on respect for human dignity, which comes from our ability to choose freely how we live our lives, and our moral right to consider others to be free, equal, and rational people and to respect their choices. The goal of this approach is to avoid actions that infringe on the rights of others. In a business context, an individual rights approach might rely on determining whether an action would infringe on the rights of an employee (or other stakeholders) and/or whether an action meets the moral obligation for equality of treatment across all people. Some common examples of rights include right to privacy, right to be compensated for work (i.e., right to not be subject to slavery), right to have fair and safe employment and so forth.

Fairness. This approach focuses on the fair and equitable distribution of good and harm, and/or the social benefits and social costs, across the spectrum of society. The goal of this approach is to treat everyone equally; if there is unequal treatment it must have a just cause (i.e., a "fair reason"). In a business context, a fairness approach might rely on first identifying any differences in treatment or outcomes across various stakeholders. Then, each difference is examined for its legitimacy. For example, paying employees at different salary levels would be "fair" if these differences were based on job performance, and "unfair" if based on being "liked by the boss."

Common Good. This approach regards all individuals as part of a larger community that shares certain common conditions and institutions upon which our welfare depends. The goal of this approach is to ensure and enhance benefits of an action for the society as a whole. Unlike the utilitarian approach that weighs the net balance of goodness and harm for a group of individuals, the common good approach asks whether an action benefits or erodes a specific element of the common good for the entire society (e.g., public safety, a just legal system, healthy ecosystem, and so forth). Determining what is deemed in the "common good" can vary across countries due to different cultural or societal values. In a business context, a *common good* approach might rely on determination of whether or not a business practice is in line with what is valued and accepted in the society (or country) within which the business operates.

Virtue. This approach focuses on individual character traits and requires us to ask whether a given action is reflective of the kind of person we are or want to be. In a business context, the virtue approach would involve asking oneself if a certain action reflects the kind of employee or leader one would like to be. Or, asking whether or not the action is what a person with high levels of integrity, honesty, compassion, and so forth would do.

It is important to note that there is not one best theory or approach to take. They each have their strengths and weaknesses. Again, the purpose of examining a situation through multiple ethical approaches is to ensure that the facts you have collected are considered from a variety of perspectives. Doing so is the only way to ensure that you have fully investigated the ethical issues involved and that you understand the real choices at hand.

Step 2: Identify Primary Stakeholders

The second step in the ethical decision making process is to understand those who could be affected by your decision; that is, the various stakeholders impacted, which can include individuals, groups, and/or organizations. This is important for ethical decision-making because it allows you to take on the different perspectives of each stakeholder ("walk in their shoes" or "see it from their side").

Although a variety of stakeholders (often all stakeholders) are likely to be affected by a decision, it is generally more useful to focus on identifying the *primary stakeholders* who could be affected. Primary stakeholders are those parties that could be *directly* impacted by a decision. In the context of business, primary stakeholders will often be you, your boss, your customers, your colleagues, and your employees. After identifying the primary stakeholders, turn your attention to secondary stakeholders, those who could be indirectly affected by a decision. Finally, list the obligations you have to each group of stakeholders. Such obligations include job requirements, responsibilities to others, and others' expectations of you.

Step 3: Increase the Number of Alternative Courses of Action

The third step in the ethical decision-making process is to expand the solution set to three or more alternatives. As we noted earlier, ethical dilemmas are especially challenging because they often involve situations that present "right versus right" choices (rather than right versus wrong). In these situations, what typically happens is that we generate only two courses of action and, to make matters more difficult, these choices are frequently "either/or" in nature. A rule of thumb in ethical decision-making is that if your thought process revolves around only two options, you're much less likely to make a good decision. Therefore, the primary purpose of this step is to think creatively and generate as many courses of actions as possible. When stuck on only two choices in an "either/or" scenario, a useful tactic is to focus on a course of action that lies in the middle - a compromise. This tactic often helps to spur ideas for other alternatives.

Step 4: Inspect the Consequences of the Alternatives

The final step of the ethical decision-making process involves determining and inspecting the consequences of each alternative course of action generated in step 3. To begin this step, it is important to not only focus on the different options you've generated but also the various stakeholders that would be impacted and *how* they would be impacted by each option.

One pitfall to be avoided in this step is listing out *all* possible consequences without regard to their probability of occurrence. In other words, it's more effective to focus on consequences that are reasonably likely to occur, versus those of very low probability. In addition, it is important to consider both short-term and long-term consequences. Once reasonable consequences have been determined for each course of action, you can then examine each by considering factors such as fairness, feasibility, risks involved, costs/benefits, respecting or violating individuals' rights, and so forth.

Once you've arrived at a choice and decided upon a course of action, there are several final "checks" or "tests" you might want to consider. These will help you determine if you've made a choice that you can "live with."

- The *"Wall Street Journal"* Test – How would I feel if my decision made front-page news in the Wall Street Journal?
- The *"Parent"* Test – Would I be proud to tell my mother or father about my decision?

- The *"Personal Gain"* Test – What have I gained in this situation? Did the chance for personal benefits get in the way of my thinking?
- The *"Platinum Rule"* Test – Am I treating others the way they would like to be treated?

Putting It to the Test: Ethical Decision Making Processes

Let's return to our example of the assistant account executive at the advertising agency, and examine how we can use the ethical decision-making process to examine the situation. Recall that a mid-level advertising executive has pressured a new hire to "fudge" a routine financial report provided to their client, a brand manager of skin care products with a large pharmaceutical company. The executive suggested, "it's just the way it's done around here." The new hire complies and the numbers are massaged to misrepresent the agency's spending of client funds.

Step 1: Investigate Ethical Issues

What exactly is the assistant account executive being asked to do? He is being asked to falsify a financial report and misrepresent the agency's spending of client funds.

Based on its client contract, the agency has a fiduciary responsibility to accurately report use of client funds. Not doing so invites a lawsuit as well as considerable harm to its reputation, which could result in the loss of other client relationships, which would erode profitability. Should this occur, those on the account team will not fare well.

Does the assistant account executive know all the facts he needs to know to make an informed decision? Yes and no. He should not need any additional information to know that falsifying a financial report is not a wise choice. However, understanding why the shortfall has occurred might enable him to see what other options are available to him besides the one his account supervisor is suggesting. Did the agency go over budget on a location shoot because it rained or because necessary production costs were simply underestimated - circumstances that could be addressed with the brand manager? Did the financial discrepancy occur at a higher accounting level and the account supervisor had not yet resolved it? Were the funds embezzled?

Have the facts been reviewed with those who could offer good advice? No, so the assistant account executive still has the opportunity to ask more questions of his account supervisor, her boss, the managing account supervisor, the account director, or the director of human resources, as well as those on the creative side who could potentially explain production-spending issues.

From a utilitarian perspective, is there a net benefit to falsifying the report? Possibly in the short term, the account supervisor's happiness will be maximized but not that of any of the other stakeholders. In the long run, even her marginal utility would not be greater than for the others unless she can quickly resolve the discrepancy because her job would be at risk. The likelihood that the budget shortfall would go unnoticed for long is not high, and the costs of discovery far outweigh the benefits.

Would the action respect the rights of others? No, the assistant account executive is being asked to do something against his better judgment, which undermines his sense of free choice and self-esteem. The brand manager has the right to expect that the agency will honor its contractual agreement with his company by adequately fulfilling their fiduciary responsibilities. Is there a good reason to make an exception and falsify the report on just one occasion? The risks and costs of discovery are too high. Would the account supervisor be pleased if the production team on the creative side falsified the financial report submitted to her? No, probably not.

Does the action represent a fair distribution of benefits and harms? No, the action could potentially put the profitability of the entire agency at risk, and there is no justification for spending client funds unaccountably.

Would the action ultimately safeguard the common good? No, it would undermine the expectation that business partners operate with trust and in good faith, which is at the very core of fair trade and commerce.

Would a virtuous person falsify a financial report? Would doing so in this instance be in accordance with the kind of person the assistant account executive aspires to be? No, the assistant account executive would be falsifying the report against his better judgment and it would be an embarrassment to the agency should it come to light.

Step 2: Identify Primary Stakeholders

Who are the primary stakeholders in this situation? The primary stakeholders are those directly affected by the course of action the account executive might take. These would include the assistant account executive himself, his boss, and the client. Other people affected include secondary stakeholders such as the immediate members of the account team and senior management, as well as the agency's partners or shareholders and all of the agency's employees.

Step 3: Increase Alternative Courses of Action

Did the assistant account executive generate multiple options for action? It doesn't appear so. The assistant account executive seems to have fallen prey to an "either/or" choice: either comply with the request to "fudge" the numbers or risk being viewed as "not a team player." There are a number of alternative courses of action that could be taken. In fact, if the assistant account executive would have gathered all the relevant information (as mentioned in step 1 above), other actions might have been revealed. For example, he could have discussed the causes of the running over budget, explored other ways the company could recoup the unbudgeted costs, explained the overrun to the client and explored ways to defray the costs, etc.

Step 4: Inspect the Consequences of the Alternatives

Were the reasonable consequences of the possible actions explored? No. Even for the "either/or" options, the assistant account executive does not seem to have explored possible consequences. For example, in the short term the account supervisor will not have to account for some misappropriation of client funds that occurred before the assistant account executive joined the agency, and that may allow time to remedy the situation. If the numbers are falsified, the assistant account executive will prove he is a "team player" and will initially secure his job. The brand manager will be unaware that there is a budget shortfall because he has not been apprised of the prior excessive spending.

In addition, the assistant account executive did not perform any final "checks" on the chosen action, which could have further informed the choice. For instance, asking questions such as: What have I gained from fudging the numbers? What did the client lose? Am I treating the client the way they would like to be treated?

Chapter Review Questions

Business Ethics Basics

1. What makes a problem or situation an "ethical issue"?

2. How are business ethics and social responsibility related?

3. What is the triple bottom line?

The Ethical Decision making Process

4. What are the four steps in the ethical decision-making process?

5. What are some examples of ethical breaches common to business?

6. What is the primary focus of each of the five approaches to (theories of) business ethics?

7. What is the difference between primary and secondary stakeholders?

8. When faced with an ethical issue, what are some ways we can increase the number of alternative courses of action?

9. What are some "tests" we can consider to weigh the consequences of our actions?

You – in the executive suite!

Ethical Decision Making

Everyone in business will, at some time, face a situation that requires ethical decision making. In this exercise you will take the material presented in this module and apply it to a series of case studies.

Activities: Approximately 30 minutes to complete.   COMPLETED

A-1: Answer all Chapter Review Questions   ☐
Your instructor will advise you on how to turn in your answers.

A-2: Consider the following cases and provide two answers for each: first note the step   ☐
in the ethical decision making process that is most relevant, second select the most
appropriate action.

Exercise # 14: Applying the Ethical Decision Making Process

Let's take all of that background on ethical decision making and apply it to some real-life situations.

Read the following cases. First decide which step of the ethical decision-making process is most relevant. Next, apply the process to choose the most appropriate action.

1. Your boss confides in you that one of your highly successful coworkers has been "padding" his expense account by billing for personal items. This action violates a company policy, which notes that termination is a possible consequence of such action. He asks you for your opinion, saying, "should I fire him or just ask him to pay back the money?" Which of the following responses would be most effective in helping your boss make an ethical decision?

   a. "Most people pad a little; consider it a bonus for his good performance."
   b. "It doesn't appear that any harm was done to individuals, he should pay back the money."
   c. "There may be additional actions beyond the ones you've presented."
   d. "People make mistakes sometimes and deserve to be heard."

2. One of your employees just told you that she is being sexually harassed at work by an employee outside your work group. Which of the following would be the most effective action to take?

   a. Review the policies and procedures in your organization for dealing with a claim of sexual harassment.
   b. Call the police to report the incident.
   c. Ask the employee to give you a full report of the details and circumstances.
   d. Ask the employee to write up a report to submit to the human resources department.

3. You are an account manager working for a major provider of sales software. You sell and service the software for sales representatives in many different industries. Your boss tells you that your programmers are contemplating changing the software's specifications to make it operate on mobile phone platforms. Some of the proposed changes however may be unpopular with your customers. You suggest to your boss that customers should be notified before any changes would take place. Your boss disagrees and says "it's better to ask for forgiveness than for permission." Which of the following is the best course of action in order to help make the best decision?

   a. Send a letter to customers before the change takes place.
   b. Follow your boss's suggestion since none of the proposed changes will eliminate the primary functionality of the device.

   c. Convene your team to discuss the possible impact of any change on all affected parties.
   d. Find legal or contractual grounds to argue that such changes made require 30-days written notice.

4. You are a Director of a large financial services firm. Your boss called you to inform you that there is a proposed layoff in your department, which would affect three of six of your employees if it takes place. Given the sensitivity of the issue, your boss asks you to keep this information absolutely confidential. Later that day, one of your employees (Shelia) who would be affected stops you in the hallway and says she's heard rumors about a layoff, remarking "I'm not going to be fired am I?" Which of the following people best represent the stakeholders for whom you are primarily obligated?

   a. Your boss and Shelia
   b. Yourself, Shelia and your other employees
   c. Your boss, Shelia and yourself
   d. Your boss, Shelia, and Sheila's family and yourself

8 Selling Your Company and Making Brilliant Business Presentations

Learning Objectives:

After reading this module and completing the associated exercises, you will be able to:

LO1: Describe the key elements of an effective presentation.

LO2: Discuss how the rule of three helps to frame a presentation.

LO3: Describe how to make a presentation more memorable and understandable.

LO4: Apply the four steps to effectively practice a presentation.

LO5: Discuss why valuation is important to business.

LO6: Compare and contrast tangible and intangible assets.

LO7: Define and describe the meaning and importance of EBIT for valuing a company.

Key Terms to Look For:

- *Book value*
- *Capital market presentation*
- *Earnings Before Interest and Taxes (EBIT)*
- *Goodwill*
- *Intangible assets*

- *Market capitalization*
- *Multipliers*
- *Overlearning*
- *"Rule of three"*
- *Shareholder presentation*

Communication and Valuation: Two Final Skills

In the introduction to Foundation, we learned that business is ideas, people, and money, configured and reconfigured in infinitely different ways to satisfy customers' needs and make a profit.

We have studied and practiced managerial skills, decision making and financial skills, and have worked on coordination and alignment of resources and the selection of tactics to achieve a goal.

We have also discussed important stakeholders, both internal and external to a business, and looked at how businesses operate in the broader economic and social environment.

When it is time to present your outcomes to peers inside and outside the enterprise, there are two more issues we need to cover. First, we need to discuss one of the most critical management skills you will need to develop: delivering strong presentations. A company's results may come down to numbers, but numbers don't tell the whole story and a strong, well-prepared presentation is your opportunity to provide context.

Second, we will look at how to put a value on a company when it comes time to sell. Different stakeholders, inside and outside of a company, have different perspectives on the value represented by that company. Its ultimate valuation, therefore, is also more than a simple number like the book value of the company's assets. You may be surprised to learn that good communication can also play a role in a company's valuation and in the sale process.

FIT for a Great Presentation

Part of the process of valuing a company often involves making presentations to employees, customers, suppliers, bankers, and the business community in general. Commonly we refer to this process as a roadshow. However it is not only when it's time to value and perhaps even sell a company that strong, persuasive presentations are critical. Whether you are trying to secure a contract with a major new customer, to convince your colleagues of a new approach or idea, or to present your annual results to shareholders, an understanding the basics of good business communication is vital.

To complete your business simulation experience, you will be asked to prepare either a:

SHAREHOLDER PRESENTATION: to convince your shareholders of your excellent stewardship of their company; or a

CAPITAL MARKET PRESENTATION: to sell your company to investors who can capture and leverage additional opportunities for the company, or to your competitors who have identified additional synergies with their own companies.

You have spent several simulated years getting your company to this point and whether you are happy with your results or feel there is more work to do, you should have plenty to say about what you have tried to achieve.

The presentation is like a playoff final for a sports team. And just as a sports team must be game or match "fit," as a business person you need to get *FIT* for your presentation. Doing so requires you to follow three essential steps:

1. Frame the message

2. Illustrate your points

3. Train for your delivery

Presentation skills are not just "nice to have" in business. With so many ideas and so much information competing for attention via so many communication technologies, the ability to make a persuasive personal presentation is an essential management skill – particularly in leadership roles.

You do not, however, have to be a polished performer or a "born showman" to deliver an excellent presentation. With careful thought and preparation, anyone can deliver a convincing presentation. Presenting is a behavior, after all, and all behavior can be learned and improved with practice.

According to Chris Anderson, a curator for TED Talks:

"I'm convinced that giving a good talk is highly coachable. In a matter of hours, a speaker's content and delivery can be transformed from muddled to mesmerizing."

It does not require an expert coach to make that transformation, just some careful attention to the basics. Now let's take a closer look at each component in the FIT model.

"F" – Frame the Message: The rule of three and being concise and precise

Steve Jobs, Apple's late CEO, was renowned for turning product launches into major news events with perfectly rehearsed and carefully pitched multi-media presentations. Jobs spent hours, and sometimes days and weeks, working on his script, choreographing the content and the visuals, and honing his message to its most essential elements.

Most of Jobs' presentations were divided into three parts, because the "rule of three" is a basic principle of successful communication. In her book *The Presentation Genius of Steve Jobs*, **Business Week's** Carmine Gallo reports:

"The number three is a powerful concept in writing. Playwrights know that three is more dramatic than two; comedians know that three is funnier than four; and Steve Jobs knew that three is more memorable than six or eight. Even if he had 20 points to make, Jobs knew that the audience was only capable of holding three or four of them in short term memory. Better that they remember three than forget everything."

So the idea here is to frame your presentation in three key parts. For example, the framework might be:

- Problem, Solution, and Call to Action for a sales presentation.

- Overview (key points you are going to make), Exposition (illustrating the key points), and Summary (repeating key points again) for an educational presentation

- Achievements (major achievements for the period), Challenges (problems management is facing), and Goals for the future for a presentation to shareholders.

Once you have a broad three-point framework, distill the key points you want to make to one short sentence each. Use the notion of an "elevator speech" – you need to be able to make your pitch in the time it would take for a short elevator ride. Alternatively, you could think of it as being able to distill your points into the 140 characters that define a tweet.

> "Steve Jobs created a single-sentence description for every product," Gallo says. "These headlines helped the audience categorize the new product and were always concise enough to fit in a 140-character Twitter post. For example, when Jobs introduced the MacBook Air in January 2008, he said that is it simply 'The world's thinnest notebook.' That one short sentence spoke volumes."

Making your key points **concise and precise** takes effort – perhaps even more time than writing out your entire presentation. As Blaise Pascal famously told a correspondent, "The present letter is a very long one, simply because I had no leisure to make it shorter."

"I" – Illustrate it: Making it memorable and comprehensible

There are three ways to enhance your presentation's message by making it easier to understand and remember – and a presentation must be both understandable and memorable in order to be convincing enough to influence others.

Tell stories and contextualize. Data or numbers do not communicate well in a presentation, but word pictures do. People love stories. Stories stick in the mind. Your key points literally become "sticky" because they are attached to a story that has an emotional impact on the audience. This doesn't mean that stories are a replacement for data or evidence of your company's value, but simply that without a good story people are unlikely to be energized by the case you're trying to make.

The same is true if you are using visual aids for your presentation, such as presentation slides. Slides with lots of information distract the audience from the speaker and the points being made. Simple visuals that add meaning to your key points are all you need. When Steve Jobs launched "the world's thinnest notebook", for example, he used a photo of the computer slipping into a manila office envelope. No need for the technical specifications of the product or comparisons with other products – no need for additional information at all.

As Walt Disney said: "Of all our inventions for mass communication, pictures still speak the most universally understood language."

When you do need to present data or numbers, it's crucial to recognize that context matters. Put simply, numbers by themselves rarely communicate. Therefore, try to give your audience some kind of analogy or context for the numbers you are presenting.

For example, in news reports you often hear or read analogies such as "the line of people was as long as five football fields" or "the flood covered an area the size of Manhattan" or "the loss was equal to the GDP of Fiji." Journalists are taught to put numbers into context so people can grasp them. This is a valuable tactic for you to use to better communicate technical details, research results, and numerical information.

In the context of your Foundation Simulation for example, a profit of $7 million may be an exceptional result, if the competition is very tough. In a simulation where most of the companies failed to make a profit, however, a profit of $30 million to the winning company might be less impressive. Whatever the number – good or bad – try to give it context.

Remember W.I.I.F.M. Before you write your presentation, put yourself in the shoes of a typical member of your audience. You are sitting out there, listening to someone talk and your major concern is: *What's In It For Me?* (W.I.I.F.M.) You wouldn't be in the audience unless you were expecting to benefit from the presentation. And, if you are in the audience under duress ("my boss made me come"), the speaker will have to work even harder to convince you of what's in it for you! Focus on benefits, tell success stories, and build a clear picture of why your key points are important using images and anecdotes. Try to make your message personal and relevant to your audience.

...And K.I.S. In all elements of your presentation – structure, language, stories, visual aids – the most important rule overall is to *Keep It Simple.*

If you have complex research data or technical information to present, consider distributing it as a handout. If your presentation can convince the audience of the importance of your information, they will eagerly seek out the background material later. (A note on handouts: If you provide your audience with material in advance of your talk, they will read it instead of focusing on your presentation. Time your distribution of handouts carefully).

"T" –Train for delivery: Perfect practice makes perfect performance

If a seasoned professional such as Steve Jobs put months into the preparation of his presentations, the rest of us should at least put a little effort into training for ours! Practice is the secret to every successful presentation.

How to best practice for an upcoming presentation? A few tips include:

- WRITE IT: Write out your presentation in full and, if you have time, memorize it. If not, distill the key points to cards and use them to keep you on track.
- READ IT: Read your draft out loud several times to ensure the words flow; then practice in front of an audience of colleagues, friends, family – anyone who can give you honest feedback.
- TIME IT: It is important to know how long you will be speaking, to ensure your message will fit into the surrounding agenda. Audiences – not to mention program organizers – loathe presenters who go on and on.
- REPEAT IT: The science of learning talks about the concept of *overlearning*, which refers to practicing beyond mastery (i.e., practicing your presentation until you are effective and then practicing a few more times). The benefit here is that your presentation can become automatic.

Don't be nervous about nerves. Again, remember that giving a presentation is behavioral and all behaviors can be learned and improved. It is also important to recognize that being nervous or anxious is completely natural. In fact, if you are not at all "amped-up" it might actually signal to your audience that you lack enthusiasm about your topic! Chris

Anderson from TED talks said in a *Harvard Business Review* report:

"In general, people worry too much about nervousness. Nerves are not a disaster. The audience expects you to be nervous. It's a natural body response that can actually improve your performance: It gives you energy to perform and keeps your mind sharp. Just keep breathing, and you'll be fine."

What all of this means is that you need to approach building and delivering a presentation in a planned and practiced manner. In fact, one beneficial outcome of practicing to the point of overlearning (as noted above) is that you may *feel* nervous but your behavior has been so honed that your audience won't even notice.

Putting It Into Practice

Once you know what the goal of your final presentation will be, either a report to your shareholders or a capital market sales pitch, begin to get your presentation FIT to deliver following the tips outlined above.

There are a number of ways to tell the story of the company you have built in the simulation. Below is a sample presentation template you can use as a guide when you begin to build a shareholder presentation for your own Foundation company.

Table 1 - Sample Outline: Shareholder Presentation

Frame it	Illustrate it
1. Achievements this year Your company's top three achievements	Story: A critical customer incident and an employee's brilliant response to it Slide: customer logo
2. Challenges What you anticipate and how you plan to deal with issues such as product placement and capacity	Story: How a specific management approach is cleverly designed to solve a problem
3. Goals for the future What you aim to achieve and how your current achievements demonstrate your ability to reach your goals.	Slide: Management team Slide: Your projected outcomes for next year in profit, ROS, ROA, and stock price.

*Note: Train for delivery: Write it, Read it, Time it, and Repeat it.

What are We Worth? - Valuing the Firm

There are several different approaches to determining the value of a company, and no single approach is universally recognized as the "right way." Every company is unique, which means those involved should consider a range of different elements before finally

New media's short-term "goodwill" toward old media

AOL Time Warner

In 2000, when AOL and Time Warner merged, the sheer size of the merger and the spectacle of a new media company buying an old media company made it a huge news story. One year later, however, came an equally spectacular story.

AOL offered Time Warner more than $150 billion to be paid for in AOL stock – 1.5 AOL shares for every Time Warner share at a time when AOL was trading at more than $70 per share. The hard assets of Time Warner were worth much less than the valuation and so the balance – estimated to be more than $120 billion – was listed as "goodwill and other intangible assets".

The intangible assets included the Warner Bros film library, its catalog of copyrighted music, CNN, *Time Magazine*, the Atlanta Braves baseball team, cable-TV franchises, and much more, including the value inherent in simply being in control of these types of assets.

A change in the accounting rules governing goodwill, however, meant that within one year, AOL Time Warner had to admit it had overpaid for Warner's intangibles. They announced a $54 billion write-off – the largest in American corporate history.

Bloomberg Businessweek reported at the time that the huge write-off: *"ought to give investors reason to pause over the volatility of stock market valuations, the vagaries of corporate accounting, and anyone's ability to judge the real, ongoing worth of a business."*

Eight years later, the entire experiment in merging the two companies was abandoned, with Time Warner spinning off AOL.

The New York Times, in an article on the 10th anniversary of the merger, reported: *"The trail of despair in subsequent years included countless job losses, the decimation of retirement accounts, investigations by the Securities and Exchange Commission and the Justice Department, and countless executive upheavals. Today, the combined values of the companies, which have been separated, is about one-seventh of their worth on the day of the merger."*

The failed valuation of goodwill left no good will at all.

---

coming up with a number that represents a company's value.

It is important to point out that a company is only valued when someone wants to sell and someone wants to buy. Often you have interested buyers for a company, but the seller's shareholders are unwilling to sell because they assume they can create even more value in the future if they retain their ownership of the company. Practically speaking, in any situation the buyer(s) and seller will need to discuss their perception of the company's value, and then negotiate in order to arrive at a final transaction price. The business and communication skills of the respective par-

ties at the bargaining table, therefore, are critically important.

The most straightforward part of the valuation is "book value," which, as we discussed in Module 5, is the value of the company's assets on the balance sheet. Book value is calculated as Owners' Equity divided by the number of shares outstanding. These are the company's tangible assets.

However, what about the strong brand the company has created? The customer loyalty it has built? The efficient and well-trained work force? Its intellectual property? These are all integral to the company's success, but they are not assets on the Balance Sheet, they are referred to as "intangible assets." The amount paid by the acquiring company over book value is referred to as "goodwill."

As mentioned, there are several ways to value a firm. A publicly traded company such as your Foundation company has a market value called "market capitalization," which is calculated as stock price multiplied by the number of shares outstanding. As we also know, the transaction value of the company – what the buyer pays for it – may be greater than or less than the capital market value. We know there is a price paid for intangible assets or goodwill, but value can be influenced by other pressures as well, including speculation on internal or external challenges, expectations for future growth, or media buzz that stimulates interest and excitement (or the opposite) for a company.

Common valuation approaches include calculations of Economic Value Added (EVA); Discounted Cash Flow (DCF); Free Cash Flow, and the very simple Public Market Value, which simply looks at what other, similar companies are being sold for in the current market environment.

One of the most often used calculations for valuation, however, involves or EBIT. We will expand on this concept because it will be useful if you are developing a capital market presentation for your Foundation company.

EBIT stands for Earnings Before Interest and Taxes. EBIT estimates the current operational profitability of the company for the current period. In this way EBIT reflects all of a company's profits before taking into account interest payments and income taxes. Analysts take this profitability measure and multiply it by a certain value to estimate the company's total value. Clearly, the big question is what value should be used as a multiplier?

For companies that are being purchased for their absolute value, the multiplier will be lower than for a company being purchased because it is a "strategic fit" with the organization making the purchase. For example, if your Foundation company was being purchased by an organization that had no presence in electronics production and saw your company as a good generator of cash, they might only pay a multiple between 4 and 8. However, if the purchaser saw your Foundation Company as an excellent fit with their current sensor/electronics portfolio, they might pay anywhere between 10 and 12 times your EBIT. For example, a possible multiplier for the Andrews company shown in Table 2 below can be estimated by dividing the market value ("market capitalization") by the EBIT. This results in a multiplier of 10 ($360 million/$36 million = 10).

Once you have determined a value, be prepared to defend it and to negotiate with your potential buyer.

To help you get started, on the following page is a sample is a sample presentation template you could use for a capital market presentation. Remember that there are, of course, many ways to tell your company's story – this is just a starting point.

Table 2

Company	Revenue	EBIT	Market Capitalization ($180 per share)	Earnings per Share
Andrews (2 million shares outstanding)	$240 million	$36 million	$360 million	$18

Table 3 - Sample Outline: Why You Should Buy My Foundation Company!

Frame it	Illustrate it
1. Why we are the company to buy? Major selling points of your company (only three!)	Story: How we achieved market domination in one segment within three years.
2. What is our future potential? What we are set up to achieve next.	Slide: Smiling picture of management team at work. Story: How a planned innovation has been designed to solve a specific customer problem.

3. What we are worth?
  The valuation (EBIT X multiple)
  Wrap up with summary of selling points and potentials
	Slide: Your R&D staff
	
	Slide: Chart that highlights your valuation compared with other similar companies with higher valuations

Note: Train for delivery: Write it, Read it, Time it, and Repeat it.

Reflection and Conclusion

Whether your Foundation company made millions of dollars in profit for its shareholders or met Big Al and had to pay back a massive emergency loan (or both!), there is one key lesson from the Foundation experience: Business is both complex and endlessly fascinating.

The Foundation experience has taken you from the very beginning – ideas, people, and money – through to the moment when with pride (or great relief) you are in a position to put a value on the company you have built, and sell it.

Put simply, you have experienced running a business from start to finish.

The simulation was designed to give you the opportunity to try and fail, and try again, in an attempt to build mastery over the concepts that are fundamental to business. Concepts such as profit, management, market segments, stakeholders, demand, risk, and so forth all become more real when they refer to *your* company and *your* results.

Now it is time to take all that new knowledge and apply it in the real world.

Best of luck in your own business adventures!

Chapter Review Questions

Presentation Basics

1. What does it mean to be "FIT" for a presentation?

2. How does the rule of three apply to presentations? Provide an example.

3. What are some ways to make a presentation memorable and understandable?

4. How can we improve an audience's understanding of numerical information?

5. What are the four steps of effective presentation practice?

Valuation

6. Why is valuation important to business?

7. What is the difference between tangible and intangible assets?

8. What is "goodwill"?

9. What is EBIT? How does this affect valuation?

You – in the executive suite!

Chief Executive Officer, making a critical presentation

Your job rotation is complete, you have had several years to run your company by managing all the various departments and have – hopefully – built a bigger, better company than the one you started with.

Whatever your financial results, the time has come to present your company's vision for the future to the outside world.

Activities: Completion time depends on the effort you invest in your future as a communicator   COMPLETED

A-1: Answer all **Chapter Review Questions**
Your instructor will advise you on how to turn in your answers.   ☐

A-2: Prepare your final presentation, in accordance with your instructor's requirements, and following the FIT model.   ☐

Exercise # 15: The Final Presentation

Your instructor will provide full details on the form of your presentation. It may be required as a video, as part of a class presentation, or delivered via an online meeting. You may be asked to put the case for buying your company before a panel of potential investors; to deliver a debriefing of the past year and future goals for your shareholders; or to present to some other audience as defined by your instructor.

As you plan your presentation, remember to carefully frame your message so it is meaningful for your audience, to illustrate the key points with simple stories, critical data in context and clear visuals, and to then train yourself to deliver.

Don't be afraid to use your imagination in this exercise. You have learned a lot about many elements of business over the course of the program and this is your chance to demonstrate some of that new knowledge. Your final numbers may be unalterable, but the story you weave around them is still to be written!

Use this opportunity to build your presentation skills because they will be important to your future success in business.

Good luck.

Appendix 1:
Foundation Business Simulation Summary Guide

The Course Road Map

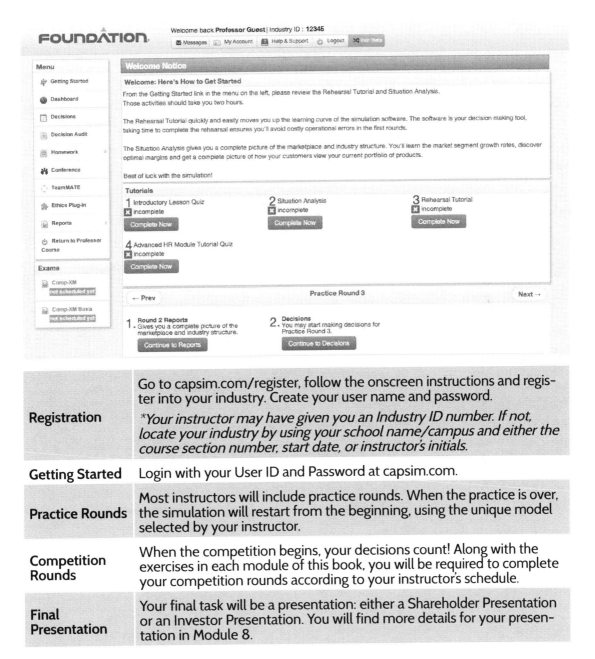

Registration	Go to capsim.com/register, follow the onscreen instructions and register into your industry. Create your user name and password. *Your instructor may have given you an Industry ID number. If not, locate your industry by using your school name/campus and either the course section number, start date, or instructor's initials.*
Getting Started	Login with your User ID and Password at capsim.com.
Practice Rounds	Most instructors will include practice rounds. When the practice is over, the simulation will restart from the beginning, using the unique model selected by your instructor.
Competition Rounds	When the competition begins, your decisions count! Along with the exercises in each module of this book, you will be required to complete your competition rounds according to your instructor's schedule.
Final Presentation	Your final task will be a presentation: either a Shareholder Presentation or an Investor Presentation. You will find more details for your presentation in Module 8.

The Foundation Reports

Found via this button on your dashboard:

1. **Round 0 Reports**
- Gives you a complete picture of the marketplace and industry structure.

> Continue to Reports

Industry Conditions Report

Why do I need this? The Industry Conditions Report covers the key parameters in your simulation model. The simulation is customizable so you will need the specific information for your model. You will need this to complete the Situation Analysis.

The Industry Conditions Report is published once, at the beginning of the simulation. It provides information you will need to produce a perceptual map, the buying criteria for customers of each market segment - both low tech and high tech - and the starting interest rate on borrowing by your simulated company.

The Foundation Interface

Found via this button on your dashboard:

2. **Decisions**
- You may start making decisions for Practice Round 1.

> Continue to Decisions

Locate and print or save your Industry Conditions Report. From your Dashboard, go to the Practice Round 1 panel and click: Reports/ Round 0 Reports/Industry Reports/Industry Conditions Report. Then click Continue. You can then print or save your report

Foundation FastTrack Report

Why do I need this? The Foundation FastTrack is an extensive year-end report of the whole industry that gives you customer buying patterns, product positioning on the perceptual map for your own and your competitors' products, production information including material and labor costs in the industry, plus publicly available financial records including cash flow statements, income statements, and balance sheets for each company in the industry.

It is published at the end of each year (round) so the current FastTrack always reflects last year's results (Round 1 FastTrack, for example, is available from the beginning of Round 2).

Where do I make management decisions for my company?

You will make decisions for your simulated company from this spreadsheet interface.

From your Dashboard, go to the Practice Round 1 panel, click Decisions and you have the option to launch either the Web Spreadsheet or the Excel Spreadsheet.

Each has a tab at the top of the screen labeled "Decisions" and a drop down menu for your R&D, Marketing, Production, HR, and Finance Departments.

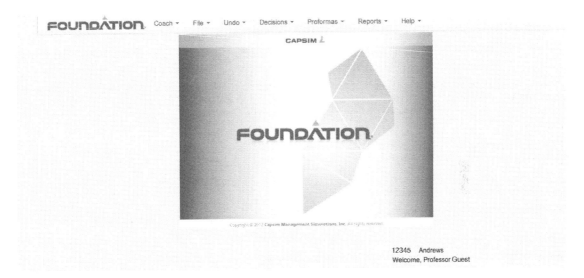

Marketing Decisions

Below is the marketing screen that you will find under Decisions/ Marketing in the top menu of your Foundation interface. You need to make *four decisions* in the marketing department: *Price, Promotion Budget, Sales Budget,* and *Your Forecast.* You may also set your *Accounts Payable* and *Accounts Receivable* terms on this screen.

Price

Customers in each market segment have different price expectations. There is a $20 spread between the lowest and highest acceptable price range in each segment. Price range is available from the Industry Conditions Report and in the Customer Buying Criteria information in the FastTrack on page 5 (low tech) and page 6 (high tech).

Sensors priced $10 above or below the segment guidelines are not considered for purchase.

Sensors priced $1.00 above or below the segment guidelines lose about 10% of their customer survey score (orange arrows in the figure below). Sensors continue to lose ap-

proximately 10% of their customer survey score for each dollar above or below the guideline, up to $9.99, where the score is reduced by approximately 99%. At $10.00 outside the range, demand for the product is zero.

What happens in a seller's market in which demand outstrips supply? When the market is undersupplied, customers will buy products with a low Customer Survey Score as long as they fit within the segment's rough cut limits. In some cases, a company can charge up to $9.99 above the price range and still sell products. However, when the price hits $10 over the range, or if the product is outside the rough cut circle on the perceptual map, customers will refuse to buy it, even if there are no alternatives.

How can you be sure of a seller's market? You can't, unless you can be absolutely certain that industry capacity, including a second shift, cannot meet demand for the segment. In that case, even very poor products will

Figure 1

Classic Price/Demand Curve (Green Bow): As price drops demand (price score) rises. Scores drop above and below the price range (orange arrows).

stock out as customers search for anything that will meet their needs.

Promotion Budget

Each product's promotion budget determines its level of awareness. A product's awareness percentage reflects the number of potential customers who know about the product. Awareness percentages are published in the FastTrack's Segment Analysis reports (pages 5-6) next the Promo Budget numbers.

An awareness of 50% indicates half of the potential customers know the product exists. From one year to the next, a third (33%) of those who knew about a product forget about it.

LAST YEAR'S AWARENESS - (33% X LAST YEAR'S AWARENESS) = STARTING AWARENESS

If a product ended last year with an awareness of 50%, this year it will start with an awareness of approximately 33%. This year's promotion budget would build from a starting awareness of approximately 33%.

STARTING AWARENESS + ADDITIONAL AWARENESS = NEW AWARENESS

The graphic below indicates that a $1,500,000 promotion budget would add 36% to the starting awareness, for a total awareness of 69% (33 + 36 = 69).

It indicates that a $3,000,000 budget would add just under 50% to the starting awareness, roughly 14% more than the $1,500,000 expenditure (33 + 50 = 83). This is because further expenditures tend to reach customers who already know about the product. Once your product achieves 100% awareness, you can scale back the product's promotion bud-

Figure 2

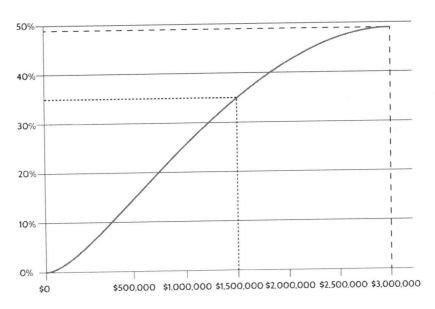

Promotion Budget: Increases in promotion budgets have diminishing returns. The first $1,500,000 buys 36% awareness; spending another $1,500,000 (for a total of $3,000,000) buys just under 50%. The second $1,500,000 buys less than 14% more awareness.

get to around $1,400,000. This will maintain 100% awareness year after year.

New products are newsworthy events. The buzz creates 25% awareness at no cost. The 25% is added to any additional awareness you create with your promotion budget.

Sales Budget

Each product's sales budget contributes to segment accessibility. A segment's accessibility percentage indicates the number of customers who can easily interact with your company via salespeople, customer support, delivery, etc. Accessibility percentages are published in the FastTrack's Segment Analysis reports (pages 5-6) next to the Sales Budget numbers.

Like awareness, if your sales budgets drop to zero, you lose one-third of your accessibility

each year. Unlike awareness, accessibility applies to the *segment*, not the *product*. If your product exits a segment, it leaves the old accessibility behind. When it enters a different segment, it gains that segment's accessibility.

If you have two or more products that meet a segment's buying criteria, the sales budget for each product contributes to that segment's accessibility. The more products you have in the segment, the stronger your distribution channels, support systems, etc. This is because each product's sales budget contributes to the segment's accessibility.

If you have one product in a segment, there is no additional benefit to spending more than $3,000,000. If you have two or more products in a segment, there is no additional benefit to spending more than $4,500,000 split between the products, for example, two products with sales budgets of $2,250,000 each (see graphic below).

Figure 3

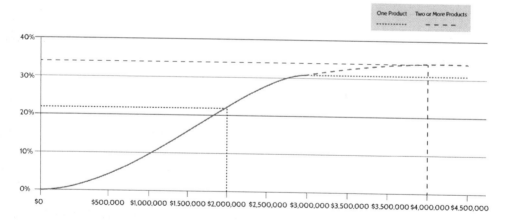

Sales Budget: For budgets above $3,000,000, the dotted red line indicates there are no additional returns for companies that have only one product in a segment and the dashed red line indicates returns for companies with two or more products in a segment. Increases in sales budgets have diminishing returns. The first $2,000,000 buys 22% accessibility. For companies with two or more products in a segment, spending $4,000,000 buys just under 35%accessibility. The second $2,000,000 buys less than 13% additional accessibility.

Achieving 100% accessibility is difficult. You must have two or more products in the segment. Once 100% is reached, you can scale back the combined budgets to around $3,500,000 to maintain 100%.

Your Forecast

The Benchmark Prediction (to the left of Your Forecast) is a computer forecast only. The Benchmark Prediction estimates unit sales assuming your product competes with a standardized, mediocre playing field. It does not use your actual competitors' products. It is useful for experimenting with price, promo, and sales budgets. It is useless for forecasting.

Use the Benchmark Prediction to help you understand how changes to your products may affect demand in the market. The prediction changes every time you make a change to a product. Therefore it can be used to estimate the impact (up or down) that the change will have upon demand. You can use it to test "best case/worst case" scenarios.

However, you should always override the Benchmark Prediction by entering your own sales forecast based on your understanding of your industry and your competitors.

If you leave Your Forecast at 0, the software will use the benchmark prediction.

A/R and A/P – Credit Policy

What are the Accounts Receivable Lag and Accounts Payable Lag? The A/R Lag (days) box defaults to 30. That means, on average, you allow customers 30 days before you expect payment. You can increase or decrease the lag. More generous terms (increasing the accounts receivable lag) may increase de-mand but it will reduce the amount of cash your company has on hand. This function is also found on the Finance page.

The accounts receivable lag impacts the customer survey score. At 90 days there is no reduction to the base score. At 60 days the score is reduced 0.7%. At 30 days the score is reduced 7%. Offering no credit terms (0 days) reduces the score by 40%.

A/P Lag (days) box also defaults to 30. That means, on average, you wait 30 days before you pay your vendors. You can increase or decrease the lag. The longer the delay, the more likely it is that vendors will withhold parts deliveries – and yet your company will have the cash available for longer. This function is also found on the Finance and Production pages.

The accounts payable lag has implications for production. Suppliers become concerned as the lag grows and they start to withhold material for production. At 30 days, they withhold 1%. At 60 days, they withhold 8%. At 90 days, they withhold 26%. At 120 days, they withhold 63%. At 150 days, they withhold all material. Withholding material creates shortages on the assembly line. As a result, workers stand idle and per-unit labor costs rise.

What does the Revenue Forecast graph tell me? It breaks down your forecast revenue (the demand you expect to achieve this round from the Your Forecast column) into variable costs, marketing, and your expected margin, per product.

What does the Unit Sales Forecast graph tell me? It shows the market segment(s) your products are forecast to sell into, and how many units are forecast to sell into each segment, per product.

Research & Development Decisions

R&D invents new products and revises existing products. The three decisions you make for each product are Performance and Size (these reposition products on the perceptual map) and MTBF (Mean Time Between Failure – the reliability rating of the product).

All R&D projects begin on January 1. If a product does not have a project already under way, you can launch a new project for that product. However, if a project you began in a previous year was not completed by December 31 of last year, you will not be able to launch a new project for that product (the decision entry cells in the R&D area of the Foundation Spreadsheet will be locked).

Performance and Size

How much does it cost to reposition a product by changing size and/or performance? Positioning affects material costs (see perpetual map graphic on the following page). The more advanced the positioning (smaller size, higher performance), the higher the cost. The trailing edge of the Low Tech segment has the lowest positioning cost of approximately $1.50; the leading edge of the High Tech segment has the highest positioning cost of approximately $10.00. Products placed on the arc halfway between the trailing and leading edges have a positioning material cost of approximately $5.75. While the segments will drift apart, and the distance between the leading and trailing edges will increase, the positioning cost range will not change. The leading edge will always be

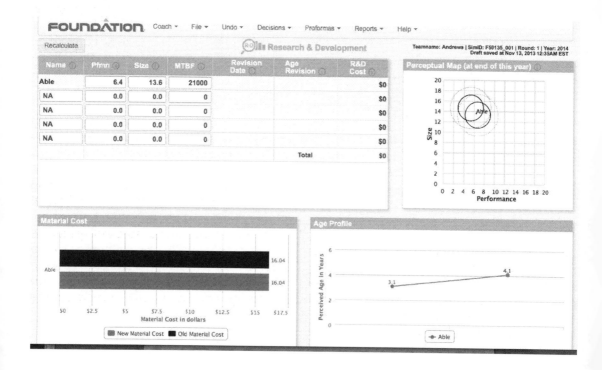

Figure 4

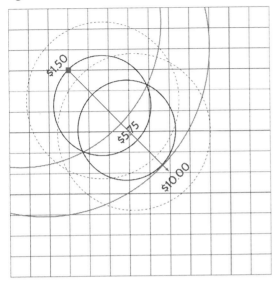

Cost of materials relative to product's positioning on perceptual map

approximately $10.00, the trailing edge will always be approximately $1.50 and the mid-point will always be approximately $5.75.

Mean Time Before Failure (MTBF)

How much does it cost to change reliability (MTBF)? The reliability rating, or MTBF, for existing products can be adjusted up or down. Each 1,000 hours of reliability (MTBF) adds $0.30 to the material cost. For example, if your product has 20,000 hours of reliability, the material cost for that product will include $6.00 in reliability costs:

$$(\$0.30 \times 20,000) / 1,000 = \$6.00$$

Improving positioning and reliability will make a product more appealing to customers, but doing so increases material costs. Material costs displayed in the spreadsheet and reports are the combined positioning and reliability (MTBF) costs.

How do I invent a new product? Click in the first cell that reads NA in the "name" column, give your new product a name, then a performance, size, and MTBF rating. The name of all new products must have the same first letter as your company name. The Production Department must order production capacity to build the new product one year in advance. Invention projects take at least one year to complete.

How long do R&D projects take? Revision Date tells you when your new or revised product will be ready for sale.

The Low Tech segment circles move on the Perceptual Map at a speed of 0.7 unit per year toward the lower right corner as products become smaller and performance improves. The High Tech segment circles move at 1.0 unit per year. You must plan to move your products (or retire them) as the simulation progresses. Generally, the longer the move on the Perceptual Map, the longer it takes the R&D Department to complete the project.

Project lengths can be as short as three months or as long as three years. Project lengths will increase when the company puts two or more products into R&D at the same time. When this happens each R&D project takes longer. Assembly line automation levels also affect project lengths.

Sensors will continue to be produced and sold at the old performance, size, and MTBF specifications up until the day the project completes, shown on the spreadsheet as the revision date. Unsold units built prior to the revision date are reworked free of charge to match the new specifications. Therefore, on the revision date, all inventory matches the new specifications.

If the project length takes more than a year, the revision date will be reported in the next Foundation FastTrack. However, the new performance, size, and MTBF will not appear; old product attributes are reported prior to project completion.

When products are created or moved close to existing products, R&D completion times diminish. This is because your R&D Department can take advantage of existing technology. Increased competence equals decreased development time.

How much does R&D cost? R&D project costs are driven by the amount of time they take to complete. A six-month project costs $500,000; a one-year project costs $1,000,000.

What determines the sensor's age? When a product is moved on the Perceptual Map, customers perceive the repositioned product as newer and improved, but not brand new. Changing a product's size or performance cuts its perceived age in half. If the product's age is 4 years, on the day it is repositioned its age becomes 2 years. Changing MTBF alone will not affect a product's age.

Production Decisions

 In Production, you set a production schedule for each product (how many units are you going to produce this year?), buy or sell production capacity, and set automation levels for each production line. You can also alter the A/P Lag.

In your Production Department, each product has its own assembly line. You cannot move a product from one line to another because automation levels vary and each product requires special tooling.

Production Schedule

How do I determine Production Schedule? Use the sales forecasts developed by your marketing department, minus any inventory left unsold from the previous year.

Buy/Sell Capacity

What is "Capacity" and how much does it cost? Capacity is the number of sensors your production lines are capable of producing in a year. First-shift capacity is defined as the number of units that can be produced on an assembly line in a single year with a daily eight-hour shift. An assembly line can produce up to twice its first-shift capacity with a second shift. An assembly line with a capacity of 2,000,000 units per year could produce 4,000,000 units with a second shift. However, second-shift labor costs are 50% higher than the first shift. (Remember, your spreadsheet does not display the additional '000' at the end of each numeral i.e., 1,000,000 appears as 1,000 in the interface).

Each new unit of capacity costs $6.00 for the floor space plus $4.00 multiplied by the automation rating. The Production spreadsheet will calculate the cost and display it for you. Increases in capacity require a full year to take effect - increase it this year, use it next year.

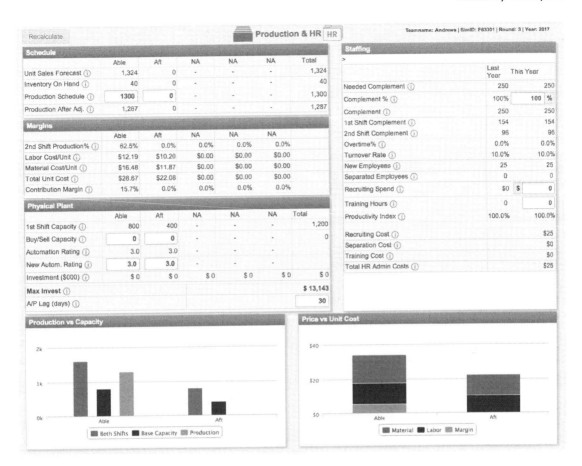

Capacity can be sold at the beginning of the year for $0.65 on the dollar value of the original investment. You can replace the capacity in later years, but you have to pay full price. If you sell capacity for less than its depreciated value, you lose money, which is reflected as a write-off on your income statement. If you sell capacity for more than its depreciated value, you make a gain on the sale. This will be reflected as a negative write-off on the income statement. The dollar value limit of capacity and automation purchases is largely determined by the maximum amount of capital that can be raised through stock and bond issues plus excess working capital.

How do I discontinue a product? If you sell all the capacity on an assembly line, Foundation interprets this as a liquidation instruction and will sell your remaining inventory for half the average cost of production. Foundation writes off the loss on your income statement. If you want to sell your inventory at full price, sell all but one unit of capacity. This signals to the software that you want to sell at full price. Next year, sell the final unit of capacity.

When do I buy capacity for a new product? All new products require capacity and automation, which should be purchased by the Production Department in the year prior to the product's revision (release) date. If you don't buy the assembly line the year prior to its introduction, you cannot manufacture your new product!

Automation

What is the Automation Rating? Automation is the level of robotics on your production lines. As automation increases, the number of labor hours required to produce each unit falls. The lowest automation rating is 1.0; the highest rating is 10.0.

At an automation rating of 1.0, labor costs are highest. Each additional point of automation decreases labor costs approximately 10%. At a rating of 10.0, labor costs fall about 90%. Labor costs increase each year because of an Annual Raise in the workers' contract.

Despite its attractiveness, two factors should be considered before raising automation:

- Automation is expensive: At $4.00 per point of automation, raising automation from 1.0 to 10.0 costs $36.00 per unit of capacity;

- As you raise automation, it becomes increasingly difficult for R&D to reposition products short distances on the Perceptual Map. For example, a project that moves a product 1.0 on the map takes significantly longer at an automation level of 8.0 than at 5.0 (see graphic below). Long moves are less affected. You can move a product a long distance at any automation level, but the project

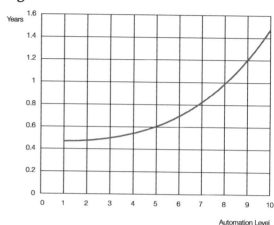

Figure 5

Time required to move a sensor on the perceptual map 1.0 unit at automation levels 1 through 10

will take between 2.5 and 3.0 years to complete.

How much does Automation cost? For each point of change in automation, up or down, the company is charged $4.00 per unit of capacity. For example, if a line has a capacity of 1,000,000 units, the cost of changing the automation level from 5.0 to 6.0 would be $4,000,000.

Reducing automation costs money. If you reduce automation, you will be billed for a retooling cost. The net result is that you will be spending money to make your plant less efficient. While reduced automation will speed R&D redesigns, by and large, it is not wise to reduce an automation level.

Finance Decisions

The Finance screen allows you to make six decisions, depending on your approach to:

1. Acquiring the capital you need to expand assets, particularly plant and equipment. Capital can be acquired via the finance screen through:
   - Current Debt
   - Stock Issues
   - Bond Issues (Long Term Debt)

2. Paying shareholders a dividend. A dividend per share can be entered once you have established your dividend policy.

3. Setting accounts payable policy (which can also be entered in the Production and Marketing areas) and accounts receivable policy (which can also be entered in the Marketing area).

4. Driving the financial structure of the firm and its relationship between debt and equity (issuing and retiring long-term debt).

Finance decisions should be made after all other departments have entered their decisions. After the management team decides what resources the company needs, the Finance Department addresses funding issues and financial structure.

Common Stock

What are the rules for stock price? Stock price is driven by book value, earnings per share (EPS), and the last two years' annual dividend.

Book value per share is shareholders' equity divided by shares outstanding. Equity equals the common stock and retained earnings

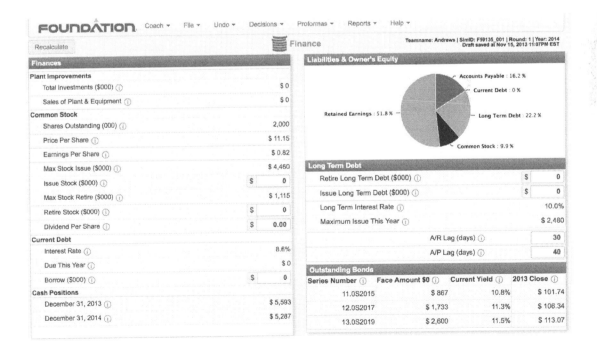

values listed on the balance sheet. Shares outstanding is the number of shares that have been issued. For example, if equity is $50,000,000 and there are 2,000,000 shares outstanding, book value is $25.00 per share.

EPS is calculated by dividing net profit by shares outstanding.

How do I issue stock? Stock issue transactions take place at the current market price. Your company pays a 5% brokerage fee for issuing stock. New stock issues are limited to 20% of your company's outstanding shares in that year.

As a general rule, stock issues are used to fund long-term investments in capacity and automation. Enter the amount in thousands of dollars ($000) in the issue stock cell.

How do I buy back stock? You can retire stock. The amount cannot exceed the lesser of either:

- 5% of your outstanding shares, listed on page 2 of last year's Courier; or
- Your total equity listed on page 3 of last year's Courier.

You are charged a 1.5% brokerage fee to retire stock.

Dividends

The dividend is the amount of money paid per share to stockholders each year. Stockholders respond negatively to a dividend per share greater than the Earnings Per Share because the policy is unsustainable and will hurt the stock price. For example, if your EPS is $1.50 per share and your dividend is $2.00 per share, stockholders ignore anything above $1.50 per share as a driver of stock price. In general, dividends have little effect upon stock price. However, Foundation is unlike the real world in one important aspect– there are no external investment opportunities. If you cannot use profits to grow the company, idle assets will accumulate.

Current Debt

What determines the limits on current debt? Your bank issues current debt in one-year notes. The Finance area in the Foundation Spreadsheet displays the amount of current debt due from the previous year. Last year's current debt is always paid off on January 1. The company can "roll" that debt by simply borrowing the same amount again. There are no brokerage fees for current debt. Interest rates are a function of your debt level. The more debt you have relative to your assets, the more risk you present to debt holders and the higher the current debt rates.

As a general rule, companies fund short-term assets like accounts receivable and inventory with current debt offered by banks.

Bankers will loan current debt up to about 75% of your accounts receivable (found on last year's balance sheet) and 50% of this year's inventory. They estimate your inventory for the upcoming year by examining last year's income statement. Bankers assume your worst case scenario will leave a three- to four-month inventory and they will loan you up to 50% of that amount. This works out to be about 15% of the combined value of last year's total direct labor and total direct material, both of which are displayed on the income statement.

Bankers also realize your company is growing, so as a final step bankers increase your borrowing limit by 20% to provide you with room for expansion in inventory and accounts receivable.

Long-term Debt

What determines the limits on bonds? All bonds are 10-year notes. Your company pays a 5% brokerage fee for issuing bonds. The first three digits of the bond, the series number, reflect the interest rate. The last four digits indicate the year in which the bond is due. The numbers are separated by the letter S which stands for "series." For example, a bond with the number 12.6S2017 has an interest rate of 12.6% and is due December 31, 2017.

As a general rule, bond issues are used to fund long-term investments in capacity and automation.

Bondholders will lend total amounts up to 80% of the value of last year's fixed assets. Each bond issue pays a coupon, the annual interest payment, to investors. If the face amount or principal of bond 12.6S2017 were $1,000,000, then the holder of the bond would receive a payment of $126,000 every year for 10 years. The holder would also receive the $1,000,000 principal at the end of the 10th year.

When issuing new bonds, the interest rate will be 1.4% over the current debt interest rates. If your current debt interest rate is 12.1%, then the bond rate will be 13.5%.

You can buy back outstanding bonds before their due date. A 1.5% brokerage fee applies. These bonds are repurchased at their market value or street price on January 1 of the current year. The street price is determined by the amount of interest the bond pays and your creditworthiness. It is therefore different from the face amount of the bond. If you buy back bonds with a street price that is less than the face amount, you make a gain on the repurchase. This will be reflected as a negative write-off on the income statement.

Bonds are retired in the order they were issued. The oldest bonds retire first. There are no brokerage fees for bonds that are allowed to mature to their due date.

If a bond remains on December 31 of the year it becomes due, your banker lends you current debt to pay off the bond principal. This, in effect, converts the bond to current debt. This amount is combined with any other current debt due at the beginning of the next year.

What happens when a bond comes due? Assume the face amount of bond 12.6S2017 is $1,000,000. The $1,000,000 repayment is acknowledged in your reports and spreadsheets in the following manner: Your annual reports from December 31, 2017 would reflect an increase in current debt of $1,000,000 offset by a decrease in long-term debt of $1,000,000. The 2017 spreadsheet will list the bond because you are making decisions on January 1, 2017, when the bond still exists. Your 2018 spreadsheet would show a $1,000,000 increase in current debt and the bond no longer appears.

What determines my company's credit rating? Each year your company is given a credit rating ranging from AAA (best) to D (worst). In Foundation, ratings are evaluated by comparing current debt interest rates with the prime rate. If your company has no debt at all, your company is awarded an AAA bond rating. As your debt-to-assets ratio increases, your current debt interest rates increase. Your bond rating slips one category for each additional 0.5% in current debt interest. For example, if the prime rate is 10% and your current debt interest rate is 10.5%, then you would be given an AA bond rating instead of an AAA rating.

Emergency Loans (Big Al)

What if my company needs to take an emergency loan? Financial transactions are carried on throughout the year directly from your cash account. If you manage your cash position poorly and run out of cash, the simulation will give you an emergency loan to cover the shortfall from Big Al the loan shark. You pay one year's worth of current debt interest on the loan and Big Al adds a 7.5% penalty fee on top.

For example, if the current debt interest rate is 10% and you are short $10,000,000 on December 31, You pay one year's worth of interest on the $10,000,000 ($1,000,000) plus an additional 7.5% or $750,000 penalty.

Emergency loans are combined with any current debt from last year. The total amount displays in the Due This Year cell under Current Debt.

You do not need to do anything special to repay an emergency loan. However, you need to decide what to do with the current debt (pay it off, re-finance it, etc.). The interest penalty only applies to the year in which the emergency loan is taken, not to future years.

Appendix 2:
The Foundation FastTrack Report

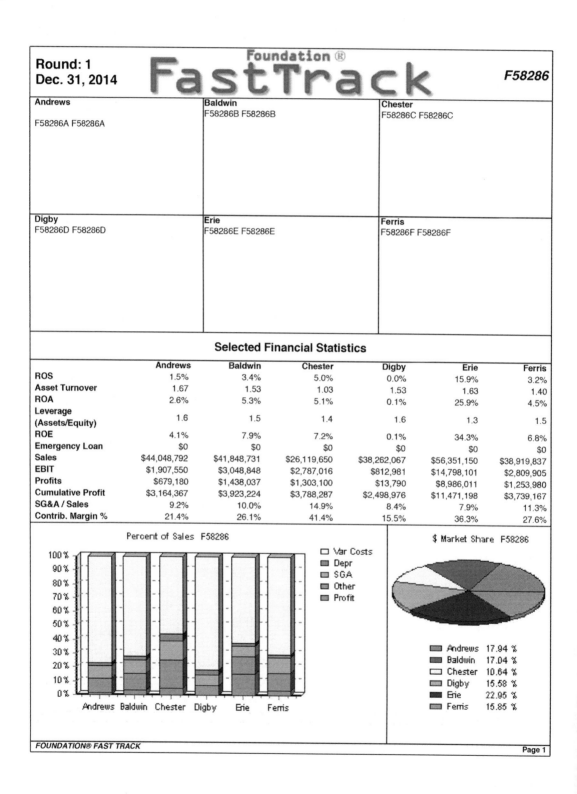

Stock & Bonds

FastTrack

F58286

Round: 1
Dec. 31, 2014

Stock Market Summary

Company	Close	Change	Shares	MarketCap ($M)	Book Value	EPS	Dividend	Yield	P/E
Andrews	$11.17	$0.02	2,269,049	$25	$7.28	$0.30	$0.00	0.0%	37.2
Baldwin	$12.57	$1.42	2,358,732	$30	$7.75	$0.61	$0.00	0.0%	20.6
Chester	$12.34	$1.19	2,358,732	$29	$7.69	$0.55	$0.00	0.0%	22.3
Digby	$9.99	($1.16)	2,269,049	$23	$6.99	$0.01	$0.00	0.0%	1411.9
Erie	$25.20	$14.05	2,394,606	$60	$10.95	$3.75	$0.00	0.0%	6.7
Ferris	$12.28	$1.13	2,394,606	$29	$7.73	$0.52	$0.00	0.0%	23.4

Closing Stock Price F58286

Legend: Andrews, Baldwin, Chester, Digby, Erie, Ferris

Bond Market Summary

Company	Series#	Face	Yield	Close$	S&P	Company	Series#	Face	Yield	Close$	S&P
Andrews						Digby					
	11.0S2015	$866,667	10.9%	101.00	A		11.0S2015	$866,667	10.9%	101.09	A
	12.0S2017	$1,733,333	11.4%	105.23	A		12.0S2017	$1,733,333	11.4%	105.49	A
	13.0S2019	$2,600,000	11.6%	111.78	A		13.0S2019	$2,600,000	11.6%	112.19	A
	10.0S2024	$2,000,000	9.9%	100.62	A		10.0S2024	$1,500,000	9.9%	101.24	A
Baldwin						Erie					
	11.0S2015	$866,667	10.9%	101.37	A		11.0S2015	$866,667	10.8%	102.02	AAA
	12.0S2017	$1,733,333	11.3%	106.27	A		12.0S2017	$1,733,333	11.1%	108.13	AAA
	13.0S2019	$2,600,000	11.5%	113.44	A		13.0S2019	$2,600,000	11.2%	116.42	AAA
	10.0S2024	$1,500,000	9.7%	103.14	A		10.0S2024	$500,000	9.3%	107.77	AAA
Chester						Ferris					
	11.0S2015	$866,667	10.8%	101.74	AA		11.0S2015	$866,667	10.9%	101.37	A
	12.0S2017	$1,733,333	11.2%	107.33	AA		12.0S2017	$1,733,333	11.3%	106.27	A
	13.0S2019	$2,600,000	11.3%	115.13	AA		13.0S2019	$2,600,000	11.5%	113.44	A
	10.0S2024	$1,000,000	9.5%	105.75	AA		10.0S2024	$2,000,000	9.7%	103.14	A

Next Year's Prime Rate 7.00%

Financial Summary

FastTrack   F58286   **Round: 1**
Dec. 31, 2014

Cash Flow Statement Survey	Andrews	Baldwin	Chester	Digby	Erie	Ferris
CashFlows from operating activities						
Net Income(Loss)	$679	$1,438	$1,303	$14	$8,986	$1,254
Adjustment for non-cash items:						
Depreciation	$960	$1,173	$1,387	$1,200	$960	$960
Extraordinary gains/losses/writeoffs	$0	$0	$0	$0	$0	$0
Changes in current assets and liablilities						
Acounts payable	($202)	($507)	($1,791)	($391)	($99)	($731)
Inventory	$2,353	$2,353	$2,353	$2,353	$2,353	$2,353
Accounts Receivable	($267)	($86)	$1,207	$209	($1,278)	$155
Net cash from operations	$3,524	$4,371	$4,459	$3,384	$10,922	$3,990
Cash flows from investing activities						
Plant improvements(net)	$0	($3,200)	($6,400)	($3,600)	$0	($6,300)
Cash flows from financing activities						
Dividends paid	$0	$0	$0	$0	$0	$0
Sales of common stock	$3,000	$4,000	$4,000	$3,000	$4,400	$4,400
Purchase of common stock	$0	$0	$0	$0	$0	$0
Cash from long term debt issued	$2,000	$1,500	$1,000	$1,500	$500	$2,000
Early retirement of long term debt	$0	$0	$0	$0	$0	$0
Retirement of current debt	$0	$0	$0	$0	$0	$0
Cash from current debt borrowing	$0	$0	$0	$0	$0	$0
Cash from emergency loan	$0	$0	$0	$0	$0	$0
Net cash from financing activities	$5,000	$5,500	$5,000	$4,500	$4,900	$6,400
Net change in cash position	$8,524	$6,671	$3,059	$4,284	$15,822	$4,090
Balance Sheet Survey	**Andrews**	**Baldwin**	**Chester**	**Digby**	**Erie**	**Ferris**
Cash	$14,117	$12,265	$8,652	$9,877	$21,415	$9,683
Accounts Receivable	$3,620	$3,440	$2,147	$3,145	$4,632	$3,199
Inventory	$0	$0	$0	$0	$0	$0
Total Current Assets	$17,737	$15,704	$10,799	$13,022	$26,046	$12,882
Plant and equipment	$14,400	$17,600	$20,800	$18,000	$14,400	$20,700
Accumulated Depreciation	($5,760)	($5,973)	($6,187)	($6,000)	($5,760)	($5,760)
Total Fixed Assets	$8,640	$11,627	$14,613	$12,000	$8,640	$14,940
Total Assets	$26,377	$27,331	$25,412	$25,022	$34,686	$27,822
Account Payable	$2,653	$2,348	$1,064	$2,463	$2,755	$2,123
CurrentDebt	$0	$0	$0	$0	$0	$0
Long Term Debt	$7,200	$6,700	$6,200	$6,700	$5,700	$7,200
Total Liabilities	$9,853	$9,048	$7,264	$9,163	$8,455	$9,323
Common Stock	$5,323	$6,323	$6,323	$5,323	$6,723	$6,723
Retained Earnings	$11,201	$11,960	$11,825	$10,536	$19,508	$11,776
Total Equity	$16,524	$18,283	$18,148	$15,859	$26,231	$18,499
Total Liabilities & Owners" Equity	$26,377	$27,331	$25,412	$25,022	$34,686	$27,822
Income Statement Survey	**Andrews**	**Baldwin**	**Chester**	**Digby**	**Erie**	**Ferris**
Sales	$44,049	$41,849	$26,120	$38,262	$56,351	$38,920
Variable Costs(Labor,Material,Carry)	$34,630	$30,916	$15,297	$32,322	$35,876	$28,186
Depreciation	$960	$1,173	$1,387	$1,200	$960	$960
SGA(R&D,Promo,Sales,Admin)	$4,051	$4,186	$3,899	$3,202	$4,472	$4,394
Other(Fees,Writeoffs,TQM,Bonuses)	$2,500	$2,525	$2,750	$725	$245	$2,570
EBIT	$1,908	$3,049	$2,787	$813	$14,798	$2,810
Interest(Short term,Long term)	$841	$791	$741	$791	$691	$841
Taxes	$373	$790	$716	$8	$4,937	$689
Profit Sharing	$14	$29	$27	$0	$183	$26
Net Profit	$679	$1,438	$1,303	$14	$8,986	$1,254

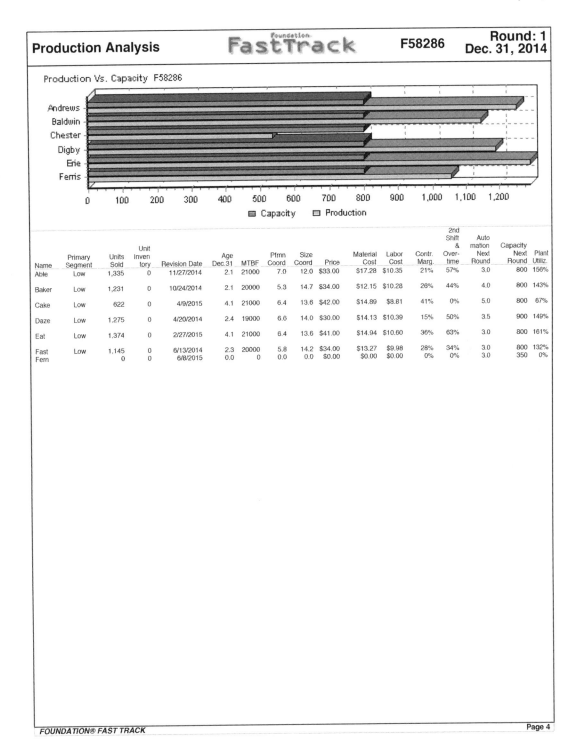

Name	Primary Segment	Units Sold	Unit Inventory	Revision Date	Age Dec.31	MTBF	Pfmn Coord	Size Coord	Price	Material Cost	Labor Cost	Contr. Marg.	2nd Shift & Over-time	Auto mation Next Round	Capacity Next Round	Plant Utiliz.
Able	Low	1,335	0	11/27/2014	2.1	21000	7.0	12.0	$33.00	$17.28	$10.35	21%	57%	3.0	800	156%
Baker	Low	1,231	0	10/24/2014	2.1	20000	5.3	14.7	$34.00	$12.15	$10.28	26%	44%	4.0	800	143%
Cake	Low	622	0	4/9/2015	4.1	21000	6.4	13.6	$42.00	$14.89	$8.81	41%	0%	5.0	800	67%
Daze	Low	1,275	0	4/20/2014	2.4	19000	6.6	14.0	$30.00	$14.13	$10.39	15%	50%	3.5	900	149%
Eat	Low	1,374	0	2/27/2015	4.1	21000	6.4	13.6	$41.00	$14.94	$10.60	36%	63%	3.0	800	161%
Fast	Low	1,145	0	6/13/2014	2.3	20000	5.8	14.2	$34.00	$13.27	$9.98	28%	34%	3.0	800	132%
Fern		0	0	6/8/2015	0.0	0	0.0	0.0	$0.00	$0.00	$0.00	0%	0%	3.0	350	0%

Low Tech Segment Analysis

F58286

Low Tech Statistics

Total Industry Unit Demand	5,544
Actual Industry Unit Sales	4,722
Segment % of Total Industry	68.1%
Next Year's Segment Growth Rate	10.0%

Low Tech Customer Buying Criteria

	Expectations	Importance
1. Price	$15.00 - 35.00	41%
2. Age	Ideal Age = 3.0	29%
3. Reliability	MTBF 14000-20000	21%
4. Ideal Position	Pfmn 5.3 Size 14.7	9%

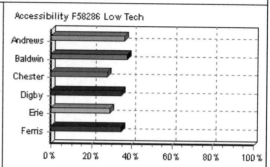

Accessibility F58286 Low Tech

Perceptual Map for Low Tech

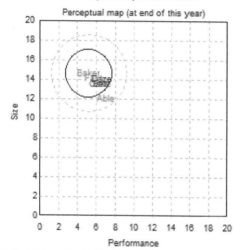

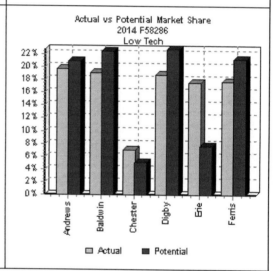

Actual vs Potential Market Share
2014 F58286
Low Tech

Top Products in Low Tech Segment

Name	Market Share	Units Sold to Seg	Revision Date	Stock Out	Pfmn Coord	Size Coord	List Price	MTBF	Age Dec.31	Promo Budget	Cust. Aware-ness	Sales Budget	Cust. Access-ibility	Dec. Cust. Survey
Able	20%	932	11/27/2014	YES	7.0	12.0	$33.00	21000	2.09	$1,100	61%	$1,100	36%	9
Baker	19%	904	10/24/2014	YES	5.3	14.7	$34.00	20000	2.14	$1,200	65%	$1,200	37%	21
Daze	19%	886	4/20/2014	YES	6.6	14.0	$30.00	19000	2.40	$1,000	58%	$1,000	35%	20
Fast	18%	837	6/13/2014	YES	5.8	14.2	$34.00	20000	2.32	$1,000	58%	$1,000	35%	19
Eat	18%	829	2/27/2015	YES	6.4	13.6	$41.00	21000	4.10	$1,300	67%	$1,300	29%	6
Cake	7%	334	4/9/2015	YES	6.4	13.6	$42.00	21000	4.10	$900	55%	$900	28%	4

High Tech Segment Analysis

FastTrack (Foundation)

F58286

Round: 1
Dec. 31, 2014

High Tech Statistics

Total Industry Unit Demand	2,592
Actual Industry Unit Sales	2,260
Segment % of Total Industry	31.9%
Next Year's Segment Growth Rate	20.0%

High Tech Customer Buying Criteria

	Expectations	Importance
1. Ideal Position	Pfmn 8.1 Size 11.9	33%
2. Age	Ideal Age = 0.0	29%
3. Price	$25.00 - 45.00	25%
4. Reliability	MTBF 17000-23000	13%

Accessibility F58286 High Tech

Perceptual Map for High Tech

Perceptual map (at end of this year)

Actual vs Potential Market Share
2014 F58286
High Tech

Top Products in High Tech Segment

Name	Market Share	Units Sold to Seg	Revision Date	Stock Out	Pfmn Coord	Size Coord	List Price	MTBF	Age Dec.31	Promo Budget	Cust. Aware-ness	Sales Budget	Cust. Access-ibility	Dec. Cust. Survey
Eat	24%	545	2/27/2015	YES	6.4	13.6	$41.00	21000	4.10	$1,300	67%	$1,300	40%	7
Able	18%	403	11/27/2014	YES	7.0	12.0	$33.00	21000	2.09	$1,100	61%	$1,100	37%	23
Daze	17%	389	4/20/2014	YES	6.6	14.0	$30.00	19000	2.40	$1,000	58%	$1,000	35%	12
Baker	14%	327	10/24/2014	YES	5.3	14.7	$34.00	20000	2.14	$1,200	65%	$1,200	38%	9
Fast	14%	308	6/13/2014	YES	5.8	14.2	$34.00	20000	2.32	$1,000	58%	$1,000	35%	9
Cake	13%	288	4/9/2015	YES	6.4	13.6	$42.00	21000	4.10	$900	55%	$900	34%	5

Market Share

FastTrack

F58286

Round: 1
Dec. 31, 2014

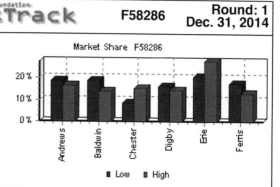

Units Sold vs Demand Chart F58286

- Industry Unit Sales
- Total Unit Demand

Market Share F58286

- Low
- High

Actual Market Share in Units

	Low	High	Total
Industry Unit Sales	4,722	2,260	6,982
% of Market	67.6%	32.4%	100.0%
Able	19.7%	17.8%	19.1%
Total	19.7%	17.8%	19.1%
Baker	19.2%	14.4%	17.6%
Total	19.2%	14.4%	17.6%
Cake	7.1%	12.8%	8.9%
Total	7.1%	12.8%	8.9%
Daze	18.8%	17.2%	18.3%
Total	18.8%	17.2%	18.3%
Eat	17.6%	24.1%	19.7%
Total	17.6%	24.1%	19.7%
Fast	17.7%	13.6%	16.4%
Total	17.7%	13.6%	16.4%

Potential Market Share in Units

	Low	High	Total
Units Demanded	5,544	2,592	8,136
% of Market	68.1%	31.9%	100.0%
Able	21.0%	19.9%	20.6%
Total	20.9%	19.9%	20.6%
Baker	22.4%	17.6%	20.9%
Total	22.4%	17.6%	20.9%
Cake	5.1%	10.6%	6.8%
Total	5.1%	10.6%	6.8%
Daze	22.8%	22.2%	22.6%
Total	22.8%	22.2%	22.6%
Eat	7.6%	12.8%	9.3%
Total	7.6%	12.8%	9.3%
Fast	21.2%	17.0%	19.8%
Total	21.2%	17.0%	19.8%

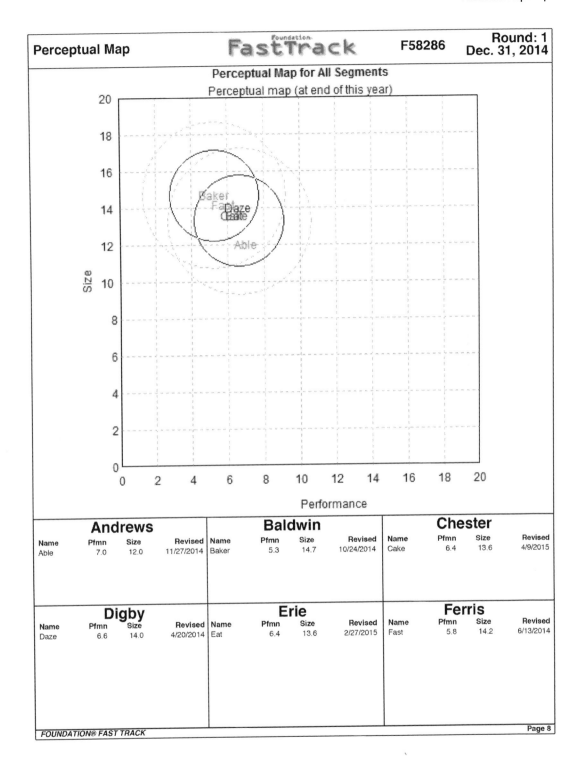

FastTrack

F58286

Round: 1
Dec. 31, 2014

Perceptual Map for All Segments
Perceptual map (at end of this year)

Andrews

Name	Pfmn	Size	Revised
Able	7.0	12.0	11/27/2014

Baldwin

Name	Pfmn	Size	Revised
Baker	5.3	14.7	10/24/2014

Chester

Name	Pfmn	Size	Revised
Cake	6.4	13.6	4/9/2015

Digby

Name	Pfmn	Size	Revised
Daze	6.6	14.0	4/20/2014

Erie

Name	Pfmn	Size	Revised
Eat	6.4	13.6	2/27/2015

Ferris

Name	Pfmn	Size	Revised
Fast	5.8	14.2	6/13/2014

HR/TQM Report	FastTrack	F58286	Round: 1 Dec. 31, 2014

HUMAN RESOURCES SUMMARY

	Andrews	Baldwin	Chester	Digby	Erie	Ferris
Needed Complement	243	226	102	234	250	207
Complement	243	226	102	234	250	207
1st Shift Complement	154	157	102	156	154	155
2nd Shift Complement	89	69	0	78	96	52
Overtime Percent	0.0%	0.2%	0.0%	0.1%	0.0%	0.0%
Turnover Rate	8.5%	8.5%	10.0%	8.9%	10.0%	8.9%
New Employees	21	19	10	21	27	18
Separated Employees	5	22	146	14	0	41
Recruiting Spend	$3,000	$4,000	$0	$4,500	$0	$1,000
Training Hours	40	40	0	30	0	30
Productivity Index	100.0%	100.0%	100.0%	100.0%	100.0%	100.0%
Recruiting Cost	$83	$96	$10	$114	$27	$37
Separation Cost	$25	$110	$730	$70	$0	$205
Training Cost	$194	$181	$0	$140	$0	$124
Total HR Admin Cost	$302	$387	$740	$325	$27	$366
Strike Days						

TQM SUMMARY

	Andrews	Baldwin	Chester	Digby	Erie	Ferris
Process Mgt Budgets Last Year						
CPI Systems	$750	$750	$500	$500	$0	$500
Vendor/JIT	$750	$0	$0	$0	$0	$500
Quality Initiative Training	$750	$0	$500	$0	$0	$500
Channel Support Systems	$0	$0	$0	$0	$0	$750
Concurrent Engineering	$0	$500	$500	$0	$0	$0
UNEP Green Programs	$0	$500	$0	$0	$0	$0
TQM Budgets Last Year						
Benchmarking	$0	$500	$500	$0	$0	$0
Quality Function Deployment Effort	$0	$0	$0	$0	$0	$0
CCE/6 Sigma Training	$0	$0	$500	$0	$0	$0
GEMI TQEM Sustainability Initiatives	$0	$0	$0	$0	$0	$0
Total Expenditures	$2,250	$2,250	$2,500	$500	$0	$2,250
Cumulative Impacts						
Material Cost Reduction	0.83%	0.40%	0.28%	0.07%	0.00%	0.28%
Labor Cost Reduction	1.84%	0.05%	1.79%	0.02%	0.00%	0.64%
Reduction R&D Cycle Time	0.00%	5.12%	5.12%	0.00%	0.00%	0.00%
Reduction Admin Costs	4.66%	8.44%	8.44%	0.00%	0.00%	1.59%
Demand Increase	0.00%	0.15%	0.00%	0.00%	0.00%	1.06%

Ethics Report		F58286	Round: 1 Dec. 31, 2014

ETHICS SUMMARY

Other (Fees, Writeoffs, etc.)	The actual dollar impact. Example, $120 means Other increased by $120.
Demand Factor	The % of normal. 98% means demand fell 2%.
Material Cost Impact	The % of normal. 104% means matieral costs rose 4%.
Admin Cost Impact	The % of normal. 103% means admin costs rose 3%.
Productivity Impact	The % of normal. 104% means productivity increased by 4%.
Awareness Impact	The % of normal. 105% means normal awareness was multiplied by 1.05.
Accessibility Impact	The % of normal. 98% means normal accessiblity was multiplied by 0.98.
	Normal means the value that would have been produced if the problem had not been presented.

	No Impact	Andrews	Baldwin	Chester	Digby	Erie	Ferris
Total							
Other (Fees, Writeoffs, etc.)	$0	$0	$0	$0	$0	$0	$0
Demand Factor	100%	100%	100%	100%	100%	100%	100%
Material Cost Impact	100%	100%	100%	100%	100%	100%	100%
Admin Cost Impact	100%	100%	100%	100%	100%	100%	100%
Productivity Impact	100%	100%	100%	100%	100%	100%	100%
Awareness Impact	100%	100%	100%	100%	100%	100%	100%
Accessibility Impact	100%	100%	100%	100%	100%	100%	100%

Annual Report

Annual Report	Andrews	F58286	Round: 1 Dec. 31, 2014

Balance Sheet

DEFINITIONS:
Common Size: The common size column simply represents each item as a percentage of total assets for that year. **Cash:** Your end-of-year cash position. **Accounts Receivable:** Reflects the lag between delivery and payment of your products. **Inventories:** The current value of your inventory across all products. A zero indicates your company stocked out. Unmet demand would, of course, fall to your competitors. **Plant & Equipment:** The current value of your plant. **Accum Deprec:** The total accumulated depreciation from your plant. **Accts Payable:** What the company currently owes suppliers for materials and services. **Current Debt:** The debt the company is obligated to pay during the next year of operations. It includes emergency loans used to keep your company solvent should you run out of cash during the year. **Long Term Debt:** The company's long term debt is in the form of bonds, and this represents the total value of your bonds. **Common Stock:** The amount of capital invested by shareholders in the company. **Retained Earnings:** The profits that the company chose to keep instead of paying to shareholders as dividends.

ASSETS		2014	2014 Common Size	2013
Cash	$14,117		53.5%	$5,593
Account Receivable	$3,620		13.7%	$3,353
Inventory	$0		0.0%	$2,353
Total Current Assets		$17,737	67.2%	$11,299
Plant & Equipment	$14,400		54.6%	$14,400
Accumulated Depreciation	($5,760)		-21.8%	($4,800)
Total Fixed Assets		$8,640	32.8%	$9,600
Total Assets		$26,377	100.0%	$20,900
LIABILITIES & OWNER'S EQUITY				
Accounts Payable	$2,653		10.1%	$2,855
Current Debt	$0		0.0%	$0
Long Term Debt	$7,200		27.3%	$5,200
Total Liabilities		$9,853	37.4%	$8,055
Common Stock	$5,323		20.2%	$2,323
Retained Earnings	$11,201		42.5%	$10,522
Total Equity		$16,524	62.6%	$12,845
Total Liab. & O. Equity		$26,377	100.0%	$20,900

Cash Flow Statement

The **Cash Flow Statement** examines what happened in the Cash Account during the year. Cash injections appear as positive numbers and cash withdrawals as negative numbers. The Cash Flow Statement is an excellent tool for diagnosing emergency loans. When negative cash flows exceed positives, you are forced to seek emergency funding. For example, if sales are bad and you find yourself carrying an abundance of excess inventory, the report would show the increase in inventory as a huge negative cash flow. Too much unexpected inventory could outstrip your inflows, exhaust your starting cash and force you to beg for money to keep your company afloat.

Cash Flows from Operating Activities	2014	2013
NetIncome(Loss)	$679	$2,485
Depreciation	$960	$960
Extraordinary gains/losses/writeoffs	$0	$0
Accounts Payable	($202)	$855
Inventory	$2,353	($2,353)
Accounts Receivable	($267)	$3,647
Net cash from operation	$3,524	$5,593
Cash Flows from Investing Activities		
Plant Improvements	$0	$0
Cash Flows from Financing Activities		
Dividends Paid	$0	($1,000)
Sales of Common Stock	$3,000	$0
Purchase of Common Stock	$0	$0
Cash from long term debt	$2,000	$0
Retirement of long term debt	$0	$0
Change in current debt(net)	$0	$0
Net Cash from financing activities	$5,000	($1,000)
Net Change in cash position	$8,524	$4,593
Closing cash position	$14,117	$5,593

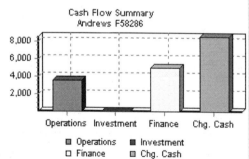

Cash Flow Summary
Andrews F58286

- ☐ Operations
- ☐ Investment
- ☐ Finance
- ☐ Chg. Cash

Annual Report		Andrews				F58286		Round: 1 Dec. 31, 2014

2014 Income Statement

(Product Name)	Able	NA	NA	NA	NA	NA	NA	NA	2014 Total	Common Size
Sales	$44,049	$0	$0	$0	$0	$0	$0	$0	$44,049	100.0%
Variable Costs:										
Direct Labor	$13,796	$0	$0	$0	$0	$0	$0	$0	$13,796	31.3%
Direct Material	$20,834	$0	$0	$0	$0	$0	$0	$0	$20,834	47.3%
Inventory Carry	$0	$0	$0	$0	$0	$0	$0	$0	$0	0.0%
Total Variable	$34,630	$0	$0	$0	$0	$0	$0	$0	$34,630	78.6%
Contribution Margin	$9,419	$0	$0	$0	$0	$0	$0	$0	$9,419	21.4%
Period Costs:										
Depreciation	$960	$0	$0	$0	$0	$0	$0	$0	$960	2.2%
SG&A: R&D	$919	$0	$0	$0	$0	$0	$0	$0	$919	2.1%
Promotions	$1,100	$0	$0	$0	$0	$0	$0	$0	$1,100	2.5%
Sales	$1,100	$0	$0	$0	$0	$0	$0	$0	$1,100	2.5%
Admin	$932	$0	$0	$0	$0	$0	$0	$0	$932	2.1%
Total Period	$5,011	$0	$0	$0	$0	$0	$0	$0	$5,011	11.4%
Net Margin	$4,408	$0	$0	$0	$0	$0	$0	$0	$4,408	10.0%

Other	$2,500	5.7%
EBIT	$1,908	4.3%
Short Term Interest	$0	0.0%
Long Term Interest	$841	1.9%
Taxes	$373	0.8%
Profit Sharing	$14	0.0%
Net Profit	$679	1.5%

Definitions: Sales: Unit Sales times list price. **Direct Labor:** Labor costs incurred to produce the product that was sold. **Inventory Carry Cost:** the cost unsold goods in inventory. **Depreciation:** Calculated on straight-line. 15-year depreciation of plant value. **R&D Costs:** R&D department expenditures for each product. **Admin:** Administration overhead is estimated at 1.5% of sales. **Promotions:** The promotion budget for each product. **Sales:** The sales force budget for each product. **Other:** Chargs not included in other categories such as Fees, Write offs, and TQM. The fees include money paid to investment bankers and brokerage firms to issue new stocks or bonds plus consulting fees your instructor might assess. Write-offs include the loss you might experience when you sell capacity or liquidate inventory as the result of eliminating a production line. If the amount appears as a negative amount, then you actually made money on the liquidation of capacity or inventory. **EBIT:** Earnings Before Interest and Taxes. **Short Term Interest:** Interest expense based on last year's current debt, including short term debt, long term notes that have become due, and emergency loans. **Long Term Interest:** Interest paid on outstanding bonds. **Taxes:** Income tax based upon a 35% tax rate. **Profit Sharing:** Profits shared with employees under the labor contract. **Net Profit:** EBIT minus interest, taxes, and profit sharing.

Variable Margins
2014 Andrews F58286

Profit History F58286

Market Share History F58286

ROE History F58286

Asset Turnover History F58286

ROS History F58286

ROA History F58286

Appendix 3
Estimating the Customer Survey Score

It is important to have a model of how the customers of a market segment make their purchase decisions. You already have some critical data: you know what product characteristics attract your customers and how important each characteristic is relative to the others. (Customer Buying Criteria are reported in the FastTrack Market Segment Analysis pages 5 and 6.) If you can systematically evaluate your product offering against customer expectations, you can assess how "desirable" your product is to customers in that segment. If you use the same system to evaluate all of your competitors' products, you should be able to predict sales for all competing products in the market. That's powerful information!

Let's start with a simple scenario and analyze a product that is not being revised during the year. Let's estimate January's Customer Survey Score (CSS) for your product Able. If your understanding is correct, it should be very close to December's CSS which you will find in the FastTrack Report on page 4, the "Production" page.

Attractiveness Score

Market research has determined an attractiveness score for each product attribute for both the Low Tech and High Tech segments. You will never have to "create" an attractiveness score. The attractiveness score will be provided to you based on this research. The attractiveness score multiplied by its importance to customers results in the CSS points for each category. The summation of these attributes equates to the Total CSS score. The following exercise illustrates this concept.

Estimating January's Customer Survey Score

To estimate a Customer Survey Score, set up a table (for each market segment) that has the product characteristics (MTBF, price etc), the importance to the CSS (percentage of the decision), the product's score (an evaluation of how close the current product offering is to the "ideal"), and the CSS points. See Table 1. Multiply the "importance" by the "attractiveness score" to give a weighted value for each. The Customer Service Score Calculations table allows you to calculate the CSS Points for the four product criteria.

Table 1 - Customer Survey Score Calculations

Market Segment	MTBF	Price	Age	Position	Total	
Importance	%	%	%	%	100%	*Customer buying criteria*
Attractiveness Score						*Tables and Graphs below*
CSS Points						*Multiply Importance x Score*

Figure 1 - From FastTrack Report - Low Tech page 5

Top Products in Low Tech Segment													
Name	Market Share	Units Sold to Seg	Revision Date	Stock Out	Pfmn Coord	Size Coord	List Price	MTBF	Age Dec.31	Promo Budget	Cust Aware-ness	Sales Budget	Cust Access-ibility	Dec. Cust. Survey
Able	20%	932	11/27/2014	YES	7.0	12.0	$33.00	21000	2.09	$1,100	61%	$1,100	36%	9
Baker	19%	904	10/24/2014	YES	5.3	14.7	$34.00	20000	2.14	$1,200	65%	$1,200	37%	21
Cake	19%	866	4/20/2014	YES	6.6	14.0	$30.00	19000	2.40	$1,000	58%	$1,000	35%	20
Daze	18%	837	6/13/2014	YES	5.8	14.2	$34.00	20000	2.32	$1,000	58%	$1,000	35%	19
Eat	18%	829	2/27/2015	YES	6.4	13.6	$41.00	21000	4.10	$1,300	67%	$1,300	29%	6
Fast	7%	334	4/9/2015	YES	6.4	13.6	$42.00	21000	4.10	$900	55%	$900	26%	4

Table 2 - MTBF Attractiveness Scores

Low Tech	14,000	15,000	16,000	17,000	18,000	19,000	20,000
High Tech	17,000	18,000	19,000	20,000	21,000	22,000	23,000
Attractiveness Score	1	17	33	50	67	83	100

To evaluate your product, you have to know its current attributes. Using page 5 and 6 from the FastTrack Report at Appendix 2, you can identify the attributes of your current product, Able, and evaluate them using the tables and graphs in this section.

Estimating Mean Time Before Failure Attractiveness

You know that your customers prefer a higher mean time before failure (MTBF). Full points (100) are awarded to the highest number in the range, and minimum points (1) to the lowest acceptable MTBF for each segment, shown in Table 2 - MTBF Attractiveness Scores.

MTBF Contribution to CSS: Able has a MTBF of 21,000 hours

- For the Low Tech market, that is above the range so it would have a score of 100 points. From the buying criteria, MTBF makes up 21% of the decision. So for the Low Tech market, a MTBF of

21,000 hours contributes 100 x 21% or 21 points to the January CSS.

- For the High Tech market, 21,000 hours has a score of 67 points. From the buying criteria, MTBF makes up 13% of the decision. So for the High Tech market, a MTBF of 21,000 hours contributes 67 x 13% or 8.7 points to the January CSS.

Estimating Price Attractiveness

Your customers prefer a lower price, so you award full points (100) to the lowest price in the range, and minimum points (1) to the highest acceptable price for each segment. See Table 3. Pricing follows a classic demand curve. *Figure 3.1.2. Pricing Score* in the Online Guide demonstrates a demand curve. The scores need to be adjusted to approximate the curve. The result is displayed in Table 3 - Price Attractiveness.

Table 3 - Price Attractiveness

Low Tech	$15	$20	$25	$30	$35
High Tech	$25	$30	$35	$40	$45
Attractiveness Score	100	70	40	20	1

Price Contribution to CSS: Able is currently being offered at a price of $33.00

- For the Low Tech market, a price of $33 would probably contribute an estimated 9 points; and price is 41% of the decision. Price contributes 3.7 points (9 x 41%) to Low Tech's January CSS.

- For the High Tech market, a price of $33 would probably contribute an estimated 52 points; and price is 25% of the decision. Price contributes 13 points (52 x 25%) to High Tech's January CSS score.

Estimating Age Attractiveness

Unlike reliability or price, the age of your product changes every month. If Able starts the year at 2.1 years old it will be 3.1 years old next December. The calculation is demonstrated in Table 4.

The Customer Survey Score is visually estimated in Figure 2.

Age Contribution to CSS: In January, Able's age is 2.2 years

- In Low Tech, an age of 2.2 would contribute 91 CSS points. Age is important to Low Tech customers contributing 29% to the CSS. So, in January, Able's age contributes 26.4 CSS points (91 x 29%) to the total Customer Survey Score.
  Note: By December, Able's age will be contributing 27.8 points (96 x 23.5%).

- In High Tech, an age of 2.2 would contribute 41 points. Age is important to High Tech customers contributing 29% to the CSS. In January, Able's attractive age contributes 11.9 CSS points (41 x 29%) to the total Customer Survey Score.
  Note: By December, Able's age will only be contributing 7 points (24 x 29%).

Estimating Position Attractiveness

The ideal position is literally a moving target – customers' expectations are changing from month to month. Also, because expectations for size and performance are interrelated, the *distance* between your product's position and customers' expectations (both for what is acceptable and for what is "ideal") is actually the hypotenuse of the triangle formed by the difference between your products position and the expected position, and difference between your product's size and the expected size. While this is important to understand, it may be too complicated to build into your decision making at this time.

Positioning Scores

Position Contribution to January's CSS: Able has a performance of 7.0, and size of 12.0.

- The Low Tech ideal starts the year at 4.8 and 15.2. Able's current performance is about 2.2 units faster than the ideal and its size is about 3.2 units smaller than the ideal for the Low Tech. It is on the edge of what is acceptable to the Low

Table 4 - Documenting Age

	Jan	Feb	Mar	April	May	June	July	Aug	Sept	Oct	Nov	Dec
Age	2.2	2.3	2.3*	2.4	2.5	2.6	2.7	2.8	2.9*	2.9	3.0	3.1

Note: The application of a 10-point scale into 12 months means that the age does not significantly change in two of the 12 months, from February to March and from August to September.

Figure 2 - Low Tech and High Tech Age CSS

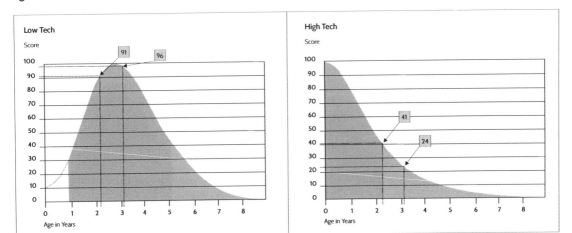

Tech customers. You estimate a CSS position score of 8 points. Position is not important to Low tech customers accounting for 9% of the CSS. So January's position contributes .72 points (8 X 9%).
***Note:** Able's Low Tech position will improve over the course of the year as the ideal spot migrates towards Able's position of 6.4 and 13.6.*

- The High Tech "ideal" position starts the year at 7.4 and 12.6. Able is 0.1 unit larger and 1.1 unit slower than the ideal point. The visual above suggests only a moderate concentration of customers in this position. You estimate a CSS position score of 35. Position is very important to High tech customers accounting for 33% of the CSS. January's position contributes 11.6 points (35 X 33%).
***Note:** In High Tech, the ideal is moving away from Able's position.*

These scores for Able are recorded in Table 5 - Able's January Customer Survey Score.

Customer Survey Score Adjustments

The "base score" calculated in Table 5 has to be adjusted. For example, investments in awareness and accessibility also influence the total CSS score.

Assessing Awareness and Accessibility: Awareness (how many people know about you product) and accessibility (how easily customers can get their hands on your product) reduce the score based on this formula:

(1 + Awareness Rating) / 2 = Awareness CSS Impact

(1 + Accessibility Rating) / 2 = Accessibility CSS Impact

For example:

If you have 61% awareness, that means 61% of your potential customers received your promotional materials and know about your product. The corollary is that 39% of customers are not aware of you. However, all customers engage in some research of their own. Of the 39% who did not receive your promotional materials, half (or 19.5%) discover your product through their own search. At decision time, 61% got your message and 19.5% discovered you through their own

Table 5 - Able's January Customer Survey Score

Low Tech	MTBF	Price	Age	Position	Total
Importance	21%	41%	29%	9%	100%
Able's Attractiveness Score	100	9	91	8	
CSS points	21	3.7	26.4	0.7	51.8†

High Tech	MTBF	Price	Age	Position	Total
Importance	13%	25%	29%	33%	100%
Able's Attractiveness Score	67	52	41	35	
CSS points	8.7	13.0	11.9	11.6	45.2

*Able's position (performance and size) takes it outside the "fine cut" for low tech, therefore the CSS raw score has to be adjusted. As Able is only in the "rough cut" for positioning, its score is reduced by a further 50%: 51.8 x 50% = 25.9.
† 51.8 (25.9 after 50% reduction)

search process. Adding these figures together indicates that 80.5% of the customers know about your product.

$$(1+.61) / 2 = 80.5\%$$

*Note: The remaining 19.5% who didn't know about your product and did not consider it for purchase are a potential source of sales growth.

Awareness is concerned with **before the sale.** Using the formula having an awareness of 61% in the Low End reduces the score by 19.5% and using an awareness of 67% in the High End reduces the score by 16.5%.

Low Tech: 19.5% of 25.9 is a loss of 5 points
High Tech: 16.5% of 45.2 is a loss of 7.5 points

Accessibility is concerned with **during the sale.** Having an accessibility of 36% in the Low End reduces the score by 32% and using an awareness of 40% in the High End reduces accessibility by 30%.

Low Tech: 32% of 25.9 is a loss of 8.3 points
High Tech: 30% of 45.2 is a loss of 13.6 points

Final Score

So to our adjusted raw scores of Low Tech, 25.9 and High Tech, 45.2 we apply the Awareness and Accessibility deductions to come up with an approximate CSS:

Low Tech: 25.9 – 5.0 – 8.3 = 12.6 points
High Tech: 45.2 – 7.5 – 13.6 = 24.1 points

Just to ensure that the scores we just calculated make sense, we should compare them with the CSS shown on pages of 5 & 6 of the FastTrack. If they compare reasonably then we can have faith that the values we calculated are valid. In this case the CSS are 9 points for the Low End and 23 for the High End. This suggests that our calculations are valid.

*Note: CSS vary throughout the year as segments and hence ideal spots drift evenly to their new positions for December 31st of the coming round. Remember that you and your competitors can improve your products during the coming round and hence boost your CSS.

Attributes in the Rough Cut: CSS adjustments

All products that fall within the ROUGH CUT parameters for position, price, and reliability will still be considered for purchase. However, if the products attributes are outside the FINE CUT parameters (all of the parameters you have been using so far), the TOTAL CSS is significantly adjusted.

For example:

If your product is priced at $36, price would contribute 0 points to your CSS score for the Low Tech market AND the adjusted score would lose another 10% of the base score. Ouch!

Customer Survey Score Adjustments

These Customer Survey Score adjustments apply to products positioned in the rough cut:

- PRICING outside the range loses about 10% (of the base CSS score) per dollar.
- MTBF set below the range loses about 20% (of the base CSS score) per 1,000 hours.
- POSITIONING outside of the fine cut circle is a 1% loss if it is just over the line, a 50% loss if it is halfway, and a 99% loss if it is on the edge of the rough cut circle.

Additional customer survey adjustments, for Accounts Receivable for example, will be discussed in Module 4.

Index

Made in the USA
Lexington, KY
03 February 2016